HOPE SPRINGS ETERNAL
IN THE PRIESTLY BREAST

HOPE SPRINGS ETERNAL IN THE PRIESTLY BREAST

A Research Study on Procedural Justice for Priests—Diocesan and Religious

"Where there's despair, let me sow hope."[1]

JAMES VALLADARES, PhD

---

[1]   St Francis of Assisi (Peace Prayer)

iUniverse, Inc.
Bloomington

Hope Springs Eternal in the Priestly Breast
A Research Study on Procedural Justice for Priests—Diocesan and Religious

The information, ideas, and suggestions in this book are not intended to render legal advice. Before following any suggestions contained in this book, you should consult your personal attorney. Neither the author nor the publisher shall be liable or responsible for any loss or damage allegedly arising as a consequence of your use or application of any information or suggestions in this book.

iUniverse books may be ordered through booksellers or by contacting:

iUniverse
1663 Liberty Drive
Bloomington, IN 47403
www.iuniverse.com
1-800-Authors (1-800-288-4677)

Because of the dynamic nature of the Internet, any web addresses or links contained in this book may have changed since publication and may no longer be valid. The views expressed in this work are solely those of the author and do not necessarily reflect the views of the publisher, and the publisher hereby disclaims any responsibility for them.

Any people depicted in stock imagery provided by Thinkstock are models, and such images are being used for illustrative purposes only.
Certain stock imagery © Thinkstock.

ISBN: 978-1-4620-7241-5 (sc)
ISBN: 978-1-4620-7240-8 (hc)
ISBN: 978-1-4620-7239-2 (ebk)

Library of Congress Control Number: 2011962041

Printed in the United States of America

iUniverse rev. date: 03/29/2012

CONTENTS

This research study is dedicated to the priests
—diocesan and religious—
of our universal Catholic Church
as a mark of
fraternal solidarity, solicitous concern, and heartfelt affection,
and with the prayerful wish
that they forge ahead
with unswerving fidelity to Christ Jesus,
the Eternal High Priest,
who has intentionally commissioned one and all
to serve as promoters of faith,
messengers of hope,
and ambassadors of God's eternal love.

May God bring to fruition
the good work that he has done
and continues to do
in and through
the pastoral ministry of each and every priest!

LIST OF ABBREVIATIONS USED IN
HOPE SPRINGS ETERNAL IN THE PRIESTLY BREAST

Ac.—The Acts of the Apostles

CD—*Christus Dominus*—Decree on the Bishops' Pastoral Office in the Church (Vatican II)

Col.—The Letter of St. Paul to the Colossians

1 Cor.—The First Letter of St. Paul to the Corinthians

2 Cor.—The Second Letter of St. Paul to the Corinthians

Deut.—The Book of Deuteronomy

Eph.—The Letter of St. Paul to the Ephesians

Exod.—The Book of Exodus

Gal.—The Letter of St. Paul to the Galatians

Gen.—The Book of Genesis

GE—*Gravissum Educationis*—Declaration on Christian Education (Vatican II)

GS—*Gaudium et Spes*—The Church Today—Pastoral Constitution on the Church in the Modern World (Vatican II)

Heb.—The Letter of St. Paul to the Hebrews

James—The Letter of St. James

Jn.—The Gospel according to John

1 Jn.—The First Letter of St. John

2 Jn.—The Second Letter of St. John

3 Jn.—The Third Letter of St. John

Lk.—The Gospel according to Luke

LG—*Lumen Gentium*—The Dogmatic Constitution on the Church (Vatican II)

Mk.—The Gospel according to Mark

Mt.—The Gospel according to Matthew

OT—*Optatum Totius*—Decree on Priestly Formation (Vatican II)

PC—*Perfectae Caritatis*—Decree on the Appropriate Renewal of the Religious Life (Vatican II)

1 Pet.—The First Letter of St. Peter

2 Pet.—The Second Letter of St. Peter

PO—*Presbyterorum Ordinis*—Decree on the Ministry and Life of Priests (Vatican II)

Ps.—The Book of Psalms

Phil.—the Letter of St. Paul to the Phillipians

Rom.—The Letter of St. Paul to the Romans

SC—*Sacrasanctum Concilium*—The Constitution on the Sacred Liturgy (Vatican II)

1 Thess.—The First Letter of St. Paul to the Thessalonians

2 Thess.—The Second Letter of St. Paul to the Thessalonians

1 Tim.—The First Letter of St. Paul to Timothy

2 Tim.—The Second Letter of St. Paul to Timothy

Tit.—The Letter of St. Paul to Titus

He who steals my purse steals trash;
T'was mine, 'tis his, it's gone;
But he who steals my good name
Takes something of great value which enriches him not at all
And leaves me very poor indeed.
—William Shakespeare

We must remember that any oppression,
any injustice, any hatred,
is a wedge designed
to attack our civilization.
—President Franklin Delano Roosevelt

He that takes truth for his guide, and duty for his end,
may safely trust to God's Providence to lead him aright.
—Blaise Pascal,
French mathematician, philosopher, physicist, and writer (1623-1662)

A person with a grain of faith in God
never loses hope,
because he believes
in the ultimate triumph of truth.
—Mahatma Gandhi

We shall repent in our generation
not so much for the evil deeds of wicked men
but for the appalling silence of the good people.
—Rev. Martin Luther King Jr.

There is no segment of the American population
with less civil liberties protection
than the average American priest.
—Dr. William A. Donohue, President of the Catholic League for
Religious & Civil Rights

FOREWORD

The clergy abuse scandal has posed the greatest threat to the traditional understanding of the Catholic priesthood since the Protestant Reformation. Now, as then, the deadliest attacks are coming from within the Church. In an attempt to ameliorate a system that allowed a small minority of the clergy to violate children and the gross negligence of some bishops who recycled these predators, the American bishops instituted the Charter for the Protection of Children and Young People in 2002. It is, unfortunately, doing the Church more harm than good.

By adhering to the charter's provisions, the American hierarchy has unwittingly undermined the Church's sacramental theology regarding Holy Orders and her ecclesiology, which depend on a priest's relationship with his bishop. This breakdown has encouraged present-day Modernists, who believe that truth is culturally conditioned and that the Faith is based merely on sentimentality, to try to remake the Church according to their own lights. Intra-ecclesial groups like Future Church, Voice of the Faithful (VOTF), and the Survivors' Network of those Abused by Priests (SNAP) have subsequently formed, challenging the hierarchical nature of the Church, her infallible teaching on the male-only priesthood, and the Western tradition of priestly celibacy.

A major factor responsible for a large number of the sex abuse cases, according to the 2011 John Jay College of Criminology Report[2] to the bishops, is attributed to the sexual confusion, which reigned in society and the Church in the 1960s and '70s. The teaching of moral relativism and the acceptance of popular psychological theories over traditional theological principles led to the excess of bad behaviour during this period.

---

[2]   WWW.philvoz.com/ABUSE.PDF

No doubt bad thinking led to bad actions. The lesson is that orthodoxy is necessary for orthopraxis.

The Dallas Charter was a response to the deep regret felt by the bishops for the perverse crimes that had occurred against minors and a recognition that strong safeguards must be in place to protect them. But the remedies that they enacted were influenced by the secular solutions of lawyers and public relations experts, which compromised the Gospel. They do not reflect justice, charity, and forgiveness towards priests. Dangerous procedural measures, such as administrative leave, zero tolerance, and a one-size-fits-all policy for accused priests and for punishing malefactors have lent themselves to violations of canonical due process and a mockery of time-tested principles of jurisprudence. This is especially evident when dioceses publish the names of defenceless deceased priests as sex abusers on their websites. But most egregious is the forced laicization imposed on those deemed to be guilty. This action clouds in the popular mind the permanency of the indelible character of Holy Orders conferred at ordination.

The present state of affairs has caused mistrust and fear in the priest-bishop relationship. The collaboration of a priest with his bishop is vital since he participates in the bishop's priesthood. Bishops, who are supposed to be fathers, brothers, and friends to their priests, have instead become mere managers with institutional damage control as their top priority. Many priests have dubbed this the *Caiaphas Principle*. A recent survey in an unpublished dissertation found that most priests don't believe that they can count on the support of their fellow priests in the event of a false accusation, presumably out of fear of retribution from their bishop or from victims' advocacy groups. This too is extremely dangerous because priests of the diocese form a presbyterate in union with their bishop. It has devastating pastoral consequences.

"Credible evidence," the nebulous standard used by diocesan review boards, has effectively made priests guilty until proven innocent. This has forced priests to shy away from human interactions, especially expressions of pastoral warmth and concern, which were the hallmarks of Jesus's public ministry. Now a fatherly touch may be interpreted as a sexual advance or an act of kindness toward a young person misconstrued as "grooming." As one priest so poignantly stated, "If I meet a woman, I'm having an affair; if I meet a man, I'm gay; and, God forbid, if I'm with a child, I'm an abuser." In the current climate, any human action of a priest is suspect. Naturally, this has had a devastating toll on the effectiveness of the ordained ministry.

In *Hope Springs Eternal in the Priestly Breast*, Fr. James Valladares shows how justice and charity have been violated by some bishops in dealing with accused priests. He examines the pertinent canons that guide the Church's justice system and finds that these are often ignored or wrongly applied. He provides true cases that highlight the injustice of the process and the agony of priests who have been subjected to the charter's draconian mandates.

The Church has incurred tremendous financial losses because of settlements rising from both legitimate and false claims. Her image has been marred by the secular media, which has taken advantage of the crisis. However, we often fail to understand how trivial these are in comparison to the damage done to the priesthood by the enactment of the charter's policies. This is *the* pressing issue that the bishops need to address.

The present scenario reported by Fr. Valladares is dark. Yet, he has surprisingly chosen a title for his book that speaks of hope. For sure, it is a hope based on Jesus' words to his disciples, *"I will be with you always."* Therefore, far from being pessimistic, Fr. Valladares presents the facts with confidence that "the truth will set us free."

For his hard work, born out of a love for the priesthood and his brother-priests, Fr. Valladares is to be commended.

Reverent Michael P. Orsi
Ave Maria School of Law
Naples, Florida

Fall 2011

ACKNOWLEDGEMENTS

Stephen L. Carter is the William Nelson Cromwell Professor of Law at Yale University. This is how he defines "integrity":

Discerning what is right and what is wrong;
Acting on what you have discerned, even at personal cost;
  Saying openly that you are acting on your understanding of right from wrong.[3]

So vitally essential is integrity in both private and public lives that, opines Carter: "The American dream may crumble—and the greatness of our democracy along with it."[4]

This perceptive, accurate and incontestable definition did challenge me to undertake a research study on procedural justice for priests—diocesan and religious.

None can deny the grievous, widespread and irreparable harm done to the credibility of priests and their ministry in the recent past. For this, each and every priest is profoundly sorry. *"A journey of a thousand miles begins with a single step."*[5]

By the same token, however, it must be admitted that there has been—and continues to be—a proliferation of false allegations against priests and for motives that range from the dubious and spurious to the specious and malicious. Once again, the harm done is grievous, widespread

---

[3]   Carter, Stephen L. *Integrity*. Basic books, New York Harper Collins, 1996. (author's summary)

[4]   Ibid.

[5]   Lao-tzu. *The Way of Lao-tzu*. Chinese Philosopher (604 BC-531BC)

and irreparable. It is, therefore, imperative that we all *judiciously discern, decisively act,* and *openly speak in the interests of truth, justice, and charity.* And that, in a nutshell, is the sole objective of this research study. Indeed, *a journey of a thousand miles* does *begin with a single step.*

At the very outset, I wish to acknowledge my gratitude to the following, who have played a key role in the progressive realization and eventual completion of this cogently important project:

- *Opus Bono Sacerdotii*—an organization (especially the president, Mr. Joe Maher, and his assistant, Mr. Pete Ferrara) that has worked strenuously to assist priests in need of defence, canonical and legal, and who have neither the personal nor financial means to plead their cause;

- Fr. Gordon Macrae—an extraordinarily heroic priest with indomitable courage, unrelenting tenacity, unwavering patience and Christ-like magnanimity, who personally and admirably reflects what Pope Benedict XVI has honestly and humbly confessed: "All of us are suffering as a result of the sins of our confreres who betrayed a sacred trust or failed to deal justly and responsibly with allegations of abuse".[6]

- Reverend Michael P. Orsi of the Ave Maria School of Law, Florida—a scholarly, courageous, and articulate protagonist for procedural justice—for his staunch support, masterful analysis of the current crisis, and invaluable commendation in the Foreword to this research study;

- Monsignor William McCarthy, Pastor Emeritus—for his unswerving fidelity to God and his unflinching commitment to his priestly vocation in the face of the cruellest twist of fate; he will always be a powerful and unmistakable witness to the mysterious but marvellous designs of our Provident God;

- Archbishop Philip Wilson, DD, JCL, of Adelaide, South Australia, for sanctioning my sabbatical leave and intended research study in the United States of America;

---

[6] *Pastoral Letter of the Holy Father, Pope Benedict XVI To the Catholics of Ireland.* 19 March, 2010. www.vactican.va/holy_father/benedict/XVI/letters/2010.

- Archbishop Jose H. Gomez, DD, STD, of Los Angeles, California, and the vicar for clergy, Msgr. Lorenzo Miranda, for so graciously welcoming me to the archdiocese and granting me the faculties to serve in the pastoral ministry and the Parish of St. Paschal Baylon, Thousand Oaks, California;
- Msgr. Craig Cox, JCD, the rector of St. John's Seminary, Camarillo, California, for his personal interest, professional advice, and morale-boosting encouragement;
- Ms. Dorothy Rabinowitz, Ms. Catharine Henningsen, Mr. Harvey L. Silverglate, Mr. Ryan MacDonald, Mr. Matt Abbott, and Mr. David Pierre Jr., whom I have never met, but whose candid, forthright, and persuasive writings have served as an added impetus in the pursuit of this vital research study;
- Fr. Dave Heney, the pastor of St. Paschal Baylon Church, Thousand Oaks, California, for his heart-warming welcome, sustained support, and generous hospitality all through my sabbatical leave, thereby ensuring the realization of this cherished dream;
- Fr. Joe Scerbo, SA; Fr. Jim Maher; and Fr. Thai Le for their fraternal support and willing assistance at all times;
- Professor Robert Cochran Jr., Director of the Herbert and Elinor Nootbaar Institute on Law, Religion, and Ethics, Pepperdine University, School of Law, Malibu, for so magnanimously accommodating me as a "visiting scholar" and generously facilitating my access to the voluminous library and its helpful resources;
- Dr. Patricia Lyons, director of the Doheny Libraries of St. John's Seminary and College, Camarillo, California, and Ms Jessica Drewitz, Public Services Librarian, Law Library at Pepperdine University School of Law, Malibu, for their outstanding professionalism and willing readiness in making the desired resources readily available to me;
- Professor Peter Wendel and Professor Mark Scarberry for kindly driving me to and from Pepperdine University, Malibu, in the absence of any other transport;
- The scores of authors whose writings have served as a treasure trove of valuable information—they have been listed at the end of this research study and duly acknowledged wherever necessary;

- Ms Jennifer Allison for willingly, painstakingly, and dexterously preparing the final draft of the manuscript and for her meticulous compliance with the precise directives of the publishers;
- Ms Margret (Midge) Mills—a seasoned research scholar and gifted writer—for her painstaking, meticulous, professional and flawless revision of the entire manuscript;
- And, finally, my dear mother (aged 95), my devoted siblings, and my closest circle of friends, who have been staunch in their loyalty, generous in their support, reassuring with their prayerful good wishes, and devotedly steadfast in their belief that *"God plus one is always a majority."*

May God bless them all!

Fr. James Valladares

St. Paschal Baylon Church
Thousand Oaks, CA, USA
Summer, 2011

INTRODUCTION

A journey of a thousand miles begins with a single step.
—Lao-tzu (philosopher, 604 BC-531 BC)

Once upon a time . . . early in 1966, I commenced my second year of theology in the Diocesan Seminary of Bombay (now Mumbai), India. As part of the curriculum in Moral Theology, we were scheduled to do a very intensive and comprehensive study of the Seventh, Eighth, and Tenth Commandments *("You shall not steal"; "You shall not bear false witness against your neighbour"; and "You shall not covet anything that is your neighbour's")* as a proximate preparation for the crucial examination that would render us eligible for the faculty to serve as ministers of the Sacrament of Reconciliation *(Ad audiendas confessiones).*

Very briefly, that particular branch was commonly referred to as *De Iure et Iustitia* (About Rights and Justice). A right was defined as something that is legitimately due to another. To take it away without authority or justification, therefore, is a violation of the person's right and a breach of the moral law. Framing it graphically, there is an invisible but inviolable link between a person and a basic right. So a failure to respect and honour the right is tantamount to breaking that invisible bond, and so offending the person and God. Stated differently, the deliberate flouting of a moral law offends God, the Supreme Lawgiver, and is, therefore, a culpable sin. For instance, each and every human being has a right to his/her life—a priceless gift that comes from God and God alone. None can take it away but God. To do so wilfully, violently and maliciously would be tantamount to murder—a grave crime that violates both the natural and the divine law. Consequently, the perpetrator must bear the entire brunt of the law—civil, moral, and divine.

Similarly, a person has a right to his reputation. Once again, there is an invisible but inviolable bond between the individual and his/her reputation. Therefore, we all are duty bound to respect another's reputation, and to refrain from any word or deed that could snap that bond and so harm the individual, often gravely and irreversibly. For instance, a very common offence is the sin of detraction, which is the unjustifiable disclosure of another's faults and failings to persons who did not know them. Even worse is the sin of calumny—the deliberate distortion of the truth, thereby poisoning the mind of the listener, and so damaging the reputation of another seriously and irreparably.

> *O! Beware, my lord, of jealousy;*
> *It is the green-eyed monster which doth mock*
> *The meat it feeds on.*
> —Shakespeare: *Othello* ac3, sc.3, l.165

> *Cruelty has a human heart,*
> *And jealousy a human face;*
> *Terror the human form divine,*
> *And secrecy the human dress.*
> —William Blake (1757-1827), "A Divine Image," 56:6

Over the past 50 years, I have observed with both surprise and consternation that while priests have their pastoral duties, which they sedulously strive to fulfil, often in the face of overwhelming odds, they have little or no claim to either rights or justice. One very senior priest, who has passed on to his Creator, would jocularly repeat: "A Catholic priest has but one right—the right to a Christian burial!"

Bound by a solemn promise of respect and obedience, a priest has no alternative but to comply with the directions of his bishop or religious superior. Should they be judicious and fair, the mutual rewards will be manifest and productive. Regrettably, not always is this the case, with the priest coming off the worse only because he is powerless, defenceless and helpless. For instance, priests have been known to be transferred because of the sinister machinations and false allegations of individuals, who either did not agree with them or had a score to settle.

What is particularly disturbing in these most unfortunate instances is the fact that the priest was denied a fair chance to defend himself and he was not even apprised of the reasons for his sudden and unjust transfer. The woeful and inexcusable assumption has always been "guilty until proven innocent"—a most reprehensible violation of the natural, canon and moral laws.

Even more deplorable is the fact that the seemingly "errant" priest was unilaterally given a particularly difficult assignment as a punitive measure, harshly and malevolently designed "to burst his bubble" or "to pull him down a peg or two." In some instances, the priest was stripped of his faculties and debarred from offering the Eucharist publicly. Even after a due investigation and the vindication of his innocence, the hapless individual was not reinstated. *The opposite of "love" is not "hate," but indifference.* And there couldn't be a more damaging blow to priestly morale.

As can be expected, the repercussions of such unjust, un-priestly, and morally reprehensible behaviour can have irreversibly injurious results that could range from loss of morale to a nervous breakdown, to a defection from the active ministry, to destructive addictions. Quite some time ago, for instance, in various parts of the United States, it had been observed that priests had been dying as a result of automobile accidents. What intrigued the investigating police was the fact that the details, in some cases, were identical—a sole driver ramming a speeding car on a highway into the concrete pylon of an overhead bridge. The article bore the intriguing but heart-wrenching caption: "Autocide!"

In an explosive expose, David Rice recounts the following gut-wrenching and tragic story:

> There was one old alcoholic priest called in to the chancery office (where the diocese is administered). "He was an 'alky,' no doubt about it," another priest remembers. "They call him in; they tell him he's a no-good alky. 'You are suspended, removed, get out of the diocese in twenty-four hours. We don't care where you go.' Maybe they just want to scare him. Well, he goes home, puts a shotgun to his mouth, and blows his head off."[7]

---

[7] David Rice, *Shattered Vows—Priests who Leave* (New York: William Morrow & Co. Inc., 1990) 16.

It is a commonly known fact that the good standing of the Catholic priest is undergoing serious appraisal in Western society. As a matter of fact, in view of the shocking revelations in the recent past, the Catholic priesthood is being undermined by a series of forces from both within and outside the Church. Even Pope Benedict XVI spoke of "the sin within."[8]

Offering the Catholic Church's strongest statement of fault to date in its widespread sexual-abuse scandal, the Sovereign Pontiff humbly and frankly confessed: "The greatest persecution of the church doesn't come from enemies on the outside but is born from the sin within."[9] This is why he confidently launched the International Year of the Priest (2009) in the 150th year of the death *(dies natalis)* of the saintly patron of the pastoral clergy, St. John Marie Vianney.

When addressing the clergy of the Diocese of Bolzano-Bressanone, for instance, our Holy Father emphasised the stringent need for reinforcing fraternal bonds within a presbyterate: "No priest is a priest on his own; we are a presbyterate, and it is only in this communion with the bishop that each one can carry out his service." [10]

In this pastorally cogent endeavour, Pope Benedict XVI unequivocally emphasised the crucial role of bishops. Speaking to the bishops of the United States of America in Washington DC, these are the Sovereign Pontiff's precise words: "If you (bishops) yourselves live in a manner closely configured to Christ, the Good Shepherd, who laid down his life for his sheep, you will inspire your brother priests to re-dedicate themselves to the service of their flocks with Christ-like generosity. Indeed a clearer focus upon the imitation of Christ in holiness of life is exactly what is needed in order for us to move forward."[11]

In so doing, our Holy Father was merely reiterating what the Fathers of the Second Vatican Council did unambiguously state in *The Decree on Priestly Life and Ministry*: "All priests share with the bishops the one

---

[8] Benedict XVI, 12 May, 2010. www.cathnews.com

[9] Benedict XVI. Op.Cit.

[10] Pope Benedict XVI, in Codes, Paul J., *Communio in the Presbyterium. Why Priests?* Address to clergy of the Diocese of Bolzano-Bressanone, August 6, 2008. Scepter.

[11] Address to bishops of the United States of America, Washington DC, April 16, 2008.

identical priesthood and ministry of Christ Jesus. On account of this common sharing in the same priesthood and ministry, then bishops are to regard their priests as brothers and friends and are to take the greatest interest they are capable of in their welfare both temporal and spiritual."[12] In a word, "no priest is a priest on his own; we are a presbyterate, and it is only in this communion with the bishop that each one can carry out his service."[13]

The current crisis of false and unsubstantiated allegations against innocent priests and religious, therefore, urgently warrants a clear and definite procedure, for the following reasons:

- This imbalance has enabled a coalition of forces to join a crescendo of sustained and damaging criticism of the Catholic Church centred on its Achilles' heel of "breach of trust" by a very small number of priests.
- Many of the rights of priests, which are protected by canon law, have been ignored.
- Some bishops/provincials have acted unjustly in dealing with priests and religious who have been accused.
- Some priests have become the victims of abuses of power, without being provided with a full understanding or advertisement of their rights. Each and every priest deserves due process of the law when he is accused.[14]
- Such a travesty of justice blatantly contravenes the specific directives of Christ Jesus, the Eternal High Priest: "You know that the rulers of the Gentiles lord it over them, and their great ones are tyrants over them. It will not be so among you; but whoever wishes to be great among you must be your servant, and whoever

---

[12] Abbott (SJ), Walter M. (Ed): The Documents of Vatican II. Geoffrey Chapman, London, 1967.

[13] Pope Benedice XVI, in Codes, Paul J., Op. Cit.

[14] "Everyone charged with a penal offence has the right to be presumed innocent until proven guilty according to law in a public trial at which he had all the guarantees necessary for his defence" (Article 11, Universal Declaration of Human Rights, General Assembly of the United Nations, adopted on December 10, 1948).

wishes to be first among you must be your slave; just as the Son of Man came not to be served but to serve, and to give his life a ransom for many."[15]

- Even Pope Benedict XVI, in addressing the American bishops, the United Nations, and all educators, spoke about the rights of every human being, *a fortiori* a priest, diocesan or religious, to receive respect and justice, as well as the need for true leaders to seek truth if they are to remain faithful to the Gospel.

- Bishops must certainly protect the laity in the diocese, but they must also protect their priests, diocesan and religious, for these are the men who are the visible face of the bishop in parishes and other ministries.

- When a bishop abuses his power, he is attacking the basis of all human rights and integrity. When used against a cleric, he is attacking one of the most defenceless of all people in the church.

- When a cleric is not told who is making the accusations, what the actual accusation is, when it happened, or other vital information, the cleric is powerless to defend himself or even prove his innocence.

- If there is no effort to ascertain the truth of an accusation or to ask for facts that are verifiable, then the bishops are opening themselves up to false accusations simply because people are seeking money at the expense of a defenceless and helpless cleric. Such a false denunciation is a canonical crime and reparation can be required (Canon 1390 §3).

- Bishops are to be in service to all the people in their diocese. By requiring minimally that the accusations be true and giving clerics the right to defend themselves, they are simply upholding the recommendations of both Blessed Pope John Paul II and Pope Benedict XVI. A failure to honour this momentous commitment cannot but result in a loss of both credibility and moral authority.

To conclude, the fathers of the Second Vatican Council in the Decree on Bishops (§16) have made it indubitably clear that "with sympathetic

---

[15] Matthew: 20: 25-28

understanding and practical help, bishops should take care of priests who are in danger of any kind or who have failed in some way."

This is particularly cogent in view of a widespread and distressing observation, which is not without a justifiable foundation: "The Catholic Church has become the safest place in the world for children, but the most dangerous place in the world for priests."[16]

---

[16] Michael Brandon, host of 'Freedom Through Truth', and quoted by Fr Gordon J MacRae in "When Priests are falsely Accused Part 2: Why Accusers Should be Named." www.thesestonewalls.com/Gordon-macrae. 20 October, 2010.

1

The Priesthood Is the Love of the Heart of Jesus[17]

On the Solemnity of the Most Sacred Heart of Jesus, Friday, June 19, 2009, Pope Benedict XVI inaugurated a "Year for Priests" in celebration of the 150th anniversary of the death *(dies natalis)* of John Mary Vianney, the patron saint of parish priests worldwide.[18] His objective was clear and definite: to deepen the commitment of all priests and to emphasise the paramount importance of an internal renewal, so as to ensure a more forceful and incisive witness to the Gospel in today's world. Wisely quoting the saintly priest, our Holy Father said: "The priesthood is the love of the heart of Jesus."[19]

This penetrating insight makes it crystal clear that a priest is indeed a very precious gift both to the Church and to God's people. Said Jesus to his first priests: "You did not choose me but I chose you. And I appointed you to go out and bear fruit, fruit that will last."[20] Fully appreciative of this gratuitous and supernatural gift, Pope Benedict adds, "How can I not pay tribute to their apostolic labours, their tireless and hidden service,

---

[17] St John Vianney. Quoted by Pope Benedict XVI in his Letter *Proclaiming A Year For Priests*, on the 150th Anniversary of the "Dies Natalis" of the Cure of Ars. Veltus.stblogs.org.2009/06/thepriesthood.

[18] He was proclaimed as such by Pope Pius XI in 1929.

[19] "Le Sacerdote, c'est l'amour du Coeur de Jesus," in *Le cure d'Ars. Sa pensée—Son Coeur*, presentés par l'Abbé Bernard Nodet, ed., Xavier Mappus, Foi Vicante (1966): 98.

[20] John 15:16

their universal charity? And how can I not praise the courageous fidelity of so many priests, who, amid difficulties and misunderstandings, remain faithful to their vocation as 'friends of Christ,' whom he has called by name, chosen and sent?"[21]

The Significance of a Gift

There are two very striking features of a genuine gift; it is gratuitous and generous. In other words, in spite of the fact that the recipient has no claim whatsoever, the benefactor gives it willingly and with no strings attached—it is gratuitous. Then the gift is given as a gesture of unfeigned goodwill, regardless of the cost to the benefactor—it is generous. Such is the priesthood: it is a gratuitous and generous gift of our Triune God.

These two features of a genuine gift are very vividly manifested in the heart-warming story of the widow in the Gospel.[22] The wealthy came forward and ceremoniously made an ostentatious display of their largesse by putting their handsome gifts into the treasury. Their sole intent was to draw attention to themselves; theirs was a gift but with a string attached: self-centred and pretentious pride. By contrast, a poor widow crept up to the temple treasury and very humbly and inconspicuously put in two small copper coins; that was all she had.

Her gift was both gratuitous and generous. First, she was under no obligation whatsoever to put in anything, as she was extremely poor and was justifiably exempt. And second, she put in all that she had because of her heartfelt gratitude to God, and God deserved nothing short of the best she could offer. Commending her generosity, Jesus said, "Truly I tell you, this poor widow has put in more than all of them; for all of them have contributed out of their abundance, but she out of her poverty has put in all she had to live on".[23]

---

[21] Pope Benedict XVI, "The Priesthood", Spiritual Thought Series, (July 2009), 65.

[22] Luke 21:1-4.

[23] Mark (12:44)

Without Me, You Cannot; Without You, I Will Not[24]

Of the many possible ways in which God could have provided for the propagation of the human race, God, in his wisdom, power, and love, chose just one. God ordained that a husband and wife would serve as the transmitters of human life into which he would breathe a spiritual and immortal soul and so bring about the birth of a newborn child. In other words, a father and a mother serve as co-creators with God in begetting new human life. Such is God's marvellous wisdom, power, and love. And therein lies the sanctity of the Sacrament of Marriage and the dignity of parenthood. It is as though God, in spite of his almighty power, wisdom, and love, is saying to the parents: "Without me, you cannot; without you, I will not."

Similarly, of the many possible ways in which God could have provided for the spiritual nurture of people, in his wisdom, power, and love, he chose just one. He decided to share his divine power, mission, and authority with mere human beings, who would serve as transmitters of his divine life in and through their priestly and pastoral ministry. In other words, God just had no alternative but to choose humans to minister to humans. And so, Christ Jesus shared his Divine Priesthood with mere mortal human beings, thereby giving them a share in his priestly, kingly and sanctifying mission. Therein lies the sanctity of the Sacrament of Holy Orders and the dignity of the sacred priesthood. Truly, the "Priesthood is the love of the heart of Jesus."[25] It is as though God, in spite of his almighty power, wisdom and love, is saying to his priests: "Without me, you cannot; without you, I will not."

The priesthood is indeed a gratuitous and generous gift of God that defies both comprehension and gratitude. Once again, of the innumerable possible ways in which God could have provided for the spiritual and pastoral care of his family, he deliberately chose one and just one; he didn't even consider a second. He decided to share his power and authority with

---

24 Anonymous.

25 St John Vianney. Quoted by Pope Benedict XVI. *Letter Proclaiming A Year for Priests on the 150th Anniversary of the "Dies Natalis" of the Cure of Ars*. www.veltus.stblogs.org.2009/06/thepriesthood

mere mortal humans, his priests, who would serve as a channel of his boundless love, his unfathomable wisdom, and his sublime power.

The priest is an "extraction from the common" to be "a consignment to the whole."[26]

Through the Sacrament of Holy Orders, a priest is brought into Christ Jesus; he enters into relations with the Father through the Son, and through a deepening of this bond, he therefore becomes capable of revealing the nature of this God to the world: not an enigmatic and terrible God, but "a God with a human face, a God who is love."[27] In explaining the term *sanctification* as "the giving over of a person to God," Pope Benedict XVI defines the essence of the priesthood as "a transfer of ownership, a being taken out of the world and given to God."[28] In a word, a priest is a visible sign of God's presence.

In virtue of the Sacrament of Holy Orders, a priest is able to enter into contact with the person of Christ Jesus, and so speak and act in his name, representing to the world this power of love through which the priesthood of Christ finds expression. And, since he carries out his ministry *in persona Christi* (*in the person of Christ Jesus*), the priest continues the saving actions of Christ Jesus, "breaking the Bread of life and remitting sins,"[29] through which he has been granted the power to reintegrate man into the very heart of God, and to offer him the possibility of redemption and forgiveness.

At the conclusion of the International Year for Priests, Pope Benedict XVI officiated at a series of services, at which approximately 15,000 priests from all over the world were present. Addressing the questions of a representative set of priests, the Holy Father said, "Christ Jesus is drawing us into himself, allowing us to speak for him. He is at all times the only

---

[26] Pope Benedict XVI. *Meeting with the Clergy of the Diocese of Bolzano-Bressanone*, Cathedral of Bressanone, August 6, 2008. www.vatican.va/holy_father/benedict_XVI/speeches.

[27] Pope Benedict XVI, "The Priesthood" (Address, March 2, 2006).

[28] Pope Benedict XVI (Homily, April 9, 2009).

[29] Pope Benedict XVI, "The Priesthood" (Homily, May 3, 2009).

real priest, yet he is very present to the world today because he draws us into himself."[30]

Next, the Sovereign Pontiff cautioned priests against a "theology of arrogance" that makes God a mere object, rather than a subject speaking to us. Instead, he said, priests must engage in a "theology stimulated by love" that seeks to dialogue with love and so come to a better knowledge of the Beloved. Finally, Pope Benedict urged priests to live out their priesthood "in a way that is so persuasive"[31] that young people may see an example of a vocation lived fully. Indeed, there is no better advertisement for the priesthood than a happy priest.

A priest continues the saving actions of Christ Jesus.

As an *alter Christus* (another Christ), the sacrifice that the priest celebrates and the absolution he gives are grounded on this Otherness that passes through him, by means of the sacrament of Holy Orders, and makes him "a humble instrument pointing to Christ, who offers himself in sacrifice for the salvation of the world."[32]

This is how the saintly Cure d'Ars, St. John Vianney, wisely described how immense a gift a priest is to his people: "A good shepherd, a pastor after God's heart, is the greatest treasure which the good Lord can grant to a parish, and one of the most precious gifts of divine mercy. Without the priest, the passion and death of our Lord would be of no avail. It is the priest who continues the work of redemption on earth."[33]

---

[30] Pope Benedict XVI. Address at conclusion of International Year for Priests

[31] Pope Benedict XVI, "Pope Answers the Questions of Priests on Prayer, Celibacy and New Vocations," *Catholic News Agency* (June 11, 2010).

[32] Pope Benedict XVI, "The Priesthood", Op.Cit. (Address, March 18, 2009).

[33] St John Vian ney, Op.Cit.

"As far as the heavens are above the earth, as far as the east is from the west . . ."[34]

If I may be permitted to be personal, on a couple of occasions, I visited my sister and her family in Virginia Beach, Virginia. This is where I would spend my annual holiday. And while there, I would assist the pastor as and when it was necessary.

One day, I got a call from the lay chaplain of the local general hospital. He explained that a lady wished to see a Catholic priest urgently, as she was not expected to survive the night. He further explained that the pastor was away and not due to return until the next day. He also explained that the pastor of the neighbouring parish was away for a few days. He turned to me, because I was the only priest available in the area. Of course, he was apologetic for turning to me, even though he knew I was on my annual holiday. Without hesitation, I assured him that I would be willing to respond, if only he would be good enough to come and fetch me, as I had no transport. Minutes later, he was at my door, and a few minutes later, I was at the bedside of the patient.

Her joy truly knew no bounds. Very candidly, she confided that she had strayed from the Catholic faith and the Catholic Church years ago, in a moment of youthful recklessness and juvenile rebellion. That was some forty years earlier. However, in that crisis, it was her earnest desire to make her peace with God, even as she prepared for the final encounter. And for that, she needed the priestly ministry of God's visible representative: a priest. In God's Divine Providence, the only priest available then was one from another continent thousands of miles away, another distant city and another nationality and culture.

None of that mattered to the patient. For her, a priest, any priest—regardless of nationality, culture or language—is indeed the love of the heart of Jesus. He is God's representative, an extension of Christ Jesus and a channel of the Holy Spirit's life-giving power and love. With great fervour and heart-warming sincerity, that good lady made her peace with God in and through the Sacrament of Reconciliation, reverently received the Sacrament of the Sick, and joyfully received the Holy Eucharist.

---

[34]   NRSV: Psalm 103

The manifest peace and inexpressible joy that descended upon her literally defy expression. The prodigal had returned home into the welcoming arms of a very merciful and forgiving Father, and the heavenly banquet had already been organised. "My daughter, whom I thought lost, has been found; and she whom all thought dead has come back to life." And that is exactly what did happen within the next few hours. Said Jesus, "I tell you there is more joy in heaven over one repentant sinner than over ninety-nine other virtuous people that have no need of repentance."[35] And God rendered that possible in and through the sacramental ministry of a priest. Indeed, a priest is the love of the heart of Jesus.

Without me, you cannot; without you, I will not.

"The priesthood is the love of the heart of Jesus," as the saintly Curé of Ars often said, and so, the Holy Father waxes eloquent in a fatherly and reassuring tribute to the priests of the world:

> This touching expression makes us reflect, first of all, with heartfelt gratitude on the immense gift which priests represent, not only for the Church, but also for humanity itself. I think of all those priests who quietly present Christ's words and actions each day to the faithful and to the whole world, striving to be one with the Lord in their thoughts and their will, their sentiments and their style of life. How can I not pay tribute to their apostolic labours, their tireless and hidden service and their universal charity? And how can I not praise the courageous fidelity of so many priests who, even amid difficulties and misunderstandings, remain faithful to their vocations as "friends of Christ," whom he has called by name, chosen and sent?[36]

Some years ago, for instance, there was a deplorable—in fact scandalous—case of bureaucratic bungling in one particular diocese. A very conscientious, industrious and highly esteemed pastor was unjustly and

---

[35] Luke 15:7
[36] Pope Benedict XVI, "The Priesthood", Op.Cit., (July 2009): 65.

vindictively removed from office because of the conspiratorial malevolence of his detractors and enemies. As a pastor, he was faithfully fulfilling his pastoral duties as clearly delineated by canon law and the Theology of the Ministerial Priesthood. His spirited defence before his bishop and that of his knowledgeable and devoted parishioners was callously ignored. *The hapless priest was declared guilty until proven innocent—if that was a viable alternative at all.*

He lost no time in referring his appeal to the Congregation of the Clergy in Rome. A very protracted and intensive investigation was conducted. *The pastor was found totally innocent, and the local bishop was instructed to have him reinstated as pastor of his parish. The bishop ignored the instruction and adamantly refused to comply.*

The priest reiterated his appeal. And once again, the Congregation urged the bishop to have the priest reinstated, but the latter stubbornly refused to do so. Compelled by circumstances, the resolute priest had no alternative but to turn to the bishop of a neighbouring diocese, who welcomed him gladly, and had no hesitation in appointing him as pastor to a local parish. Subsequently, it was reported that the new appointee was greatly loved, highly respected, and most gratefully appreciated by his parishioners, in much the same way that he had been in his own diocese.

This isn't the first, and it certainly will not be the last instance, corroborating the prediction of Christ Jesus, "Truly I tell you, no prophet is accepted in his own hometown . . . Servants are not greater than their master. If they persecuted me, they will persecute you . . . Blessed are you when people revile you and persecute you and utter all kinds of evil against you falsely on my account. Rejoice and be glad, for your reward is great in heaven, for in the same way they persecuted the prophets who were before you."[37] "Priests will put nothing before the love of Christ Jesus."[38]

In yet another diocese, three priests had their faculties withdrawn in the not-too-distant past. Two have reportedly had them reinstated, after a long time. No public announcement has been made. *Both have repeatedly and publicly protested the injustice of the procedures, which have resulted in irreparable harm to their reputations and ministries.* One has retired, now a physical and psychological wreck; the other has resumed

---

[37] Luke 4:24; John 15:20; Matthew 5:11.
[38] Pope Benedict XVI, Angelus (June 5, 2005).

his ministry outside the diocese, by sheer force of complex and irreversible circumstances. The third has not been officially dismissed, nor has he had his faculties formally revoked. Being in *limbo*, he went on to graduate as a nurse, and is presently serving in a large public hospital. *To this day, he has no idea as to his personal or priestly status.*

In his message for the 47th World Day of Prayer for Vocations, Pope Benedict XVI focussed on the theme: "Witness Awakens Vocations." By referring to the prophets, Jesus himself, and John the Baptist, the Holy Father calls us back to the reality that sharing in the ministry of Christ Jesus exposes us to misunderstanding, rejection and persecution. Like Christ Jesus, we have the choice to give witness faithfully or look for some course that avoids the pain, at the risk of compromising the message. "Bad men need nothing more to compass their ends, than that good men should look on and do nothing."[39]

Admittedly, the entire faithful share in the mission of the Church, by virtue of their baptism. Nevertheless, we, in the ordained ministry, contribute in a very unique way to the life of the Church, especially through the sacramental ministry we celebrate and the leadership we are called to exercise. It is in this context that the Sovereign Pontiff highlights St. John Mary Vianney, Curé of Ars, as a model of a priest and a pastor, especially for his focus, commitment and prayer.[40]

As all are aware, these are extremely difficult times for all involved in the pastoral ministry. This adverse and most unfortunate situation has been further compounded by the irresponsible and inexcusable tendency to tar all with the same brush. What has been particularly disconcerting is the unscrupulous and avaricious tendency in some to fabricate untruths, and to exploit a questionable situation, to their personal and financial advantage.

Reportedly, there have been recurring instances all over the world, where the individual priest or religious has not been supported by his bishop or superior, who callously relegates him to both isolation and oblivion. In a word, priests are both defenceless and helpless. As is patently clear, this is a deplorable travesty that does more harm than good; it also

---

[39]   John Stuart Mill. Inaugural Address, at St Andrew's. 1867.

[40]   Bishop Les Tomlinson, "Sharing in the Ministerial Priesthood of Christ," *The Swag*, 18, no. 2 (Winter 2010): 13.

does little to help generate a climate that is favourable to the promotion of vocations to the priesthood and the religious life.

"You Have Not Chosen Me; No, I Have Chosen You"[41]

Blessed Columba Marmion, who has written a magnificent book on the Sacred Priesthood, once said: "There could be no more fatal error for the priest than to underestimate the sacerdotal dignity. He must, on the contrary, have a very high conception of it."[42]

This is because the Sacrament of Holy Orders, like the Sacraments of Baptism and Confirmation, imposes upon the newly ordained an indelible spiritual mark known as a sacramental character, thereby giving him a new configuration to Christ Jesus and a specific standing in the Church—hence the saying: "Once a Christian, always a Christian; once a priest, always a priest."

In commissioning his first priests, Christ Jesus said to them, "As the Father has sent me, so am I sending you."[43] In other words, Christ Jesus was commissioning his first priests and their successors to continue his God-ordained mission; and in order that they may successfully and effectively achieve their mission, he empowered them with the requisite divine power and authority. So the power and authority that a priest enjoys give him a share in the very priesthood of Christ Jesus and can, therefore, enable him to do what only Christ Jesus can.

For instance, at every Eucharistic sacrifice, the priest, acting in the name of his people and with the sacred power invested in him by Christ Jesus, pronounces the words of Consecration over the bread and the wine. In doing so, he is well aware that he is the visible representative of Christ Jesus, and that he, through the power of the Holy Spirit, will transform the bread and wine into Christ's very own Body and Blood. What a sublime privilege and singular joy for a priest to say: "This is my Body! This is my Blood!" And the priest, a mere human being, can do that, thanks to Christ Jesus, who has marvellously shared his sacred priesthood with him, in

---

[41] Luke 15:19.

[42] Columba Marmion, Quoted by David L. Toups. www.sknirp.com/toup

[43] John 20:21

spite of his frailties, imperfections, and personal unworthiness, and who is continually at work in and through him.

In his memorable Post-Synodal Apostolic Exhortation, *Pastores Dabo Vobis* (I will give you shepherds), Blessed Pope John Paul II very aptly referred to the ministerial priesthood as both "a mystery" and "a gift." And the reason is patently clear:

> We derive our identity ultimately from the love of the Father; we turn our gaze to the Son, sent by the Father as high priest and good shepherd. Through the power of the Holy Spirit, we are united sacramentally to him in the ministerial priesthood. Our priestly life and activity continue the life and activity of Christ Jesus himself. Here lies our identity, our true dignity, the source of our joy, the very basis of our life.[44]

As is well known, at every Eucharistic sacrifice, the priest consecrates the bread and wine into the Body and Blood of Christ Jesus. This is a stupendous miracle, which God alone can perform. And yet, the priest dares to say, "This is my Body! This is my Blood!" Instantaneously, both are transformed into the Body and Blood of Christ Jesus—a miraculous change that is best designated by the word *transubstantiation*.

The Council of Trent summarizes the Catholic faith by declaring:

> Because Christ our Redeemer said that it was truly his body that he was offering under the species of bread, it has always been the conviction of the Church of God, and this holy Council now declares again, that by the consecration of the bread and wine there takes place a change of the whole substance of the bread into the substance of the body of Christ our Lord and of the whole substance of the wine into the substance of his blood. This change the holy Catholic Church has fittingly and properly called *transubstantiation*."[45]

---

[44] Pope John Paul II, *Pastores Dabo Vobis* #18, 37.

[45] Council of Trent (1551): DS 1642.

And the priest, a mere human being, can do that thanks to Christ Jesus, who has marvellously shared his sacred priesthood with him, in spite of his frailties, imperfections and personal unworthiness!

"The Eucharist is a Verb as well as a Noun." So said Fr. Tim Shillcox, a seminary professor.[46] In other words, a priest is meant to be a man of sacrificial love, to be the bread that is broken for others, to be the wine that is poured out and shared with others in and through his pastoral ministry. This is living the Mass, which he celebrates daily. We verbalise Eucharist by witnessing it. In the poignant words of St. Paul: "Offer your bodies as a living sacrifice."[47] This is spiritual worship. In a word, a priest's existence must be wholly dedicated to God and to others; he must become a sacrificial gift.

Again, each time a priest administers the Sacrament of Reconciliation, he acts with the power and the authority of Christ Jesus and says to the penitent: "I forgive you of your sins in the name of the Father, and of the Son and of the Holy Spirit." None but God can forgive sins, and the priest, a mere human being, dares to do that each time he administers the Sacrament of Reconciliation, because the sacramental character, that indelible stamp, ensures that he enjoys and will always enjoy the power and authority of Christ Jesus himself. "As the Father has sent me, so am I sending you . . . Then Jesus called the twelve together and gave them power and authority over all demons and to cure diseases, and he sent them out to proclaim the kingdom of God and to heal."[48]

This is the reason why the sacred priesthood differs essentially from the common priesthood of the baptised. To quote the precise words of the Catechism of the Catholic Church: "While the common priesthood of the faithful is exercised by the unfolding of baptismal grace . . . the ministerial priesthood is at the service of the common priesthood . . . The ministerial priesthood is a means by which Christ Jesus unceasingly builds up and leads his Church. For this reason it is transmitted by its own sacrament, the sacrament of Holy Orders" (§1547).[49]

---

[46] Alfred McBride O. Praem, *A Priest Forever*, Cincinnati, OH: St. Anthony Press, 2009, 48.

[47] Romans 12:1.

[48] John 20:21; Luke 9:1-2.

[49] The Catechism of the Catholic Church

A crucial and radical difference

On September 17, 2009, Pope Benedict XVI met a group of bishops from Brazil who had just completed their *ad limina* visit. During his address, he highlighted the distinctive role of priests in the Church. He said:

> "The particular identity of priests and laity must be seen in the light of the essential difference between priestly ministry and the 'common priesthood' of the baptised. Hence it is important to avoid the secularization of the clergy and the 'clericalisation' of the laity."[50]

> Lay-people certainly need to give expression to "the Christian view of anthropology and the social doctrine of the Church." Priests, on the other hand, "must distance themselves from politics in order to favour the unity and communion of all the faithful, thus becoming a point of reference to everyone."[51]

> A shortage of priests does not "justify a more active and abundant participation of the laity" since "the greater the faithful's awareness of their own responsibilities within the Church, the clearer becomes the specific identity and inimitable role of the priest as pastor of the entire community, witness to the authenticity of the faith, and dispenser of the mysteries of salvation in the name of Christ the Head."[52]

> So, "the function of the clergy is essential and irreplaceable in announcing the Word and celebrating the Sacraments, especially the Eucharist. For this reason, it is vital to ask the Lord to send workers for his harvest; and it is necessary

---

[50] Pope Benedict XVI. Address to bishops from Brazil. 17 September, 2009.

[51] Ibid.

[52] Ibid.

that priests express joy in their faithfulness to their priestly identity."[53]

Indeed, it has been rightly said that a happy priest is the best advertisement for the sacred priesthood. Stated differently, actions always speak louder than words, and people are always more influenced by what they see than what they hear. "The best possible way of attracting men to the priesthood is the witness of life given by priests themselves."[54] So if priests show themselves to be happy and fulfilled in their ministry, other men will more easily hear the Lord's call and respond generously. This certainly is one positive dividend we all can expect from the Year for Priests.

Conclusion

In his homily at the Chrism Mass, Holy Thursday, April 13, 2006, Pope Benedict XVI said,

> The world needs God—not any god but the God of Jesus Christ, the God who made himself flesh and blood, who loved us to the point of dying for us, who rose and created within himself room for man. This God must live in us and we in him. This is our priestly call; only in this way can our actions as priests bear fruit.[55]

St. John Vianney once said, "When people want to destroy religion, they begin by attacking the priest; for when there is no priest, there is no sacrifice; and when there is no sacrifice, there is no religion."[56]

---

[53] Ibid.

[54] Paul M. Conroy, *The Pastoral Review* (May/June 2010): 16.

[55] Pope Benedict XVI, "The Priesthood" (July 2009): 3.

[56] St John Vianney. Op.Cit.

2

Rights Are a Matter of Justice and Charity

Rights come from wrongs—
when a society realizes
it is trampling on the rights of an underprivileged group,
it creates a right to protect that minority group.
—Alan Deshowitz, a constitutional lawyer, author, and law professor

Then the Pharisees met together to try to think of some way to trap Jesus into saying something for which they could arrest him. They decided to send some of their men along with the Herodians to ask him this question: "Sir, we know you are very honest and teach the truth regardless of the consequences, without fear or favour. Now tell us, is it right to pay taxes to the Roman government or not?"

But Jesus saw what they were after. "You hypocrites!" he exclaimed. "Who are you trying to fool with your trick questions? Here, show me a coin." And they handed him a penny.

"Whose picture is stamped on it?" he asked them. "And whose name is this beneath the picture?"

"Caesar's," they replied.

"Well, then," he said, "give it to Caesar if it is his, and give God everything that belongs to God."

His reply surprised and baffled them, and they went away.[57]

Ask . . . Seek . . . Knock

A story, it has been rightly said, is the shortest distance between reality and truth. Of this, none was more aware than the greatest storyteller and the wisest teacher this world has ever known—Christ Jesus. Well aware of the finitude of humans and their inability to meet every need, Christ Jesus urged one and all to "ask . . . , seek . . . , and knock . . ." assuring them that "whosoever asks will unfailingly receive, whosoever seeks will always find and whosoever knocks will assuredly have the door open to him/her."[58] In a word, the humble, trusting and persistent prayer of a faithful person will never go unanswered.

To emphasise his point, Christ Jesus narrated the following poignant story. "There was a city judge," he said, "a very godless man, who had great contempt for everyone.[59] A widow of that city came to him frequently to appeal for justice against a man who had harmed her.[60] The judge ignored her for a while, but eventually she got on his nerves. "I fear neither God nor man," he said to himself, "but this woman bothers me. I'm going to see that she gets justice, for she is wearing me out with her constant coming!"[61]

---

[57] Matthew 22:15-22.

[58] Matthew 7:7

[59] The judge is reminiscent of Josephus's description of King Jehoiakim, who was "neither religious toward God, nor kind toward men." In short, the judge is corrupt.

[60] The widow is one of the typical needy of the Bible (Exodus 22:21-24). Since her case is brought before an individual, it is probably a litigation concerning money, perhaps an inheritance. She kept coming, asking for vindication, so that finally the judge answers.

[61] The root meaning of "wear me out" is "beat me under the eye" (the same verb is translated "pommel" in 1 Corinthians 9:27, but Jesus probably intends the figurative idea.

Then the Lord said, "If even an evil judge can be worn down like that, don't you think that God will surely give justice to his people who plead with him day and night? Yes! He will answer them quickly!⁶² But the question is: When I, the Messiah, return, how many will I find who have faith and are praying?"⁶³ In a word, rights are a matter of both justice and charity.

A Global Challenge

Human rights are becoming the language of the entire world in the realm of politics, international relations, and law. In the opinion of many scholars, it is now the dominant discourse of our day, and it is becoming more broadly so daily.

So very important has been the issue of human rights in the eyes of the global community that the United Nations (UN) declared the years 1995 through 2004 as the UN Decade of Human Rights Education. As a matter of fact, human rights education is expanding so extensively that courses and terminal degree programs have been established everywhere.

However, the study of human rights should not be undertaken for mere intellectual stimulation or curiosity, but principally so that all persons at appropriate levels and in both academic and non-academic contexts inculcate and enhance a culture wherein the dignity of the human person is respected and his/her fundamental rights are dutifully upheld. After all, human rights are the birthright of humanity, and their protection is the first responsibility of all, without exception. In other words, they are inherent attributes of the human personality, and their purpose is the legal protection of the inherent human dignity of each individual human being. So very vital is the universal protection of human rights that life itself can be at stake if they are not preserved.

---

⁶² In the application, the Lord uses the typical argument from the lesser to the greater. If an unrighteous judge hears the pleas of a woman because of her persistence, how much more will God respond to the continued prayers of his people. The emphasis is on the speedy vindication of God's chosen.

⁶³ Luke. 18:1-8

17

A Definition of Terms

The Latin word for duty, *officium*, suggests that duty is related to one's office (i.e. an official role or position). Indeed, Webster's defines a duty as "obligatory tasks, conduct, service, or functions that arise from one's position (as in life or in a group)."

In speaking of rights, it must be noted that legal philosophy, judicial opinion, and canonical tradition commonly hold that rights "correlate" with duties. In fact, there are those who see these two terms as simply opposite sides of the same coin. For them, assertions of rights "are merely the shadows cast by (other people's) duties."[64]

Canonical tradition generally maintains the close connection between rights and duties. Thus, Pope Paul VI said that "the basic rights of the baptized are not efficacious, nor can they be exercised, unless one recognizes the duties connected with them by baptism."[65] Pope John Paul II echoed these words when he spoke of the "hoped-for reciprocity between the rights and duties of the Christian faithful."[66]

In the light of this close connection between rights and the duties of office, the placement of the canons on the removal and transfer of pastors after those on administrative recourse is appropriate. While administrative recourse may be used affirmatively to vindicate and defend rights in the Church, the removal or transfer of pastors is related to the performance of their official duties and obligations. Since the "Christian faithful have the right to receive assistance from the sacred pastors out of the spiritual goods of the Church and the sacraments" (c. 213), it follows that there should be some procedure to remove a

---

[64] A duty or legal obligation is that which one ought or ought not to do. *Duty* and *right* are correlative terms. When a right is invaded, a duty is violated.

[65] Paul VI, "The Function or Juridical Structures in the Life of the Church: Address to the Judges of the Sacred Roman Rota," February 4, 1977, *Acta Apostolici Sedis* 69 (1977): 149.

[66] John Paul II, "The Function of the Sacred Rota Increases through Exemplary Quality of Work Accomplished: Address to the Tribunal of the Sacred Roman Rota," February 26, 1983, *Acta Apostolici Sedis* 75 (1983): 556.

pastor who is not fulfilling this duty or to transfer one whose ministry is badly needed elsewhere.

A Salient Point to Ponder

Dear Joe,[67]

Disaster has struck! In mid-February, I was terminated from my teaching job. It seems the Head of Human Resources from the School was speaking to another employee about how I was a very successful hire for the School. This person—unnamed to me—told the Head of HR something to the effect of, "I can't believe you hired him. You should look at his past." I was fired the next day. The School contends that I misrepresented information on my employment application.

Actually, this is untrue. Our faculty is unionized, and the Union is standing behind me. I have filed a grievance to regain my job, but I do not know if I will go back. I am sure my reputation has been defamed. So, I am back to "square one." This whole mess is an over-reaction to the news going on in Philadelphia, where I am teaching.

Joe, this situation is another "gut punch." How can these lawyers get away with what they are doing? I wish people would think with reason and wisdom and not with emotion. This is so unfair! Why does the world hate me? I am innocent and cannot defend myself. Many want to help, but there is nothing they can do. God help the Church!

Joe, I hope and pray God infuses your movement and work with the mighty impact of Pentecost. But I have to tell you, I am getting to the point where I am too broken to care anymore. Thanks for listening and caring!

Fr. David

---

[67] Joe Maher is the president of *Opus Bono Sacerdotii*, an organization that is championing the cause of priests who have been falsely accused and relegated to a state of "limbo."

Most regrettably, Fr. David, like countless other hapless and helpless priests, was pronounced guilty until proven innocent. This is a blatant violation of the natural, canon, and moral laws, which declare categorically and unequivocally that a person is innocent until proven guilty.[68] With just one stroke of the pen, a gifted and promising priest was declared "accused, convicted and condemned." As a consequence, his reputation was destroyed irretrievably, his prospects for the future marred irreparably, and his priestly morale crushed cruelly and mercilessly. What an abominable injustice! Said Jesus: "Never criticize or condemn—or it will all come back to you. Go easy on others; then they will do the same for you. For if you give, you will get!"[69]

Catharine A. Henningsen once interviewed a pre-eminent canon lawyer and asked one simple question: "What can an accused priest do to clear himself?" He replied, "In the present environment, absolutely nothing!" Ms. Henningsen then pointed out some of the many violations of canon law that she had seen in the church's treatment of accused priests and asked the canon lawyer, "Why aren't the penalties stipulated in canon law being imposed on the bishops who violate the rights of their priests?" And he said to her, "It's not that canon lawyers aren't aware of the abuses. We are. It's because the thugs (sic) are in charge."[70]

That caught her attention, and it is her stated hope that it has caught that of others as well, for, she candidly and courageously says, "I do not believe that the abuse of priests we are seeing now will change until all of us raise our voices to say we will not tolerate abuse in any form. *Voice of the Faithful* has, as one of its goals, the support of priests of integrity. And I'm here to argue that that goal needs to be expanded to support the rights of all priests to due process."[71]

---

[68] Article 11: "Everyone charged with a penal offence has the right to be presumed innocent until proven guilty according to law in a public trial at which he had all the guarantees necessary for his defence" (Universal Declaration of Human Rights, adopted and proclaimed by the General Assembly of the United Nations on December 10, 1948).

[69] Luke 6:37-38.

[70] Catherine Henningsen, "The Second Wave of Abuse: the Fate of our Accused Priests," *Voice of the Faithful* (VOTF) February 5, 2004.

[71] Ibid

Without mincing her words, Ms Henningsen continues:

> I believe that we are witnessing a second wave of abuse on
> the part of many of the bishops and that that abuse is now
> being directed at the priests accused of paedophilia. Across
> the country, priests are disappearing never to be heard from
> again. And their bishops are trampling their legal rights for
> reasons that have little to do with either canon or civil law.
> The abuses I am about to delineate for you are not taking
> place because canon law offers insufficient protection for
> the rights of accused priests, but because our bishops either
> through ignorance or wilfulness, are ignoring canon law.[72]

And she does not stop there.

> I am here today to argue that we cannot substitute the abuse
> of children with the abuse of accused and innocent priests.
> In the abuses I am about to outline for you, I believe you
> will agree that we have arrived at a point in our handling
> of these cases where canon and civil law are being eroded
> to the detriment, and I think diminishment, not only of
> who we are as human beings, but of who we claim to be as
> Christians.[73]

Procurators for Litigation and Advocates (Cc.1481-1490): "If an
Ordinary contemplates either administrative or judicial action against an
accused cleric, he must provide him with a canonical advocate" (c.1481).

> An advocate is a person approved by ecclesiastical authority
> who safeguards the rights of a party in a canonical process by
> arguments regarding the law and the facts. Besides providing
> advice and technical assistance, preparing the evidence, etc.,
> an advocate may be present at the examination of the parties,
> witnesses, and experts (c. 1561), may review the documents

---

[72]   Ibid.

[73]   Ibid.

produced by the parties (c. 1678 §1, 2°), and is, of course, expected to write a brief (c. 1601).

A procurator or proxy is one who, by legitimate mandate, performs judicial business in the name of someone else. Stated differently, the procurator is a representative of the party and is, in effect, the *alter ego* of the party.

In his famous 1944 allocution to the Rota, Pope Pius XII outlined the functions of the advocate and also noted that the advocate "must not withdraw himself from the sole and common final purpose: the discovery, the ascertainment, the legal affirmation of the truth of the objective fact" (CLD—3, 617).[74]

The right to a competent defence is basic to both the civil and canon law systems, yet in many cases, like that of Fr. David, clerics facing disciplinary or penal actions are not advised to obtain the assistance of a canon lawyer, much less provided one.

One of the most noteworthy features of the 1983 Code of Canon Law is the inclusion of listings of the rights and obligations of Christians (e.g. cc.208-231 and 273-289). The identification and articulation of rights are only the first steps toward ensuring that these rights are honoured. Without adequate means of vindicating and defending rights, the effect of recognizing them would be nugatory.

The importance of effective procedures for protecting rights quickly became evident in the early history of the United States. Defending the broad powers given to courts of justice in the new Constitution of the United States, Alexander Hamilton wrote: "Without this all the reservation of particular rights or privileges would amount to nothing."[75]

This realization was not, however, an original discovery of the American Federalists. It had already been recognized by the great medieval canonist,

---

[74] *Canon Law Digest*, ed. T. Bouscaren and J. O'Connor (1975-1986).

[75] A. Hamilton, J. Madison, and J. Jay, *The Federalist: A Commentary on the Constitution of the United States*, 78.

Henry de Susa Cardinal Hostiensis, who observed: "It is of little use to have rights in society unless there is someone to administer justice."[76]

Effective and practical ways must also be provided to pursue claims of injustice in the Church today. Archbishop Zenon Grocholewski, Prefect of the Supreme Tribunal of the Apostolic Signatura, has pointed out: "The proclamation of the rights of the faithful in the Church would be in vain if there were not the possibilities of an adequate defence of such rights."[77] If this is true of the rights of the laity, how much more true should it be of priests, both diocesan and religious?

Protective measures or "prior process" to prevent violations of rights before they occur include confining, structuring and checking authority to help prevent both rigid juridicism and discretionary arbitrariness.[78] Once again, if this is true of the laity, how much more true should it be of priests, both diocesan and religious?

Unfortunately, in an imperfect world, there are no measures that can wholly prevent wrongs from occurring. Accordingly, when harm does happen, Canon 221, §1, states that the "Christian faithful can legitimately vindicate and defend the rights which they possess in the church" before the competent ecclesiastical authority. Having provided this guarantee, the Church must then ensure that its procedures for vindicating rights are effective.

As then-Bishop Joseph L. Bernardin said, when he was general secretary of the United States Catholic Conference and the National Conference of Catholic Bishops:

> In this age when the question of human rights and freedoms
> looms so large in the thinking of people the world over,

---

[76] Quoted in C. Gallagher, *Canon Law and the Christian Community: The Role of Law in the Church According to the Summa Aurea of Cardinal Hostiensis* (Rome: Typis Pontificiae Universitatis Gregorianae, 1978), 162.

[77] Z. Grocholewski, "Aspetti Teologici dell'Attivita Giudiziara della Chiesa," *Il Monitore Ecclesiastico,* Rome 1876-1948; *Monitor Ecclesiasticus,* Rome (1948): 110, (1958): 197.

[78] J. Beal, "Protecting the Rights of Lay Catholics," *The Jurist,* Washington, 47 (1987): 132-133.

surely the Church should exert her leadership by ensuring those rights and freedoms among her own members. We should not be afraid, therefore, to examine closely our legal apparatus to see if it will stand the test of today's needs and aspirations. We must listen to those who insist that our procedures are not adequate. Then, on the basis of actual fact rather than emotion or an effort to prove some preconceived idea, we must decide whether changes are needed and, if so, what kind. Only in this way will the Church's credibility in this area remain intact.[79]

Forty-two years later, this is a morally binding and inescapable imperative for one and all in the Church—the Mystical Body of the Christ—and especially for her priests, both diocesan and religious.

Conclusion

The draft protocols[80] regarding clergy misconduct emphasise two crucial points: first, that the accused cleric immediately seek canonical counsel; and second, if it concerns a criminal offence, he should seek civil counsel before saying or doing anything else. Neither was done when a cleric was abruptly and unceremoniously removed from a posting in a parish.

Second, the draft instructs a cleric: "If you have been accused, your bishop or superior will encourage an atmosphere of mutual courtesy and respect and seek your co-operation with him, and his agents, in dealing with the accusation." [81]

Third, the document *Towards Healing* clearly states "the process is always a serious matter, and the accused cleric's livelihood and reputation are always at stake, even when the allegations themselves may appear trivial." Further, the stated feature article unambiguously reminds a cleric: "You should be aware that the law of the Church and the *Towards Healing*

---

[79] J. Bernardin, "Due Process in the Church," *Homiletic and Pastoral Review* 69 (1969): 756-757.

[80] *The Swag*, "Draft Protocols regarding Clergy Misconduct", April 2011. www.theswag.org

[81] Ibid.

protocols give you certain rights in the process, and you may have to remind the Church authority to respect these rights." [82] This was done only to be met with a veiled threat: "the matter could get 'messy' if it went to the Industrial Court."[83] The cleric had no alternative but to comply under duress.

The stated article recommends: "Carefully choose a support person to accompany you to this meeting (in connection with an allegation). It is best not to attend alone. It is also recommended that you request the details of the accusation in writing." [84] This was flatly denied. A request to seek legal advice was cynically and unscrupulously spurned. The cleric was guilty until proven innocent, which did not happen. In spite of being totally innocent, no apology was proffered to the cleric, nor was he reinstated. The ensuing scandal has alienated both parishioners and non-parishioners, left them frustrated and angry, and shattered the unity and harmony that had earlier served as a powerful witness to the local community.

Finally, the stated article continues: "The accused priest should not resign as Parish Priest, or from any other office, or even step aside, without first having the benefit of canonical advice. The Church authority is required to approve and provide a canonical advisor for you."[85] Once again, this obligation was not met. The cleric was ordered to leave within a week. To add insult to injury, a public announcement was made, so that the unfortunate cleric was subjected to the shame of warped and malicious innuendos. He was totally defenceless and helpless.

Said Fr. Richard John Neuhaus, in a very frank and forthright article entitled "In the Aftermath of Scandal": "The niceties of Canon Law, due process, and elementary decency have in many instances taken a beating. As one cardinal archbishop said after Dallas (2002), it may be necessary for some priests to suffer injustice for the good of the Church. In the course of history, Caiaphas has not been without his defenders."[86]

---

[82] Ibid.

[83] Ibid.

[84] Ibid.

[85] Ibid.

[86] Richard John Neuhaus, "In the Aftermath of Scandal," *First Things* (February 2004): 58-61.

3

An Irrepressible Hunger—An Insatiable Thirst

Blessed are those who hunger and thirst for justice,
they shall have their fill.
—Matthew 5:6

One of the most popular authors of fictional thrillers, who is universally acclaimed as a masterful and captivating novelist, is John Grisham. I have thoroughly enjoyed the few books of his I have personally read. However, the one that made an indelible impact on me was *The Innocent Man*, Grisham's first non-fiction work. In a nutshell, it is the actual story of Ron Williamson, his wrongful conviction for a murder he did not commit, his gruelling and horrific twelve years on death row, and his eventual acquittal.

In 1971, there was a draft for the major league. Ron Williamson was signed with the Oakland A's and bid farewell to his native Ada, Oklahoma. Regrettably a bad arm, addictions and mental health issues shattered his dream and compelled him to return home.

In 1982, a twenty-one-year-old cocktail waitress named Debra Sue Carter was raped and murdered in Ada. In spite of an intensive investigation, no arrests were made, and the case was unresolved. Five years later, Ron Williamson and Dennis Fritz were charged with the murder, despite the lack of any compelling and conclusive physical evidence linking them to the crime. Williamson was convicted and spent twelve harrowing years on death row. He was eventually exonerated just days before his execution, and on the basis of DNA evidence.

Some critics, customarily attuned to Grisham's penchant for mounting suspense and gripping thrillers, have dismissed *The Innocent Man* as boring, slow-moving and far too factual. Said one critic, "I had imagined that he (Grisham) would apply his skill for writing page turning legal suspense to a true story, captivating readers with a tale too amazing to be fiction. Within the first 100 pages of *The Innocent Man*, I knew my expectations would not be met."[87] Another adds, "Grisham's challenge was to build suspense despite readers knowing the outcome of the story from the beginning. Truman Capote mastered this in his classic, *In Cold Blood*. Grisham doesn't even come close."[88]

Nonetheless *The Innocent Man* is a powerful story. The details Grisham provides about incorrect convictions, shoddy police work, and impulsive prosecution certainly make a case for some sort of judicial reform. Perhaps even more compelling is the story of Williamson's mental decline and society's inability to deal with his mental illness. In many ways, Williamson's story, both before and after his imprisonment, is just as tragic as the time he spent on death row. The first critic candidly admits, "I feel bad saying *The Innocent Man* is boring since it is a true and awful story. If you are expecting typical Grisham, though, you will be bored. The writing is detailed, but dry. It is a very straightforward account with no dialogue or suspense."[89]

"Blessed are those who hunger and thirst for justice, they shall have their fill."[90]

An Irrepressible Hunger—An Insatiable Thirst

"Blessed are those who hunger and thirst for justice, they shall have their fill."[91]

As with the words of any great speaker, these too must be interpreted in their proper context. By today's standards and living as we do in times of both prosperity and abundance, those precise words of Jesus may be

---

[87] Book review. www.bestsellers.about.com
[88] Ibid.
[89] Ibid.
[90] Matthew 5:6
[91] Ibid

incomprehensible, even strange. But to his listeners 2,000 years ago, they were both pertinent and poignant.

A working man, the breadwinner of a family, would earn just enough to provide the barest essentials for his family and just for a day. Said William Barclay, a reputed biblical scholar, "A working man's wage was the equivalent of three pence a day, and, even making every allowance for the difference in the purchasing power of money, no man ever got fat on that wage. A working man in Palestine ate meat only once a week, and in Palestine the working man and the day labourer were never far from the border-line of real hunger and actual starvation."[92]

It was still more so in the case of thirst. Today, we have easy access to clean, running water at the mere turning of a tap. Simultaneously, we can carry clean drinking water for ready access at any time and in any place. This certainly was not the case in the days of Jesus. Those were days when scorching heat and turbulent dust storms would compel people to resort to the only safeguard—covering their heads and faces with their shawls and turning their backs against the blinding fury of the swirling dust. As a consequence, their nostrils would be invaded by the suffocating sand, and their throats would be parched with an imperious thirst. At such critical times, the only thing on their minds was finding something to slake their thirst.

Today, a person can very easily satisfy his/her hunger with an inexpensive snack or slake his/her thirst with a cool or hot drink that is both easily and cheaply available on every corner. This was not possible in the days of Jesus. Neither food nor drink was easily available, so that a hungry and thirsty person could collapse either from gnawing starvation or extreme thirst.

Christ Jesus Was Both an Intellectual and an Intelligent Man

As a wise and insightful teacher, Christ Jesus uses the known to lead his listeners to the unknown, to steer them from the earthly to the heavenly, and to raise them from the human to the divine. He said, "Blessed are those who hunger and thirst for justice, they shall have their fill."[93] In other

---

[92] www.bibletools.org
[93] Matthew 5:6

words, Jesus is both posing a question and throwing a challenge: "How eagerly do you desire justice? Do you want it as earnestly as a starving man desires food and a thirsty man craves water? How intense is your desire for true justice?"

Robert Louis Stevenson once spoke of "the malady of not wanting."[94] That is to say, people often are knowingly and intentionally indecisive. They have an instinctive desire for goodness, but that desire is wistful and nebulous, rather than precise and intense. And should an actual opportunity for true goodness be offered them, they will be unwilling to make the necessary effort or personal sacrifice in much the same way as the proverbial cat would like to have the fish without wetting its paws.

And so Jesus very rightly poses the question and challenge: "How very eagerly do you desire true goodness? Is your desire as intense and insistent as food is to the hungry and water is to the thirsty?" The innocent Ron Williamson, in spite of the alleged charge of rape and murder, his declining mental health, and his impending execution, literally yearned both for justice and freedom. And who would dare to guarantee him either—or better still, both?

In every human being, there is an irrepressible desire for justice and an insatiable quest for a fair deal. Robert Louis Stevenson once spoke of even those who had sunk to the lowest depths as "clutching the remnants of virtue in the brothel and on the scaffold."[95] In other words, even though a person may be well aware of his/her moral turpitude or an incriminating offence, he/she secretly knows what is right and earnestly wishes that he/she had done it instead.

This is why Sir Norman Birkett, a famous lawyer and judge, spoke of "the inextinguishable in every man."[96] And he said this after listening to the innumerable heart-rending stories that compelled seemingly good people to become convicted criminals. So even the worst of men are "condemned to some kind of nobility." And goodness, "the implacable hunter," is always at their heels.

---

[94] Stevenson, R.L. *The Master of Ballantrae*, "IX Mr Mackellor's Journey with the Master".

[95] Ibid: *Across the Plains*, "II Pulvis at Umbria".

[96] Quoted by William Barclay. www.cconline.faithsite.com

"Every saint has had a past—every sinner has a future."

The true wonder of man is not that he is a sinner, but that even in his sinfulness, he is haunted by goodness and that even while wallowing in the mud, he can never refrain from wholly forgetting the stars. In the book of 1 Kings, we read that David always wished that he could build the Temple of God—a cherished ambition that was never actually realized. As a matter of fact, it was both denied and forbidden him. But God said to him, "You did well to consider building a house for my name; nevertheless you shall not build the house, but your son, who shall be born to you, shall build the house to my name."[97] In a word, God judges us not only by our achievements but also by our dreams. "Blessed are those who hunger and thirst for justice, they shall have their fill."[98] In God's unfathomable goodness and divine providence, a person who earnestly desires to pursue what is right and just will be unfailingly blessed.

Finally, the rich significance of this beatitude lies in a closer examination of the text in Greek. It is a rule of Greek grammar that verbs of *hungering* and *thirsting* are followed by the genitive case. The genitive case, as is well known, signifies possession, and, in English, is expressed by the word *of* (e.g., "the hat of the man," or "the bag of the woman").

Stated differently, the genitive that follows the verbs of *hungering* and *thirsting* in Greek is called the *partitive genitive* or the *genitive of the part*. So, for example, *hungering for* can be translated, "I hunger for of bread," which means "I hunger for a part of the bread, not the whole loaf." Similarly, *thirsting for* can be translated "I thirst for of water," which means "I thirst for some of the water or a drink of water, but not all the water in the tank."

But in this beatitude, most unusually, *righteousness or justice* is in the direct accusative, and not in the normal genitive. Now, when verbs of *hungering* and *thirsting* in Greek take the accusative instead of the genitive, the meaning is that the hunger and the thirst is for the whole thing. So to say "I hunger for bread" (in the accusative) means "I want the whole loaf, so intense is my hunger." And to say, "I thirst for water" (in the accusative)

---

[97] 1 Kings. 8:18
[98] Matthew 5:6

means "I want the whole pitcher of water and not just a part of it, so insatiable is my thirst."

"Blessed are those who hunger and thirst for the whole of justice or complete righteousness, they shall have their fill" [99]—a complete satisfaction, no less.

And so, this beatitude can be rightly translated: "O the bliss of the man who longs for total righteousness (justice) as a starving man longs for food, and a man perishing of thirst longs for water, that man will be truly satisfied!"

A Scandalous Miscarriage of Justice

Fr. Lance was appointed as pastor by his bishop. Though initially apprehensive, the dutiful priest submitted in obedience. No profile or preliminary instructions were issued by the bishop to better prepare the appointee for his new assignment. His predecessor was equally evasive, so that the new incumbent had to literally "walk by faith and not by sight."[100]

Over the first two years, the new pastor was amazed to see how deficient the catechetical instruction in the local parish school was. The candidates for the Sacraments of Reconciliation, the Eucharist and Confirmation were blissfully ignorant and inadequately prepared. The situation was further compounded by the fact that the majority of both staff and students were not Christian. So, to all intents and purposes, the sole Catholic members on the staff were the principal and the religious education coordinator (REC).

As a conscientious pastor, Fr. Lance conferred with the REC. Her grounding in the Catholic faith was elementary and, by her own admission, she was ill-suited for the position but constrained to accept it by sheer force of circumstances. Very sincerely, Fr. Lance offered to extend his fullest co-operation.

At his request, the REC rather reluctantly produced the curriculum for religious instruction in the school. It was issued by the Catholic Education Office (CEO). The presentation was voluminous and impressive, but the

---

[99] Matthew 5:6
[100] 2 Corinthians 5:7.

31

content was, to say the least, very abstract and suspect. If a tree is known by its fruit, then the current curriculum was certainly not producing the desired results. If out of the abundance of the heart, the mouth speaks, the current curriculum was a dismal failure. And if a good person brings good things out of a good treasure, then the current curriculum was certainly a sharp disappointment.[101]

For one thing, it was far from intelligible to Fr. Lance. How much more, then, to the members of the staff, who enjoyed no grounding in the Catholic faith whatsoever, and who even had no religious affiliation? "And everyone who hears these words of mine and does not act on them will be like a foolish man who built his house on sand. The rain fell, and the floods came, and the winds blew and beat against that house, and it fell—and great was its fall!"[102]

Fr. Lance expressed his grave concern about the content and the objectives. This was reported to the school Principal, who misconstrued the priest's assessment as a needless interference, and relayed her displeasure to the director of Catholic education. He, in turn, spitefully informed the vicar general and the bishop, both of whom did later come down with a very heavy hand on the dutiful but unsuspecting priest. As a matter of fact, the subsequent conspiratorial malevolence and vindictive intrigue literally defied comprehension. The die, as with the hapless Ron Williamson, had been irreversibly cast.

> At that time Herod the ruler heard reports about Jesus; and he said to his servants, "This is John the Baptist; he has been raised from the dead, and for this reason these powers are at work in him." For Herod had arrested John, bound him, and put him in prison on account of Herodias, his brother Philip's wife, because John had been telling him, "It is not lawful for you to have her." [103]

---

[101]   Matthew 12:33-37.
[102]   Matthew 7:26-27
[103]   Matthew 14:1-4

The Teaching of the Church on Catholic Education

Canon law very clearly and emphatically states that, because of its very nature, catechesis must be found in various elements of Catholic education in general and, in particular, in the formation offered by Catholic schools.[104] Further, the fathers of the Second Vatican Council explicitly indicated the differences among educational formats in general, the content and means of Christian education, and the specific function of Catholic schools.

"Christian education is especially directed toward ensuring that those who have been baptized, as they are gradually introduced to a knowledge of the mystery of salvation, become daily more appreciative of the gift of faith which they have received."[105] The all-important purpose, then, is to ensure that students in a Catholic educational institution will be inspired by the spirit of Christ Jesus and, in turn, serve as the "salt of the earth" and "the light of the world" by actively contributing to the good of society as a whole. And in this regard, the pastor has a very important role to play. As a matter of fact, the obligation of Canon 794 §2 is "to arrange all things so that all the faithful may enjoy a Catholic education."[106]

More precisely, the pastor is called upon by Canon 796 §1 *"to greatly value schools."* This is an explicit obligation, but very generally stated. Further, as a member of the faithful, the pastor would share the same personal obligation as the other faithful. In addition, as pastor of a parish, he is responsible for the Catholic education of all in the parish.[107] In this, Fr. Lance was merely fulfilling his crucial role as an extension of his bishop who "is to have serious pastoral concern for students" of Catholic institutions of education—schools and universities. In a word, "where the diocesan bishop does establish that kind of a parish, the regular canonical obligations and rights of pastors would become the responsibilities and prerogatives of the pastor of such a parish."[108]

---

[104]   Cc. 528 §1; 793 §§1–2; 794 §2; 801, 804 §1.

[105]   *Gravissimum educationis,* n. 1.

[106]   C. 794 §2.

[107]   C. 800 §2.

[108]   Edward A. Sweeny, JCD, PhD, *The Obligations and Rights of the Pastor of a Parish—According to the Code of Canon Law* (2002) 87.

As a diligent and hardworking pastor, Fr. Lance was both loved and admired by one and all in his parish. Both Catholics and non-Christians in the region held him in high esteem. This was particularly true of those non-Christian parents whose children were attending the local parish school. However, the poisoned relationship with his bishop kept deteriorating, in spite of repeated attempts to resolve the matter fairly and amicably.

> Though Herod wanted to put John the Baptist to death, he feared the crowd, because they regarded him as a prophet. But when Herod's birthday came, the daughter of Herodias danced before the company, and she pleased Herod so much that he promised on oath to grant her whatever she might ask. Prompted by her mother, she said, "Give me the head of John the Baptist here on a platter."[109]

Official letters, prompted by a genuine pastoral concern, to key members of the Catholic Education Office (CEO) were either ignored or treated with scant respect. No attempts were made to resolve the deteriorating situation and in the best interests of the students and the parish as a whole. "Just as the twig is bent, the tree's inclined."[110]

Letters to the bishop passed unheeded. Later, it was discovered that they were being intercepted; the person responsible confessed it in an unguarded moment.

"A bishop should always welcome priests with a special love since they assume in part the bishop's duties and cares and carry the weight of them day by day so zealously. He should regard his priests as sons and friends." [111]

The innocent and conscientious Fr. Lance was accused, convicted, and condemned. His repeated and earnest attempts to resolve the impasse were spurned and rejected. Never again did he enjoy the position of pastor. Blacklisted by the CEO, he was never permitted to serve as chaplain to any Catholic school in the diocese. *Justice delayed was justice denied!*

---

[109] Matthew 14:5-8

[110] Alexander Pope. "To Lord Cobham", in *Epistles to Several Persons.* 1734. See also, Proverbs 615.5

[111] Vatican II, Decree to Bishops #16b.

"*Et tu, Brute!* Then fall, Caesar!"[112]

> The king (Herod) was grieved, yet out of regard for his oaths and for the guests, he commanded it (the head of John the Baptist) to be given (on a silver platter as desired by Herodias). He sent and had John beheaded in the prison. The head was brought on a platter and given to the girl, who brought it to her mother.[113]

"Cowards die many times before their deaths; the valiant never taste of death but once."[114]

A Pastoral Imperative

> Canon 528 §1 very clearly and unequivocally states:

> The Pastor has the obligation of ensuring that the word of God is proclaimed in its entirety to those living in the parish. He is, therefore, to see to it that the lay members of Christ's faithful are instructed in the truths of the faith, especially by means of the homily on Sundays and holydays of obligation and by catechetical formation . . . He is to have special care for the Catholic Education of children and young people.

More precisely, this canon establishes the following:

- A pastor is a teacher to those entrusted to his pastoral care.
- His duty is to bring the Gospel message to all those living in the parish.
- He has a special obligation to reach those who have given up the practice of the faith.
- This he does by two forms of proclaiming God's word: preaching and teaching.

---

[112] Shakespeare, *Julius Caesar*, act 3, scene 1, line 77.

[113] Matthew 14:9-11

[114] Shakespeare, *Julius Caesar*, act 2, scene 2, line 32.

- For this, he must enlist the support of others—especially lay people.
- In particular, he has a positive duty to facilitate the provision of Catholic schools and to ensure, so far as he can, that they are, in fact, available for all the people of the parish.

Catholic Education

Canon 793 §1 unambiguously states that "Catholic parents have also the duty and the right to choose those means and institutes which, in their local circumstances, can best promote the Catholic Education of their children." This was denied Fr. Lance and, as a consequence, his Catholic parishioners. "Pastors of souls have the duty of making all possible arrangements so that all the faithful may avail themselves of a Catholic Education."[115] *Parents, after all, are the first educators of their children.* "Since parents have conferred life on their children, they have a most solemn obligation to educate their offspring. Hence, parents must be acknowledged as the first and foremost educators of their children."[116]

Fr. Lance's local parish school had much earlier been established by the pastor, who enlisted the services of a congregation of women religious, with the official approval of the diocesan bishop. As such, and by Canon 801, the CEO and the local administration had the duty "to keep faithfully to the stated mission and to earnestly strive to devote themselves to Catholic Education." This is the essential and all-important mission of every Catholic school.

In this regard, neither the CEO nor the local administration is autonomous. Canon 804 §1 expressly states: "The formation and education in the Catholic religion provided in any school, and through various means of social communication, is subject to the authority of the Church. It is for the Bishops' Conference to issue general norms concerning this field of activity and for the diocesan bishop to regulate and watch over it." Fr. Lance was on an official assignment as pastor, and he had been commissioned by none other than his bishop, who negligently failed to effectively support him in the exercise of his pastoral duty.

---

[115] Canon 794 §2.

[116] Decree on Education, Vatican II, #3.

Further, Canon 803 §2 explicitly enjoins that "Instruction and education in a Catholic School must be based on the principles of Catholic doctrine, and the teachers must be outstanding in true doctrine and uprightness of life." It stands to reason that a teacher is employed on the basis of his/her academic qualifications, expertise, competence and experience and with the specific purpose of teaching an assigned subject. Why, then, should the teaching of the Catholic doctrine in a Catholic school be an exception?

Canon 794 §2 unequivocally reminds pastors of souls of their duty to make all possible arrangements, so that all the faithful may avail themselves of a Catholic education. Even more, Canon 794 §1 reminds one and all that the Church has, in a very special way, the duty and the right of educating, for it has the divine mission of helping all to arrive at the fullness of Christian life. So the duty of pastors of souls is to do all in their power to provide for a Catholic education that corresponds to the right of the faithful to an authentically Christian formation. To this, Fr. Lance was devotedly and consistently true.

Finally, Canon 800 §2 directs Christ's faithful to promote Catholic schools, doing everything possible to help in establishing and maintaining them. This had been done by generations before Fr. Lance. As a pastor, canonically appointed by his bishop, he was merely perpetuating a well-established tradition in accordance with the stipulations of canon law, the teachings of the Catholic Church, and his unswerving commitment to his priestly vocation and pastoral ministry.

"Everyone then who hears these words of mine and acts on them will be like a wise man who built his house on rock. The rain fell, the floods came, and the winds blew and beat on that house, but it did not fall, because it had been founded on rock."[117]

The Priestly Ministry and Vatican II

"All priests, both diocesan and religious, participate in and exercise with the bishop the one priesthood of Christ Jesus and are thereby meant to be prudent co-operators of the Episcopal order. In securing the welfare of souls, however, the first place is held by diocesan priests who . . . dedicate

---

[117] Matthew 7:24-25

themselves to its service by way of pasturing a single portion of the Lord's flock."[118] This was Fr. Lance's prime and consistent objective, in dutiful obedience to his bishop, who expressly appointed him as parish priest.

The fundamental flaw that precipitated the unfortunate and disruptive crisis was a mistaken notion of the theology of the priesthood. The *Catechism of the Catholic Church* very clearly states that the ministerial or hierarchical priesthood of bishops and priests and the common priesthood of all the faithful participate "each in its own proper way, in the one priesthood of Christ."[119] While being "ordered to one another," they differ essentially.[120]

In what sense? While the common priesthood of the faithful is exercised by the unfolding of baptismal grace . . . *the ministerial priesthood is at the service of the common priesthood.* The ministerial priesthood is a *means* by which Christ Jesus unceasingly builds up and leads his Church. For this reason, it is transmitted by its own sacrament, the sacrament of Holy Orders.[121] A persistent refusal by members of the school staff and the CEO to acknowledge this essential difference, and the baffling failure of the bishop to intervene authoritatively, marred every possibility of a fruitful dialogue and harmonious relationship with the pastor and the local parishioners. The damage done was irreparable.

"The function of the bishops' ministry was handed over in a subordinate degree to priests so that they might be appointed in the order of the priesthood and be co-workers of the Episcopal order for the fulfillment of the apostolic mission that had been entrusted to it by Christ Jesus."[122]

---

[118] Vatican II, Decree on the Bishops' Pastoral Office in the Church (Christus Dominus), #28.

[119] LG 10 §1.

[120] LG 10 §2.

[121] CCC §1547.

[122] PO §2.

4

Justice Delayed Is Justice Denied

Polonius: What do you read, my lord?
Hamlet: Words, words, words.
—Shakespeare, *Hamlet*, act 2, scene 2, line 195

In 2002, the United States Conference of Catholic Bishops (USCCB)[123] issued a document entitled *Essential Norms for Diocesan / Eparchial Policies Dealing with Allegations of Sexual Abuse of Minors by Priests and Deacons*.[124] This charter is a reaction to a crisis in the Church, namely the sexual abuse of children by clergy.

A Psychiatrist's Observation

Dr. Donald Ruedinger, MD, MDiv, is a retired psychiatrist, who has worked extensively with priests and has been a consultant to several bishops and religious superiors on these issues for over 35 years. It is his candid opinion that the implementation and interpretation of the charter has significantly undermined any trust between priests and bishops or their religious superiors. And the reason is patently clear: "In many cases, due process has not been followed and many priests have been basically abandoned by their bishops."[125]

---

[123] www.usccb.org
[124] Ibid.
[125] www.justiceforpriests.org

"Even more," continues Dr. Ruedinger, "many bishops seem to overreact out of anger, frustration and/or fear. Given the difficult task of balancing justice for the victim and the priest this might be understandable, but never excusable. Once an allegation has been filed against a priest, he would be foolish to put his trust in his bishop to protect his rights. Many priests have realized this too late."[126]

A second very serious concern, according to Dr. Ruedinger, is the creeping and expanding interpretation of what constitutes sexual abuse. So, for instance, allegations that should be considered sexual harassment or boundary violations are being treated as if they were sexual abuse. One primary school principal, for instance, was dismissed because he had shared some suggestive photographs over the Internet with a selected group of recipients. What began as an innocent, though imprudent, prank ended disastrously. A female recipient showed the pictures to a friend, who found them supposedly inappropriate and offensive. Her report was entertained and the principal dismissed when, in reality, a firm reprimand, issued confidentially would have been more appropriate and satisfactory. For one thing, it was not an instance of sexual abuse in the strict sense of the term. Something similar could happen to a priest or religious, with far-reaching and irreversible results. "But if you had known what this means, 'I desire mercy and not sacrifice,' you would not have condemned the guiltless." [127]

Consequently, much clearer definitions of sexual abuse must be adhered to by bishops, counselling centres and facilities that evaluate priests. *This is the principal reason why Dr. Ruedinger emphatically urges priests to insist on getting the allegations in writing, and with all the details possible. No vagueness should be allowed, much less be part of a decision.*

A third grave concern, according to Dr. Ruedinger, is the impulsive leap from "a credible allegation" to "a presumption of guilt."[128] As is well known, almost all allegations appear sound and credible when they are presented. For instance, allegations of bullying can be irresponsibly and unscrupulously bandied by individuals who wish to reinforce a complaint

---

[126] Ibid.

[127] Matthew 12:7

[128] www.justiceforpriests.org

against a priest. The situation is even more complex when the supposed victim is a female and shrewdly manipulates it "to cry wolf."

Dr. Ruedinger very wisely adds a precautionary note: "Many alleged victims have had professional help and advice on how to make their allegations sound credible."[129] Regrettably, once an allegation is deemed credible, then the charter initiates what can only be perceived by the priest as punitive actions. He is "temporarily" removed from the active ministry. This is a slur that will remain permanently attached to his name no matter the outcome of the investigation. Ironically, the burden of proof rests with the hapless priest; he has the odious, complex, and protracted task of proving that the allegations are untrue. In a word, he is guilty until proven innocent—if ever!

On his blog *These Stone Walls*, Fr. Gordon MacRae[130] relates the heart-rending story of James "Jamie" Bain—yet another grim reminder of the flawed assumption of guilty until proven innocent—if ever! In a Florida courtroom in 1974, 19-year-old Jamie Bain was sentenced to life in prison for kidnapping and raping a nine-year-old boy. It was a heinous crime, and Jamie endured gruesome treatment in prison because of it.

Thirty-five years passed. Then, a week before Christmas, Jamie walked out of a Florida courtroom a free man, after it was proven that he had no connection whatsoever to the crime. He had turned 54 in prison.

DNA evidence preserved from the crime scene absolutely excluded Jamie Bain as a suspect in the crime. For 35 years, the real criminal walked free, while Jamie suffered decades of being labelled a child rapist in prison. On the steps of the courthouse, after his chains were removed, he faced a small group of family and reporters. He asked to be taken home to his 77-year-old mother. She was 42 when Jamie was taken off to prison. He also asked for a Dr. Pepper. It had been 35 years.

Across the nation, 247 wrongfully convicted prisoners have been released after preserved DNA evidence proved that the wrong person was serving the prison sentence. Most were convicted of sexual assault, and many served **20 years or more** in prison before being exonerated.

---

[129] Ibid.

[130] www.GordonMacRae.net, *These Stone Walls: Musings from Prison of a Priest Falsely Accused.*

In the case of Jamie Bain, the sole evidence against him was an eyewitness identification by the traumatized nine-year-old victim of the awful crime. The boy described his attacker's bushy sideburns. His uncle, a high school principal at the time, said, "That sounds like Jamie Bain."[131] That was all it took. When a photo lineup was placed before the boy, he picked out Jamie Bain. Now, 35 years later, there are lingering questions about how much police detectives steered the boy toward that photo.

The most sordid aspect of this story is the behaviour of prosecutors long after the trial. Multiple petitions to have the DNA evidence re-tested were thrown out of court when prosecutors vehemently opposed them. The Innocence Project got involved with their own attorneys and, finally, the DNA was tested. A prosecutor conceded to the judge that Jamie Bain had no connection to this crime.

"I'm not angry," Jamie Bain said on the courthouse steps. "I've got God."[132] I'd say it's the other way around. God's got Jamie Bain. What else could have preserved his soul and his mind for 35 years of mistreatment in prison?

Yet Another Heartbreaking Travesty—the Story of Bernard Baran[133]

In addition to the 247 men exonerated by re-tested DNA evidence, there are also exonerations, when no real crime was ever committed at all. In June of 2010, a Berkshire County, Massachusetts, judge announced that all charges were being dropped against Bernard Baran, who also went to trial for child rape at the age of 19. He was released at the age of 44, after spending 24 years in prison for a crime that now appears never to have taken place at all. The judge who released him declared that Bernard's lawyer at trial was incompetent, and prosecutors withheld crucial evidence of Bernard's innocence.

That evidence consisted of videotapes of interviews with the child "victims." The tapes showed them insisting that no sexual assaults ever

---

[131] Ibid.
[132] Ibid.
[133] Gordon MacRae, *These Stone Walls: Musings from Prison of a Priest Falsely Accused.*

took place, while interrogators kept asking the same questions over and over, until the children changed their story. All the children's denials were edited out of the tapes before they were presented to Bernard's defence lawyer—and to the jury.

Bernard Baran was himself raped and beaten during his more than two decades of wrongful imprisonment. The National Center for Reason and Justice[134] sponsored Bernard Baran's new appeals and helped win his release. The NCRJ also sponsors the defence of Fr. MacRae, and he is most grateful for their advocacy. He highly recommends spending some time at their website and at a new related blog, *Friends of Justice*.

Sometimes, the prosecutorial misconduct in sexual abuse cases is just a subtle form of "spin." In one now thoroughly discredited sexual abuse case that has been widely written about—the Massachusetts case against the Amirault family—the spectre of child pornography rose to the surface. When not a shred of evidence for it was found, the prosecutor said to the news media, "the fact that child pornography wasn't found doesn't mean it never existed."[135] So, *the absence of evidence is evidence of evidence!*

The Inefficacy of Mediation Processes

Unfortunately, mediating persons prove ineffective, principally because they align themselves with the bishops and religious superiors. "They seem to have lost their objectivity in the search for the truth," avers Dr. Ruedinger, "or they have been afraid to keep their recommendations in line with the results of their evaluations."

Reportedly in one instance, nothing definite could be proved against a priest even after intense interrogation of the complainant, the defendant and the witnesses. Nevertheless, neither the agency nor the mediator made an objective report, which had been explicitly pledged to the defendant. *What is even more disturbing is the fact that the mediator even failed to explain why she was unable to abide by her given assurance—a blatant breach of trust and professional integrity.* The agency had been employed by the bishop and duly paid, and *that is all that eventually mattered!*

---

[134] www.ncrj.org
[135] Gordon MacRae. Op.cit.

> No one can serve two masters; for a slave will either hate the
> one and love the other, or be devoted to the one and despise
> the other. You cannot serve God and wealth.[136]

The agency purportedly is committed to the highest ethical standards of truth and justice!

Writing in an issue of *The Swag*, a quarterly magazine of the National Council of Priests of Australia, Susan O'Connor, the director of the Office for Employment Relations, has entitled her article: "Workplace Bullying—There's Just No Place for It." [137]

Among her recommendations, she wisely advises:

- Do not wait until someone reports bullying. If you see it, act on it.
- Non-victimisation—Ensure that anyone who raises issues of bullying is not going to be victimised. The person about whom the complaint is made as well as any witnesses must also be protected from victimisation.
- Neutrality—Remain impartial through the investigation process.
- Communication (of process and outcomes)—Keep all parties involved informed on the process and the outcomes.
- *Confidentiality—An accusation of bullying can be potentially defamatory, especially if confidentiality is not observed and a person's reputation unjustly damaged. Discussions, information and records related to complaints should remain factual and confidential.*[138]
- Documentation—All formal investigations should be documented. Records of all informal investigations should also be maintained.[139]

---

[136] Matthew 6:24
[137] *The Swag*, Vol.18, No.2—Winter 2010, p.34
[138] Ibid. Emphasis added.
[139] Ibid.

A Gross Miscarriage of Justice

The following distressing report by Daniel Burke ever strikingly illustrates the woeful state of priests who are wrongly accused, publicly maligned, and unjustly punished, with no qualms of conscience whatsoever. The caption reads: "Accused Catholic priests left in limbo." [140]

Somewhere in the Vatican, there is a thick file with the Rev. James Selvaraj's name on it. It's been there since 2006.

A native of southern India, Selvaraj was a guest priest in the Diocese of Trenton, New Jersey, when he was accused of endangering the welfare of a child in late 2005. Shortly thereafter, Trenton Bishop John Smith removed Selvaraj from ministry.

Within three months, a grand jury declined to indict the priest, citing insufficient evidence. New Jersey's attorney general expunged the charge from Selvaraj's record.

But more than four years after secular authorities exonerated Selvaraj, Smith and the Vatican have refused to restore his salary, priestly duties, or—most important, Selvaraj says—his reputation.

"I am really angry, really furious," said Selvaraj, a slight 50-year-old with a friendly demeanour. "This is what happens to an innocent priest?"

The Catholic Church has been castigated in recent months for moving slowly to remove abusers from the priesthood. Pope Benedict XVI himself, while he was a cardinal in charge of a Vatican office that handled abusive clergy, stalled for years before moving to defrock serial child molesters in the United States, according to documents recently made public.

But the Vatican moves just as slowly, if not slower, to return innocent clergy to ministry, according to priests and canon lawyers. Meanwhile, priests like Selvaraj live for years in a state of limbo, evicted from parishes and rectories, prohibited from presenting themselves as clerics or administering sacraments, and branded all but guilty in the public eye.

As many as 300 American priests claim innocence and are waiting for the Vatican to restore them to duty, according to the Rev. Michael Sullivan, a Minnesota priest and member of Justice for Priests and Deacons, an independent group of canon lawyers who defend Catholic clergy.

---

[140] Daniel Burke, *National Catholic Reporter*, 6 May, 2010. Religion News Service. May 5, 2010.

Among such priests, Selvaraj is fortunate. Former parishioners have stood by him, raising $70,000 to pay living expenses and legal fees, offering him places to stay, and inviting him to perform occasional private Masses. The diocese pays his health and car insurance, Selvaraj says.

But other priests aren't so lucky, said Joe Maher, executive director of *Opus Bono Sacerdotii*, a Michigan-based support group for accused priests. "I know priests who are living out of hotels, eating one meal a day," he said.

Many priests say they recognize the difficulty of the Vatican's task—most allegations concern decades-old events, making it hard to determine guilt or innocence, and the Vatican has relatively few employees to process the thousands of accusations that surfaced after the sex abuse scandal exploded in 2002. Meanwhile, no bishop wants a priest to abuse children on his watch.

But some priests say the get-tough rules approved by U.S. bishops in 2002 swing the pendulum too far in the other direction, trampling their rights to due process and good reputations. Where once abuse victims were silenced and sacrificed for the sake of the Church, they say, now innocent priests are overlooked casualties of the crisis.

"The way the bishops once treated victims, that's the way they treat priests now," said the Rev. Michael Maginot, an Indiana priest and canon lawyer who is representing Selvaraj. "They are willing to throw any priest under the bus."

"It Can Be Done"

At the height of the crisis in 2002, U.S. bishops vowed to act quickly on "credible" accusations of abuse of a minor by immediately removing the priest from his parish and informing the public and local authorities of the charge.

Priests say an announcement that a priest has been suspended is often tantamount to a guilty verdict in the public and the pews. Selvaraj's removal was front-page news in the local paper. "The media crucified me," he said. His father had to undergo heart surgery after he read the news in India, Selvaraj said.

Canon law says Catholics have the right to privacy and a good reputation. But the U.S. bishops and victims' advocates say the sex abuse guidelines are necessary to protect children and are no stricter than in other occupations where employees are placed on temporary leave when a crime is suspected.

False accusations are rare, according to a 2004 study conducted by the John Jay College of Criminal Justice. Just 1.5 per cent of 5,681 sex abuse allegations lodged against Catholic priests from 1950 to 2002 were deemed false after investigations. *Clergy advocates say bogus accusations ballooned after 2002, especially after victims began receiving large monetary settlements.*

In 2009, 21 allegations of child sex abuse were made against Catholic priests, according to a report conducted for the U.S. Bishops' Conference. Four were determined to be unfounded, one accusation was recanted, and eight are still under investigation.

If a priest is falsely accused, the bishops' guidelines say that every effort should be made to restore his reputation, said Teresa Kettelkamp, executive director of the U.S. Bishops' Abuse Prevention office.

"It's nearly impossible," she said, like pouring feathers out a pillow from the top of a mountain and trying to collect them, "but it can be done."

"For instance, the bishop could say Mass with the priest and use his homily to talk about how the allegation was unfounded, or he could meet with the local media to get the word out," Kettelkamp said. "Anything he can do to show his support for the priest." For instance, on March 7, 2004, jubilant parishioners assembled in St. Francis de Sales Church, in Troy, New York, to greet their priest, Rev. Donald Ophals, who had been exonerated of charges of sexual abuse after nearly a year.[141]

"After the grand jury exonerated me, Smith did none of that," Selvaraj said. Instead, Smith tried to pack the priest off to India.

"We Have Nothing Further to Add"

Selvaraj was popular in Trenton, where he was sent in 1999 by his Indian bishop to gain experience. He liked the diocese, and officials

---

[141] Stephen J. Rolsetti, "Post-Crisis Morale among Priests," *America*, 191, no. 6:8-10. Fr. Rosetti is the president of St. Luke Institute in Silver Springs, Maryland. He is a psychologist and consultant to the U.S. Catholic Bishops' ad hoc Committee on Child Sexual Abuse.

convinced him in May 2005 to apply to be "incardinated"—formally accepted as a permanent priest, in Trenton.

Four months later, Selvaraj was visiting an after-school program run by his parish, St. Raphael-Holy Angels, in Hamilton, New Jersey, when he took an 11-year-old girl's hand and helped her write her name in Tamil, his native language, on a blackboard.

An adult eyewitness—a close friend of the girl and her mother—swore in a deposition that she stood inches away and saw Selvaraj do nothing wrong. The girl's mother was "over-protective of the child," the witness said and was disgusted that the church "always brings us Puerto Ricans, blacks and Indians" as priests.

The mother accused Selvaraj of molesting her daughter. Diocesan attorneys encouraged the priest to make a deal with prosecutors and return to India, Selvaraj recalls. Instead, he decided to stay and fight. Hours before he was arraigned on December 1, 2005, Smith told Selvaraj that he would never again be a priest in the Diocese of Trenton, the priest recalls. "My life was ruined," he said.

After the grand jury exonerated Selvaraj, Smith refused to take him back. Instead, he wrote a letter telling parishioners at St. Raphael-Holy Angels that Selvaraj would be sent back to India. More than 650 parishioners signed a petition asking Smith to reinstate Selvaraj, said long-time parishioner, Lou Monticchio. Smith refused.

In a letter to Selvaraj's canon lawyer, Smith said the priest had done nothing to warrant "even the preliminary investigation." The decision to send Selvaraj back to India was not a penalty, Smith said, but a precaution.

"Because of his overly friendly personality he has been warned on several occasions to be cautious concerning outward signs of friendship and affection toward young people," the bishop wrote. "Our contemporary national culture and particularly the present church situation demand such caution. Father James does not seem to fully understand these cautions and their implications."

Selvaraj said he was never warned about his conduct with young people. Asked for clarification about Smith's decision, diocesan spokeswoman Rayanne Bennett said, "We are confident that the process undertaken in this matter was appropriate and handled in a just and responsible way toward all parties involved. We have nothing further to add."

"No Justice, No Truth"

Priests have little recourse to challenge bishops' actions, clergy say.

Some priests have sued their bishops in civil courts for defamation, invasion of privacy, or intentional affliction of emotional distress after they were removed from ministry. But citing church-state separation, secular judges have been wary of wading into clergy personnel matters.

Other priests, like Selvaraj, have turned to the Vatican for help, only to be frustrated by bureaucratic delays, ambiguous responses and a lack of transparency about the appeal process.

Selvaraj began writing to the Vatican in 2006, asking the Congregation for the Doctrine of the Faith (CDF) to force Smith to reinstate the priest's ministry, salary and good name. "I want him to restore my dignity," the priest said, "so wherever I go this won't haunt me."

For nearly three years, Selvaraj got no response. Maginot, his canon lawyer, believes the CDF decided Selvaraj's case during that time, but only informed Smith of the ruling, which the bishop buried in a file. "The problem is, they never communicate with us," Maginot said of the CDF. "If they gave us a copy of what they give the bishop, they could never get away with this."

Selvaraj and Maginot kept writing appeals—to the CDF, the Vatican's supreme court, and finally, to Benedict himself. A top Vatican secretary responded by telling Selvaraj to take the case "to the competent Roman dicastery"—in other words, back to the CDF, the office that had failed to return his correspondence.

Finally, in December 2008, Smith sent Selvaraj a letter from the CDF saying that, because Selvaraj was not yet incardinated in Trenton, the bishop does not have to allow him to be a priest in his diocese. According to a copy of the letter provided by Selvaraj, the CDF also said that, because the sex abuse charge was unfounded, there was nothing for them to review. The letter said nothing about restoring Selvaraj's name or salary.

Selvaraj has appealed again to the CDF. In the meantime, he dons a cleric's collar at private Masses or when counselling former parishioners, but he is not permitted to present himself publicly as a priest—the only vocation he's ever known. Selvaraj says his faith in God remains strong, though his faith in the Catholic Church wavers.

"Before I started this case, I had great hope and faith that Rome would take the side of truth and justice and produce a decision," Selvaraj said. "Now, I see the politics all around the church. There is no justice, no truth."

Returning to the article by Susan O'Connor, the director informs us that, by common law, an employer has a duty of care. This was incumbent on Bishop John Smith of Trenton, as it is on every bishop.[142]

Should the employer "reasonably foresee" the risk of harm to the employee and do nothing to prevent it, the employee may bring a civil law claim in tort for negligence. Of this, Bishop Smith is clearly liable even if he adamantly refuses to have Fr. James Selvaraj reinstated. "With sympathetic understanding and practical help, the bishops should take care of priests who are in danger of any kind or who have failed in some way" (Decree on Bishops, Vatican II, #16). As the local Ordinary, Bishop Smith enjoys the prerogative to have the priest incardinated in the diocese or not, even though the former would have been the most effective move to undo the pervasive scandal and colossal harm. Said Fr. Michael Sullivan, JCL, a priest of the Archdiocese of St. Paul, Minneapolis, Minnesota: "The abuse of power is driving a wedge between bishops and priests."

Fr. Michael Sullivan continues:

When a bishop shows an abuse of power he is attacking the basis of all human rights and integrity. When used against a cleric, he is attacking one of the most defenceless of all people in the church . . . If there is no effort to ascertain the truth of an accusation or to ask for facts that are verifiable, then the bishops are opening themselves up to false accusations simply because people are seeking free money at the expense of the cleric. Such a false denunciation is a canonical crime (Canon 1390 §3) and reparation can be required.[143]

---

[142]   Susan O'Connor (Director, Office of Employment Relations), "Workplace Bullying—There's Just No Place for It". March 2010., *The Swag*, Spring 2011.

[143]   Michael Sullivan. *justiceforpriests.org/pdf* January 2010.

Toward the end of the Rite of Sacerdotal Ordination, the ordinand kneels before the ordaining prelate, places his hands in those of the bishop, and trustfully promises both respect and obedience to the prelate and his successors. In other words, while committing himself to the service of God and his people in a certain diocese and under the pastoral leadership of the bishop, a priest is entering into a bilateral agreement in which both parties have their rights and duties. A deliberate failure to honour this mutual agreement by either party is not only a breach of trust, but a violation of a binding contractual agreement and, therefore, morally wrong. And this mutual bond persists undimmed and unchanged even when a priest serves in a diocese other than his own.

The Decree on Priestly Life and Ministry from the Second Vatican Council expressly says: "All priests share with the bishops the one identical priesthood and ministry of Christ. On account of this common sharing in the same priesthood and ministry, then bishops are to regard their priests as brothers and friends and are to take the greatest interest they are capable of in their welfare both temporal and spiritual." Stated differently, while, on the one hand, bishops must certainly protect the laity in the diocese, on the other, *they must also protect their priests and deacons for these are the men who are the visible face of the bishop in parishes and other ministries.* If a priest cannot turn to his own bishop as a compassionate, supportive, and caring father and friend, then what is his next option?

With a sharp decrease in vocations to the priesthood and religious life in the Western world and dwindling numbers of those in the pastoral ministry, it isn't uncommon for dioceses to invite priests from countries that can afford to share their priestly personnel. This is consonant with the precise directives of the fathers of the Second Vatican Council: "The spiritual gift which priests received at their ordination prepares them not for any limited and narrow mission but for the widest scope of the universal mission of salvation 'even to the very ends of the earth.' Hence priests belonging to dioceses which are rich in vocations should show themselves willing and ready, with the permission or at the urging of their own bishop, to exercise their ministry in other regions" (Decree on Priests #10).

And this missionary thrust was ordained by none other than the Supreme High Priest, Christ Jesus, "the Shepherd and Bishop of our souls who so constituted His Church that the people whom He chose and purchased by his blood would be due to have its priests always to the end of time" (Decree on Priests #11).

So when a priest leaves his diocese in order to serve another with the sanction of his own bishop and the official reception of another bishop, it stands to reason that he is duly prepared for his ministry and clearly informed of the pastoral expectations of the people he is assigned to serve, the special challenges of his given ministry, the support he can count on—personal, financial, medical, social, and pastoral—and the boundaries within which he can work effectively. And once again, the most trustworthy friend of this priest should be his bishop, who can extend his paternal care either personally or through a nominated and responsible delegate. As the saying goes, "Forewarned is forearmed."

Further, the Fair Work Act, adds Ms. O'Connor, prohibits an unfair or unlawful dismissal.[144]

In view of the fair and thorough investigation of the alleged case against Fr. James Selvaraj and the unanimous declaration of his innocence, the bishop has violated the principles of natural justice and pastoral charity in refusing to duly reinstate the priest. The high esteem in which the priest was and continues to be generally held clearly indicates that he was and still is both respected and trusted. Consequently, a public statement like the following—"We are confident that the process undertaken in this matter was appropriate and handled in a just and responsible way toward all parties involved. We have nothing further to add"—is as evasive as it is dishonest. Fr. Selvaraj has been proved to be absolutely blameless.

And, concludes Ms. O'Connor, where an employee "resigns" as a result of bullying, a tribunal may be asked to determine whether in fact the employee had no option but to resign in the circumstances. [145]The big question now is: to whom does the helpless and victimised priest turn?

Justice Delayed Is Justice Denied

How very pertinent is the humble, candid, and courageous admission of our most Holy Father, Pope Benedict XVI: "The greatest persecution of the church doesn't come from enemies on the outside but is born from the sin within the church." *(L'Osservatore Romano)*

---

[144] Susan O'Connor. Op.Cit.
[145] Ibid.

5

In Quest of Both Truth and Justice

This is what the Lord Almighty says: "Administer true justice;
show mercy and compassion to one another."
—Zechariah 7:9

The Wisdom of Ages and Sages

In ancient Greece, the scholar and intellectual Socrates was reputed to hold knowledge in high esteem. One day, an acquaintance met the great philosopher and said, "Do you know what I just heard about one of your friends?"

"Hold on a minute," Socrates replied. "Before telling me anything, I'd like you to pass a little test. It's called the triple-filter test."

"Triple filter?" asked the man.

"That's right," Socrates continued. "Before you talk to me about my friend, it might be a good idea to take a moment and filter what you're going to say. That's why I call it the triple-filter test. The first filter is truth. Have you made absolutely sure that what you are about to tell me is true?"

"No," the man said, "actually I just heard about it and wanted to tell it to you."

"All right," said Socrates. "So you don't really know if it's true or not. Now let's try the second filter, the filter of goodness. Is what you are about to tell me about my friend something good?"

"No; on the contrary, it is bad."

"So," Socrates continued, "you want to tell me something bad about him, but you're not certain it's true. You may still pass the test though, because there's one filter left: the filter of usefulness. Is what you want to tell me about my friend going to be useful to me?"

"No, not really," replied the man.

"Well," concluded Socrates, "if what you want to tell me is neither true, nor good, nor even useful to me, why tell it to me at all?"

Forgiveness Is an Indispensable Prerequisite

Every priest and religious has often reflected on, closely examined, discussed, and preached on the parable of the unmerciful servant.[146] As always, the frank and forthright Peter broached a legitimate but difficult question: "Lord, if another member of the church sins against me, how often should I forgive? As many as seven times?" In his personal estimation, that was more than magnanimous.

Equally frank and forthright was Jesus' unhesitating reply: "Not seven times, but, I tell you, seven times seventy."[147]

Peter's question was not altogether unwarranted. It was the rabbinic teaching that a man must forgive his brother three times. Rabbi Jose ben Hanina said, "He who begs forgiveness from his neighbour must not do so more than three times." [148]

Rabbi Jose ben Jehuda is even more precise: "If a man commits an offence once, they forgive him; if he commits an offence a second time, they forgive him; if he commits an offence a third time, they forgive him; the fourth time they do not forgive him."[149]

The biblical basis was taken from the prophet, Amos. In the opening chapters of the book of Amos, there is a series of condemnations on the various nations for three transgressions and for four.[150] From this, it was deduced that God's forgiveness extends to three offences and that he visits the sinner with punishment at the fourth. If that was the yardstick

---

[146] Matthew 18:21-35.
[147] Matthew 18:21-22.
[148] www.forthefainthearted.com
[149] Ibid.
[150] Amos 1:3, 6, 9, 11, 13; 2:1, 4, 6.

established by God, then a man was as gracious if he forgave three times and no more.

Peter thought he was being exceptionally magnanimous in exceeding the rabbinic limit of three, multiplied by two for good measure and, to make assurance doubly sure, he added one. Without mincing his words, Christ Jesus pulled the rug from beneath his feet in setting the ideal much higher than Peter had ever contemplated—the Christian must forgive seventy times seven. In a word, there is no numerical limit to forgiveness. The authentic Christian will forgive unreservedly and constantly.

And then Christ Jesus, the ingenious teacher, related the powerful parable of the unmerciful servant, which spoke more eloquently than any scholarly discourse on forgiveness. A master willingly condoned his servant of an enormous amount of money on his plea for clemency and time. Both were readily given.

The servant had barely walked out of his master's presence when he chanced upon a colleague who owed him an infinitesimal fraction of what he himself owed. The colleague fell on his knees and begged for both clemency and time as he was unable to repay the debt there and then. Flaring into a violent temper, the unmerciful servant throttled him and then had the pleading colleague jailed until such time he was able to pay the debt.

Of course, this was reported to the master, who lost no time in summoning the vengeful debtor and said to him: "You wicked slave! I forgave you all that debt because you pleaded with me. Should you not have had mercy on your fellow slave, as I had mercy on you?' And in anger his lord handed him over to be tortured until he would pay his entire debt."[151]

With his spellbound listeners hanging onto his words, Christ Jesus solemnly added, "So my heavenly Father will also do to every one of you, if you do not forgive your brother or sister from your heart." [152] In a word, nothing we have to forgive can even faintly or remotely compare with what we have been forgiven—thanks to the redeeming death of Christ Jesus, our Crucified Lord and Risen Saviour!

---

[151] Matthew 18:32-34

[152] Matthew 18:35

We Must Forgive if We Expect to Be Forgiven

Throughout the New Testament, there is one recurring and inescapable truth stated: *we must forgive if we expect to be forgiven.* As a matter of fact, the converse is terrifying in its irreversible consequences: *the one who fails to forgive his fellow man cannot hope to be forgiven by God.*

Said Jesus himself, "Blessed are the merciful, for they shall obtain mercy."[153] And then, for emphasis, Christ Jesus repeated, "For if you forgive men their trespasses, your heavenly Father also will forgive you; but if you do not forgive men their trespasses, neither will your Father forgive your trespasses."[154] Having heard this solemn statement himself, the apostle James wrote: "For judgement is without mercy to one who has shown no mercy."[155] In a word, divine and human forgiveness go inextricably hand in hand.

The ingenuity of Christ Jesus, as the Way, the Truth, and the Life, shines through most marvellously in and through this masterful parable. The first servant owed his master 10,000 talents, which is the equivalent of £2,400,000. That is an enormous debt, even by current standards! It was more than the total budget of the richest province, which stood around 600 talents, or approximately £120,000. And the debtor was forgiven with one spontaneous and magnanimous gesture.

By contrast, his fellow servant or colleague owed him a trifling 100 denarii. A denarius is worth about four pence in value; and therefore the total debt was less than £5. In short, the amount due was approximately one five-hundred thousandth of his own debt! A ridiculous trifle! And so, *we must forgive if we expect to be forgiven.* In the words of Rev. Jay Hughes, "Our willingness to forgive others must reflect God's willingness to forgive us—which, like God's himself, is without limit."[156]

---

[153] Matthew 5:7

[154] Matthew 6:14-15

[155] James 2:13

[156] Rev. Jay Hughes, ThD, *Justice for Priests and Deacons*, Vol. 1, no. 1 (Sept. 2007), 6.

Example Is Better than Precept

In 1754, a young woman named Neria Caggiano accused St. Gerard, a 28-year-old Redemptorist brother, of lecherous conduct. She had been dismissed from a convent and was seeking revenge on the one who had recommended her there. St. Alphonsus Ligouri, the founder of the Redemptorists, called St. Gerard in to answer the accusation. Rather than defending himself, Br. Gerard remained silent, not seeking to do any damage to his accuser's reputation. The superior thought he had no choice but to discipline him severely; he forbade him from all contact, not to mention pastoral work, with outsiders and even denied him the privilege of receiving Holy Communion. These were very severe penalties for Br. Gerard, which he offered up for his accuser's conversion and salvation. He simply said, "There is a God in Heaven. He will provide." [157]

Several months later, Neria became dangerously ill and thinking that she might die, realized she could not go to her particular judgment with such a calumny on her conscience. She wrote a letter to St. Alphonsus confessing that she had invented the charges. The founder, overjoyed at the innocence of his spiritual son, fully restored him, but St. Gerard's example of trust in God even in the midst of terrible accusations and penances quickly became a model not only for his religious family but for the whole Church; he is now the patron saint of those falsely accused.

The second and complementary camp we see in the life of St. John Vianney. He was accused, among other types of debauchery, of impregnating a young woman who lived near the Church in Ars. His instinctive response was to forgive and pray for his accusers as well as for the young woman. But he also came to recognize that it was not merely his own reputation that was suffering because of the calumnies, but also the reputation of the priesthood. For that reason, he undertook a defence, lest by failing to do so, he would give any plausibility to the vile rumours. The truth eventually came out. His serenity in the midst of the false allegations and his firm confidence that the truth would emerge, however, were lessons his parishioners never forgot.

Saints are distinguished by their heroic virtue—and responding to false accusations as the saints above did is clearly heroic. It is totally

---

[157] www.catholicity.com

understandable that those who have been falsely accused may undertake a vigorous defence of their reputation, as some like Cardinal Joseph Bernardin of Chicago and Cardinal George Pell of Sydney have, so as not only to clear their names and remove the stigma from the priesthood and their entire ministry, but also to dissuade others from making similar false accusations in the future. But, whatever one's external strategy is, the interior strategy of total confidence in God in union with Christ Jesus in the midst of calumny is the type of heroism to which God calls all his priests.

Jesus said in the Sermon on the Mount, "Blessed are you when they revile you . . . and utter every kind of evil against you falsely on my account. Rejoice and be glad, for your reward will be great in heaven."[158] Among the greatest in heaven will be those who have suffered false accusations, in union with the Lord Jesus, who was—we should never forget—killed through false accusations, but rose triumphant on the third day.

To Every Right, There Is a Corresponding Responsibility

Should a complaint be made against a priest, it is for the bishop to ascertain the veracity and the gravity of the complaint. It could be minor or a mere misunderstanding that could easily be rectified by a judicious intervention with both the complainant and the priest. This interchange must be held in the strictest confidence—*sub sigillo secreto.*

Said Christ Jesus very wisely and judiciously in relation to reproving another who sins: "If another member of the Church sins against you, go and point out the fault when the two of you are alone. If the member listens to you, you have regained that one. But if you are not listened to, take one or two others along with you, so that every word may be confirmed by the evidence of two or three witnesses."[159] This fair and just arrangement has a six-fold advantage.

First, it safeguards the rights of the complainant and the priest as well as their reputations—both are assumed to be innocent until proven guilty. Second, it ensures justice for both. Third, it is a striking and edifying demonstration of the ideal that Christ Jesus did propose in the parable

---

[158] Matthew 5:11-12
[159] Matthew 18:15-16

of the unmerciful servant. Fourth, it can bring about a closure for both and a resumption of a new stress-free future. Fifth, it avoids the tedium, complexity, and expense of a long, drawn-out legal battle. Even Christ Jesus wisely recommended: "Come to terms quickly with your accuser while you are on the way to court with him, or your accuser may hand you over to the judge, and the judge to the guard, and you will be thrown into prison."[160] And sixth, it concretely realises a vital moral premise declared by Pope John Paul II: "How can you perceive of justice without the right to defence?"[161]

If, however, the matter is grave, the complaint must be presented to the bishop by the complainant in writing. He/she must be informed in no uncertain terms that a copy will be shown to the priest concerned and that the complainant could be legally responsible for the consequences should the allegations be unfounded or false. This is an essential step in the initiation of the process. The complainant may need time to discuss the matter with his/her legal advisor. It should be readily given.

The bishop must make it clear and definite to the complainant that no action can be taken unless the complaint is made in writing. Negatively, this is intended to avoid needless misunderstandings and distortions, but, more positively, it is to ensure objectivity and reliability. The case ceases if the complainant refuses to comply with this essential pre-requisite.

If, after due deliberation, the complainant still wishes to pursue the stated allegations, the bishop must personally reiterate the next step in the process: that he will deliver the statement to the priest concerned in the presence of a canon lawyer and a civil lawyer. Both lawyers should be provided by the bishop himself and at the expense of the diocese. The priest concerned should be allowed to bring along a priest friend or another trustworthy person, who can serve as an authentic witness. Once again, at this stage, all transactions should be held in the strictest confidence—*sub sigillo secreto.*

With the aid of both the canon lawyer and the civil lawyer, the priest should make a written response in defence, which should be presented to the bishop. Of course, should the allegations be false or slanderous, it is for the civil lawyer and the canon lawyer to determine the next line

---

[160]   Matthew 5:25

[161]   www.justiceforpriests.org Newsletter, May 2011.

of action. And this must be communicated to the bishop. A formal legal process can then be initiated.

At this stage, the priest cannot—and should not—be removed from his office, until it is patently clear that there are grave canonical reasons for such a drastic decision. Also, all communications related to the matter must be provided *in writing* and be shown to the priest, so that he can legitimately defend himself. So many priests have been wrongly punished for reports that are at best baseless and at worst malicious. And regrettably, so many bishops have been prejudiced and unbending in their line of action against an innocent priest. *This is why it is paramount that every priest is shown the allegations that are made, who is making them, and the reasons why they are being made. In a word, there is absolute need for both transparency and accountability in the quest for truth and justice.*

No priest can be obliged to undergo a psychological test or evaluation. In other words, it is his prerogative to refuse to comply should he deem it unnecessary and a needless invasion of his privacy. Of course, there could be times when it will be beneficial to a priest in need. For instance, a priest who struggled with alcoholism for years was buoyed by the concern of his bishop and personally agreed to engage in a process of rehabilitation. He was very candid in asserting that at times it is important for the bishop to be quite frank and courageous and to confront the individual priest with the truth. As the saying goes, "A stitch in time saves nine." Once again, there is the paramount need for confidentiality.

What about the intervention of a mediator—personal or professional? Experience has proved that a mediator or intermediary, as a paid individual, is inclined to favour those who enlist his/her services. In other words, swayed by the financial income, it is extremely difficult for a mediator or intermediary to be impartial and objective. And, of course, such a person is always selected by the bishop; the priest has neither the financial resources nor the personal clout to engage one of his own. *Instances in which a priest is wrongly accused do not constitute a case for mediation, but a stringent demand for truth and justice.* And these can best be administered by competent, honest and courageous persons, who will sedulously work for the most desirable outcome without fear or favour.

Finally, in view of the shocking revelations of sexual abuse in the recent past, priests the world over have been emphatically told what is not permissible and insistently reminded about their obligations for both discretion and transparency. And so, should a priest breach this sacrosanct code of conduct, he renders himself liable to prosecution and to the full force of the law. Of this one and all are fully aware, and will most assuredly be both cautious and diligent.

A significant factor in facilitating this new climate of trust and hope is the interpersonal relationship that priests enjoy with their bishop. As a father and friend, the bishop should ensure that at all times his priests can repose in him the confidence that will bolster priestly morale and so engender the most desirable outcomes for the diocese as a whole. "Administer true justice; show mercy and compassion to one another."[162]

Bishops are Accountable

This process has been strenuously defended and strongly emphasised by Catharine Henningsen of *Voice of the Faithful* (VOTF) in an address that she made on February 5, 2004. Without in any way denigrating the gravity of the sexual abuse of minors by priests and religious, she vehemently champions the cause of due process for accused priests. To quote her precise words:

> I believe that we are witnessing a second wave of abuse in part of many of the bishops and that that abuse is now being directed at the priests accused of paedophilia. Across the country, priests are disappearing never to be heard from again. And their bishops are trampling their legal rights for reasons that have little to do with either canon or civil law.[163]

And so, Ms Henningsen very rightly recommends:

That said, according to Canon Law, the following procedure should be followed whenever allegations of sexual misconduct are made against a priest:

---

[162] Zechariah 7L9

[163] Catharine Henningsen, "The Second Wave of Abuse: the Fate of Our Accused Priests," BishopAccountability.org.

1. The allegation should always be made in writing by the plaintiff and signed by the plaintiff in the presence of a Notary Public.
2. If the bishop deems the allegations have merit, he should proceed according to the norms of canons 1717-1715 which outline the requirements of prior investigation. If he then decides to proceed further with the case, the accused is to be given a copy of the allegation and the proofs (Canon: 1720:1).
3. The good reputation of the people involved should be protected, and also their right to privacy and confidentiality (This is according to Canon 220). The good reputation of a person is always presumed unless the contrary is proven.
4. The accused priest has the right to defend his rights. This presupposes that his rights are known. Note: there is no equivalent of our civil Miranda Law in canon law, but accused priests should be immediately informed of their right to both civil and canonical counsel and their right to remain silent. Ideally, a priest should be informed of the allegations in the preliminary meeting with the ordinary/bishop and then come back to answer the charges on another day with both canon and civil counsel.
5. The accused priest has the right to advocacy according to Canon 1481:1. The accused in a penal trial must always be provided with an advocate (Canon 1482:2).
6. The Code of Canon Law says that an advocate must have reached the age of majority; may be either a man or a woman, cleric or layperson; enjoy a good reputation; be Catholic unless otherwise provided and have a doctorate in Canon Law or be otherwise qualified.
7. During this process, the priest should continue to receive his salary and sustenance (Canon 281).
8. There should be a list of competent canonists and civil attorneys provided to the accused. The Diocese should also pay the legal fees and expenses incurred in these cases.[164]

And so, Ms Henningsen insists:

---

[164] Henningsen, Ibid.

I am here today to argue that we cannot substitute the abuse of children with the abuse of accused priests . . . I believe you will agree that we have arrived at a point in our handling of these cases where canon and civil law are being eroded to the detriment, and I think diminishment, not only of who we are as human beings, but of who we claim to be as Christians.[165]

Bishop—Father and Pastor

In the document on bishops, the fathers of the Second Vatican Council expressly said: "In exercising his office of father and pastor, a bishop should stand in the midst of his people as one who serves. Let him be a good shepherd who knows his sheep and whose sheep know him. Let him be a true father who excels in the spirit of love and solicitude for all . . ."[166] More precisely, "a bishop should always welcome priests with a special love since they assume in part the bishop's duties and cares and carry the weight of them day by day so zealously. He should regard his priests as sons and friends."[167]

And this is incumbent on the bishop by virtue of the fact that, although priests do not possess the highest degree of the priesthood and, although they are dependent on the bishop in the exercise of their power, they are nevertheless united with the bishops in sacerdotal dignity.[168] The document on bishops elucidates this special bond thus: "Pastors, however, cooperate with the bishop in a very special way, for as shepherds in their own right they are entrusted with the care of souls in a certain part of the diocese under the bishop's authority."[169]

---

[165] Henningsen, Ibid.
[166] CD #16(a).
[167] CD #16(c).
[168] LG #28.
[169] CD #30.

"I Was in Prison and You Visited Me"[170]

With trustful confidence and unwavering hope, the Psalmist reassures us: "The Lord is merciful and gracious, slow to anger and abounding in steadfast love. He will not always accuse, nor will he keep his anger forever. He does not deal with us according to our sins, nor repay us according to our iniquities. For as the heavens are high above the earth, so great is his steadfast love toward those who fear him; as far as the east is from the west, so far he removes our transgressions from us."[171]

Christ Jesus has made it crystal clear that, in the last analysis, God will judge us, not according to our sins, but in accordance with our reaction to human need. Stated differently, God's judgement will not depend on the knowledge we have gleaned, or the fame that we have acquired, or the fortune that we have amassed, but on the help that we have given the helpless, the defenceless and the powerless. "When I was hungry, you gave me food; when I was thirsty, you gave me drink; when I was naked, you clothed me; when I was sick, you visited me; and when I was in prison, you came to me."[172] *The most startling revelation is the fact that Christ Jesus lives in these helpless, defenceless and powerless persons.* And so, in reaching out to them with genuine concern and selfless good will, we are actually doing it to Christ Jesus himself, who guarantees us an unfailing reward both here and hereafter.

The story is told of Martin of Tours, a Roman soldier and a Christian. One cold winter day, as he was entering a city, a famished and shivering beggar stopped him and asked for alms. Martin instantly dug into his pockets and realised with regret that he had no money. However, around his shoulders he wore a frayed soldier's cloak. So he cut it into two and tenderly laid one half around the shivering shoulders of that poor beggar. That night, Martin had a dream in which he saw Christ Jesus amid the angels and the saints wearing the frayed cloak that he had earlier shared with the poor beggar. Reportedly, one of the angels said to Jesus, "Master, why are you wearing that battered old cloak?" Without hesitation, Jesus replied, "Because my servant, Martin, gave it to me."

---

[170] Matthew 25:36.

[171] Psalm 103:8-12

[172] Matthew 25:31-46

"Truly I tell you, just as you did it to one of the least of these who are members of my family, you did it to me . . . Come, you that are blessed by my Father, inherit the kingdom prepared for you from the foundation of the world."[173]

The Pastoral Care of Priests by Their Bishop

Canon 369 states very clearly and definitely that a diocese is a portion of the people of God, which is entrusted to a bishop to be nurtured by him, with the cooperation of the *presbyterium*, in such a way that, remaining close to its pastor and gathered by him through the Gospel and the Eucharist in the Holy Spirit, it constitutes a particular Church. Stated differently, the bond between a bishop and his priests must always be close, paternal, trustful and supportive. After all, if a bishop is to fulfil his onerous pastoral responsibilities, as shepherd, teacher, and leader, then he must effectively rally the whole-hearted support of all in the *presbyterium*.

The text of this canon is taken almost verbatim from the Second Vatican Council.[174] The emphasis is on the community and the *presbyterium* gathered around the bishop, rather than on the geographical area assigned to a bishop. The relationship between the bishop, presbyterium and people is described in fundamentally dynamic terms: it is the bishop's responsibility to gather the people in the Holy Spirit; the means proposed for this are the proclamation of the Gospel and the celebration of the Eucharist. So the bishop's authority in these areas is not simply a responsibility entrusted to him, but a fundamental part of his role as diocesan bishop. When the people of God are so gathered and animated, the one Church founded by Christ Jesus is truly present and active.

In view of this momentous pastoral responsibility, Canon 384 goes on to emphasise that:

- A bishop should have special concern for his priests, to whom he is to listen as his helpers and counsellors.

---

[173] Matthew 25:34
[174] CD 11.

- He is to defend their rights and ensure that they fulfil the obligations proper to their state.
- He is to see that they have the means and the institutions needed for the development of their spiritual and intellectual life.
- He is to ensure that they are provided with adequate means of livelihood and social welfare in accordance with the law.

Since the cooperation of the presbyterate is essential to the pastoral care of the faithful in the particular Church (Canon §369), the law obliges the diocesan bishop to demonstrate special care and attention towards his priests.

- First, he is required to seek their advice *informally* as "sons and friends," and *formally* through structures such as the Council of Priests and the College of Consultors.
- Second, he must defend all their rights—those accruing both from natural justice and from the law of the Church.
- Third, he must make sure his priests have what they need to carry out their obligations.
- Fourth, he must provide whatever is necessary for their ongoing spiritual and intellectual formation (Canon §279), in whatever way this can best be done in the local circumstances.
- And fifth, he must make sure that all his priests have "remuneration that befits their condition" (Canon 281 §1); this provision is to be regulated by particular law (Canon 1274) as is the provision for what the priest needs by way of social welfare for "infirmity, sickness or old age" (Canon 281 §2).

6

The Canonical Rights of Priests

We hold these truths to be sacred and undeniable;
that all men are created equal and independent,
that from that equal creation they derive rights,
inherent and inalienable,
among which are the preservation of life and liberty,
and the pursuit of happiness.
—Thomas Jefferson (1743-1826), Declaration of Independence

Justice has certainly been turned on its head when men who stand to gain hundreds of thousands of dollars for making a false claim are automatically called "victims" by Church leaders now, while priests accused, without evidence, of acts taking place decades ago are just as quickly called "priest-offenders" and "slayers of souls."

Noted Boston criminal defence and civil liberties lawyer, Harry Silverglate, had something quite pointed to say about the onslaught of decades-old claims that have fractured and polarized the Church over the past eight years: "There is considerable doubt about the veracity of many of the new claims, quite a few of which were made after it became apparent that the Church was willing to settle sex abuse cases for big bucks."[175]

For instance, a New Hampshire diocese faced accusations of abuse from 62 individuals. Rather than spending the time and resources looking

---

[175] Harvey Silverglate, "Fleecing the Shepherd," *Boston Phoenix* (December 10-16, 2004).

into the merits of the cases, "Diocesan officials did not even ask for specifics such as the dates and specific allegations for the claims," New Hampshire's local newspaper, *Union Leader,* reported. Getting money from the diocese could not have been any easier for the complainants. It was almost as simple as a trip to an ATM machine. "I've never seen anything like it," a pleased and much richer attorney for a plaintiff admitted.[176]

Fr. Gordon MacRae reports the alluring proposition of a prisoner who brazenly approached him with an insidious bargain and the implicit hope that it would not be turned down. He asked Fr. MacRae to find out the name of a priest—any priest—who might have been serving in the area where he lived as a child around 1972 or so. He went on to explain that he had heard "on the grapevine" that the Church would settle with a handsome financial compensation, if he accused a priest of sexually abusing him back then. Without batting an eyelid, the inmate volunteered some of the money to Fr. MacRae if he complied with his treacherous proposition. Of course, Fr. MacRae categorically refused and dismissed the sinister plot as a joke.

But it wasn't. Two years later, Fr. MacRae read in a local newspaper that the same lawyer referred to earlier—who said, "I've never seen anything like it!"—was representing a prison inmate "whose life had been ruined" when he was sexually abused by a now 80-year-old priest in that same community in 1972! It was, of course, the same guy who had approached him. Promptly, Fr. MacRae wrote to a lawyer for his diocese informing him that he had firsthand knowledge of that scam.

Further, Fr. MacRae urged him and the diocese not to settle this fraudulent claim, but to expose and publish the name of the accuser because he had information that would clear the accused priest and expose this fraud. He received no reply. In the honest confession of one prison inmate: "People are so gullible. No one would think a person could accuse a priest just for money. I know a lot of people who would do it in a heartbeat."[177]

---

[176] David F. Pierre Jr., *Double Standard—Abuse Scandals and the Attack on the Catholic Church*, 125.

[177] Gordon MacRae, Op.Cit.

The Stark and Disturbing Truth

On February 5, 2004, Catharine A. Henningsen delivered an address entitled "The Second Wave of Abuse: the Fate of Our Accused Priests." Again without mincing words, this is how she began:

> I'm here tonight to address what I believe is the most under-reported aspect of the paedophilia crisis: The lack of due process for accused priests . . . I believe that we are witnessing a second wave of abuse on the part of many of the bishops and that that abuse is now being directed at the priests accused of paedophilia. Across this country, priests are disappearing never to be heard of again. And their bishops are trampling their legal rights for reasons that have little to do with either canon or civil law. The abuses I am about to delineate for you are **not** taking place because canon law offers insufficient protection for the rights of accused priests, but because our bishops, either through ignorance or wilfulness, are ignoring canon law.[178]

In an interview with a pre-eminent canon lawyer, Ms Henningsen asked a simple question: "What can an accused priest do to clear himself?" This was the candid and alarming reply: "In the present environment, absolutely nothing!" She then went on to list some of the many violations of canon law that she had personally witnessed in the church's treatment of accused priests, and she asked, "Why aren't the penalties stipulated in canon law being imposed on the bishops who violate the rights of their priests?" And once again, this was the prompt and unambiguous answer: "It's not that canon lawyers aren't aware of the abuses. We are. It's because the thugs (sic) are in charge."[179]

In a word, concludes Ms Henningsen,:

---

[178] Catharine Henningsen, *Voice of the Faithful,* Op.Cit. February 5, 2004.
[179] Ibid.

I do not believe that the abuse of priests we are seeing now will change until all of us raise our voices to say we will not tolerate abuse in any form . . . In our rush to ensure that no child is ever sexually victimized by a priest again, and in the bishops' somewhat knee-jerk reaction to the fully justified public outrage at priest-paedophilia, we have unwittingly allowed another form of abuse to surface: that against our accused priests. We cannot substitute the abuse of children with the abuse of accused priests.[180]

The Right to One's Reputation and Privacy

Canon 220 states: "No one may unlawfully harm the good reputation which a person enjoys or violate the right of every person to protect his or her privacy."

Two rights are recognised and protected here: the right to one's good name or reputation and the right to one's privacy—this latter having been inserted only after the final draft was submitted to the pope.[181] No one may "unlawfully" infringe either right. The right to one's good reputation is manifestly based on the natural law, rooted in the dignity of the human person, and acknowledged as such by Vatican II,[182] but a person may by his or her own conduct obviously forfeit this right. The innocent but hapless 80-year-old priest was unscrupulously and callously denied both *the right to his reputation and the right to his privacy.*

The right to one's privacy is equally given protection against unlawful invasion. This right certainly includes, but extends beyond, the protection of one's personal correspondence. Just how far it extends will depend upon that delicate balance which must be maintained between the inherent rights of the individual and the demands of the common good. This could well become a critical issue in the matter of candidates for the priesthood or for the religious life.[183]

---

[180] Ibid.
[181] For the history of the drafting of this canon, cf. RCom SPD 30 at Cann 32, 33; Sch 1982 36 at Can. 220.
[182] Cf. GS 26-27; Fl I 927, 929-930, 956.
[183] See Canon 241m, 642.

The canon carries an implied warning to superiors and others that, while observing the criteria laid down by the Church, they must seriously take into account these basic rights of the individual.[184] Pope John Paul II, in his annual address to the Roman Rota in 1989, said that one couldn't conceive of a just judgment unless the right of defence has been given. Once again, the diocesan authorities denied the unfortunate 80-year-old priest the right to defence; nor did they heed the legitimate intervention of Fr. MacRae in the interests of both truth and justice.

False allegations are falsely assumed to be rare. For instance, twelve falsely accused men appeared on CNN's *Larry King Live* with *Innocence Project* attorney Barry Scheck on October 6, 2010. [185]They had just been exonerated following an average of 20 years in prison accused of sexual assaults they had nothing to do with. Their stories, and the hundreds of others, constitute the theme of a notable film *Conviction*.

Adds Fr. Gordon MacRae:

> Justice has certainly turned on its head when men who stand to gain hundreds of thousands of dollars for making a false claim are automatically called 'victims' by Church leaders now, while priests accused without evidence from decades ago are just as quickly called 'priest-offenders' and 'slayers of souls'.[186]

The Right to Lawful Defence

Canon 221 §1 states: "Christ's faithful may lawfully vindicate and defend the rights they enjoy in the Church before the competent ecclesiastical forum in accordance with the law."

"The Obligations and Rights of all Christ's Faithful": this title (Canon 208-223) and the next (Canon 224-231) introduce a major innovation into the Church's law and constitute a particularly significant part of the code. Here, for the first time in legislative form, is spelled out what

---

[184]   See Canon 43 §2, 1352 §2, 1361 §3, 1390 §2, 1455 §3.

[185]   www.innocenceproject.org

[186]   Gordon MacRae, Op.Cit. October 23, 2010.

might be called a *charter* of the obligations and of the rights which obtain throughout the Church. The present title provides such a charter in respect of *all* Christ's faithful, both clerics and lay, while the following title gives an additional charter in respect of lay members. In Canon 273-289 and the Canon 662-672, equivalent, additional charters in respect of *clerics* and of *religious* are set out.

Regrettably, it must be admitted that this has not been the case with innumerable falsely accused clerics in the course of the past decade. How does a priest accused from ten, twenty or thirty years ago defend himself, or ever restore his reputation, when a diocese simply writes a cheque with no other evidence of guilt than the claim itself?

Comments Fr. Gordon MacRae: "And unlike the lawsuits filed by the accusers of Bishop Eddie Long, the lawyer who was given a $5.2 million cheque by my diocese—the first of several rounds of mediated settlements with the same lawyer who proclaimed, 'I've never seen anything like it! Didn't even file the claims in a court of law.' He simply wrote a letter demanding settlement, and got it. Not much later, the *Concord Monitor* reported on another case handled by that same lawyer with amazing results."

So Canon 221 upholds the right of defence. Such a right provides that a competent canon lawyer be made available and that the person have access to all the accusations, the evidence, and information about one's canonical rights. The effectiveness of this innovation will be measured in great part by the extent to which the rights themselves are recognised in practice, and are officially vindicated, when threatened or abused. The application of this canon is pivotal in this regard.

It is a formal statement that all may lawfully *vindicate* and *defend* the rights they enjoy in the Church—and precisely "before the competent ecclesiastical forum" (i.e. the appropriate tribunal[187] or organ of administrative recourse[188]). True, the code stresses that recourse to such a forum should never be the first step;[189] yet, it insists that everyone in the Church has the right to which this canon refers. Tribunals in the Church have hitherto—for the most part—been concerned with cases of alleged

---

[187] See Canon 1404-1416, 1671-1673.
[188] See Canon 1732-1739.
[189] See Canon 1446, 1733 §1.

nullity of marriage. This canon clearly signals the need for a wider vision of judicial or quasi-judicial service to all the people of God.

In his book *Contrary to Popular Opinion*,[190] noted civil liberties lawyer and Harvard Law professor Alan Dershowitz wrote no less than four essays defending why justice requires that accusers in sexual assault claims should be identified along with the accused. This is especially so when accusers bring civil lawsuits or other demands for compensation from a deeper pocket than that of the accused person himself. When accusers have a monetary motive, and the courts issue conflicting rulings allowing them to proceed decades later, but exclusively against Catholic priests, then the names of accusers should be scrutinized as well. This was rashly ignored in the case of Fr. Gordon MacRae, who was falsely accused, and unjustly and unjustifiably imprisoned for a crime that he never committed. As a consequence, his accuser walked away with $200,000, while the innocent priest lost his freedom.

The Right to Be Defended According to the Provisions of the Law

Canon 221 §2 states: "If any members of Christ's faithful are summoned to trial by the competent authority, they have the right to be judged according to the provision of law, to be applied with equity."

So, if summoned before an ecclesiastical tribunal, any member of the faithful has the right to the "due process of law" (i.e. no one can be judged in a manner which is unjust or arbitrary). Every case must be judged "according to the provision of law," which is to be found in detail in the Code of Canon Law.[191] And those provisions must be applied with canonical equity:[192] true justice must always be tempered by compassion and administered in a humane fashion in accordance with the spirit of the Gospel.

Canon 221 §3 states: "Christ's faithful have the right that no canonical penalties be inflicted upon them except in accordance with the law." In other words, with this canon, the protection of the rights of the faithful is extended into the domain of penal law. If no penalty is stated in the law,

---

[190] Pharos Books, 1992.
[191] Book VII, Judicial Procedures.
[192] See Canon 19.

then none can be imposed—except as permitted by the limited provision of Canon 1399.

The Right to the Pastoral Care of the Diocesan Bishop

Canon 384 states: "In exercising his pastoral office, the diocesan Bishop is to have a special concern for the priests, to whom he is to listen as his helpers and counsellors. He is to defend their rights and ensure that they fulfil the obligations proper to their state. He is to see that they have the means and the institutions needed for the development of their spiritual and intellectual life. He is to ensure that they are provided with adequate means of livelihood and social welfare, in accordance with the law."

Since the cooperation of the presbyterate is essential to the pastoral care of the faithful in the particular Church,[193] the law obliges the diocesan Bishop to demonstrate special care and attention towards his priests.[194] He is required to seek their advice *informally* as "sons and friends,"[195] and *formally*, through structures such as the Council of Priests[196] and the College of Consultors.[197] In particular, the Bishop takes on certain obligations towards his priests:

1. He must *defend all their rights*, those accruing both from natural justice and from the law of the Church;
2. He must make sure they have what they need to carry out their obligations;
3. He must provide whatever is necessary for their ongoing spiritual and intellectual formation,[198] in whatever way this can best be done in the local circumstances;
4. He must make sure that all his priests have "remuneration that befits their condition"[199]; this provision is to be regulated by

---

[193] See Canon 369.
[194] See Canon 107-117, 118-119, 197.
[195] CD 16: Fl I 573.
[196] See Canon 495.
[197] See Canon 502.
[198] See Canon 279.
[199] See Canon 281 §1.

particular law[200] as is that for whatever the priests need by way of social welfare for "infirmity, sickness or old age."[201]

In one diocese, a falsely accused priest felt so deprived of basic civil and canonical rights that he filed a suit against his bishop. On September 27, 2010 the *Wall Street Journal (WSJ)* ran a brief news story by reporter Valerie Bauerlein, titled "Influential Pastor Pledges to Fight Sexual Allegations". Among the *Journal's* vast online global readership, it was the fifth most viewed article for that day. Reportedly, the compelling reason that prompted such a notable response was the unanimous feeling: "Finally, one of them is fighting back." In a post on September 10, 2010, entitled "A Thorn in the Flesh," Michael Brandon, who hosts *Freedom through Truth*, wrote about a profoundly troubling observation: "The Catholic Church has become the safest place in the world for children, but the most dangerous place in the world for priests."

Added Fr. Gordon MacRae in his post "Are Civil Liberties for Priests Intact?":

> I laid out what some have called a compelling case for how the Church's sex abuse scandal has become like an ATM machine for lawyers and litigants at the expense of basic civil liberties for the priests accused.[202]

Procurators and Advocates

Canon law states:

> A party can freely appoint an advocate and procurator for him or herself. Apart from the cases stated in §§2 and 3, however, a party can plead and respond personally, unless the judge considers the services of a procurator or advocate to be necessary.

---

[200] See Canon 1274.

[201] See Canon 21 §2.

[202] Gordon MacRae, Op.Cit. October 20, 2010

> In a penal trial the accused must always have an advocate,
> either appointed personally or allocated by the judge.

> In a contentious trial, which concerns minors or the public
> good, the judge is *ex officio* to appoint a legal representative
> for a party who lacks one; matrimonial cases are excepted.
> (Canon 1481 §1-§3)

An advocate is a person approved by the diocesan bishop and appointed by a party to safeguard the rights of that party by arguments regarding the law and the facts. The general principle of the canon is that advocates and procurators are optional to the parties, unless the judge or the law demands otherwise. The judge may do so in order to protect the rights of a person whom he foresees may otherwise not be sufficiently safe-guarded. In penal trials, the law demands that the accused person must have an advocate, either chosen personally, or appointed by the judge. And in contentious trials, which concern minors or the public good, the law again demands a "legal representative" *(defensor)* and if there is none such, the judge is to appoint one.

The Right to Due Provision by the Diocesan Bishop

Canon 1350:1 states that if a canonical penalty has been imposed, the priest still has a right to those things which are necessary for a decent living. *In imposing penalties on a cleric, except in the case of dismissal from the clerical state, care must always be taken that he does not lack what is necessary for his worthy support. And if a person is truly in need because he has been dismissed from the clerical state, the Ordinary is to provide in the best way possible.*

According to Canon 281 §1, clerics have the right to receive sufficient remuneration in order to provide for their necessities, taking due account of the nature of their office and the conditions prevalent in society. The fact that a cleric incurs a penalty, whether automatically or otherwise, does not affect that right, provided that the penalty involved is not dismissal from the clerical state. Whatever other punishment is inflicted upon a cleric, it may never be to the detriment of "his worthy support."

Dismissal from the clerical state, however, involves the extinction of the cleric's strict right to support. Yet it does not remove all the obligations of the Ordinary towards the cleric concerned. The Code reminds the Ordinary of his duty to make sure that the dismissed cleric is provided for "in the best way possible." In actual practice, this provision of law is to be interpreted as generously as the circumstances of all concerned will permit, bearing in mind that "equity and evangelical charity"[203] may never be overlooked.

Canon 1347:2 states that a censure cannot be imposed validly unless the person has been given a warning and suitable time to repent. A censure cannot validly be imposed unless the offender has beforehand received at least one warning to purge the contempt and has been allowed suitable time to do so. The offender is said to have purged the contempt if he or she has truly repented of the offence and has made, or at least seriously promised to make, appropriate reparation for the damage and scandal.

Since the purpose of medicinal penalties is the reform of the offender, the law requires that every effort be made to attain this end before the imposition of the penalties. Thus, the validity of a censure[204] is made contingent upon the issuing of a warning to the offender by the appropriate ecclesiastical authority. The law requires that at least one warning be given, urging the offender to "purge the contempt" and providing a suitable time in which to repent.

The meaning of the technical term *purging contempt* consists of two elements:

1. The repentance of the offender (i.e. an expression of genuine regret and sorrow concerning the offence committed);
2. The making of appropriate restitution for any damage done or scandal caused, or at least the making of a serious promise to do this.

To conclude, on February 5, 2004, Catharine Henningsen, then editor of SALT, the op-ed page of the Catholic Church, clearly and emphatically said the following:

---

[203] See Canon 702 §2.
[204] See Canon 1331-1335.

I am here today to argue that we cannot substitute the abuse of children with the abuse of accused priests. I believe you will agree that we have arrived at a point in our handling of these cases where Canon and Civil Law are being eroded to the detriment, and I think diminishment not only of who we are as human beings, but of who we claim to be as Christians.[205]

---

[205]   Catherine Henningson, www.bishop-accountability.org "The Second Wave of Abuse: The Fate of Our Accused Priests". VOTF Norwalk, CT, 5 February, 2004.

7

The Protection of the Canonical Rights of Priests

When a bishop demonstrates an abuse of power
he is attacking the basis of all human rights and integrity.
When used against a cleric, he is attacking
one of the most defenceless of all people in the church.
When a cleric is not told who is making the accusation,
or what the actual accusation is . . .
the cleric is powerless to defend himself or even prove his innocence.
The abuse of power is driving a wedge between bishops and priests.
—Rev. Dr. Michael Higgins MA, DD, JCL

Sad but True

Fr. Damien owned a rental. Constrained by circumstances, and pushed to the end of his tether, he evicted the tenant. Vindictively, she accused the priest of sexual misconduct. The bishop never investigated the allegation but proceeded to censure the priest with an order of suspension, so that he could not function as a priest in the diocese. Regrettably, the letter did not give any reason for the suspension. No provision was made for his personal or medical care. Sometime later, the tenant relented, and signed a document stating that the allegation had been fabricated as an act of spitefulness.

"Come to terms quickly with your accuser while you are on the way to court with him; or your accuser may hand you over to the judge, and the judge to the guard, and you will be thrown into prison. Truly I tell you, you will never get out until you have paid the last penny."[206]

Fr. Errol was summoned by his bishop and informed that a parishioner had made a complaint against him, alleging that he was overly friendly with a female member of the family. No further information was given. As a matter of fact, the bishop directed the priest to undergo psychological testing. Even more, the bishop offered to assist the priest with the process of laicization, although that was not necessary nor did the priest ask for it. As the lesser of two evils, the priest submitted to psychological testing, with the hope that he could be vindicated in his cause and continue his pastoral ministry in the diocese. Finally, Fr. Errol was bound by confidence, under the pain of legal action.

"So when you are offering your gift at the altar, if you remember that your brother or sister has something against you, leave your gift there before the altar and go; first be reconciled to your brother or sister, and then come and offer your gift."[207]

An Analysis of Fr. Damien's Case

This is what Canon 208 explicitly states: "Following from their rebirth in Christ Jesus, there is a genuine equality of dignity and action among all of Christ's faithful. Because of this equality they all contribute, each according to his or her own condition and office, to the building up of the Body of Christ" (Canon 208).

This canon contains an explicit statement of the fundamental equality of all the faithful, rooted as it is in their common baptism. More explicitly, and in the specific words of the Second Vatican Council: "Although by Christ's will some are established teachers, dispensers of the mysteries and pastors for others, there remains, nevertheless, a true equality between all with regard to the dignity and to the activity which is common to all the faithful in the building up of the Body of Christ."[208] In a word, all forms of discrimination in the basic rights of the person are thus rejected. And so, *priests have the same rights as the members of the laity.*

---

[206] Matthew 5:25-26
[207] Matthew 5:23-24
[208] Lumen Gentium#32

Further, priests have additional rights, by virtue of their incardination in a diocese, or an institute or the consecrated life. Consequently, *bishops have a bounden duty to protect and care for their priests and staunchly uphold their rights.*

Fr. Damien's bishop patently and blatantly violated his right as enunciated in Canon 221: "Christ's faithful may lawfully vindicate and defend the rights they enjoy in the Church before the competent ecclesiastical forum in accordance with the law." To begin with, the bishop did not contact Fr. Damien and confidentially inform him of the allegation.

Second, the bishop denied him access to his defence. As a matter of fact, the bishop himself should have made this necessary assistance, by providing competent defence by a canon lawyer.

Third, both the priest and his defence canon lawyer should have access to the allegations and the substantiating evidence, so that they could be duly contested. In 1989, the late (and now Blessed) Pope John Paul II unequivocally said that one cannot conceive of a just judgement until and unless the person's right to a defence is firmly upheld. In a penal trial, for instance, the accused must always have an advocate, either appointed personally or allocated by the judge. This was not even considered in the case of Fr. Damien. Consequently, he could not—and should not—have been formally accused in the absence of incriminating evidence and proven culpability.

No provision was made by the bishop for the financial support of Fr. Damien. This is a clear case of dereliction of duty. This is how canon law frames it: "[A bishop] is to have special concern for the priests, to whom he is to listen as his helpers and counsellors. He is to defend their rights and ensure that they correctly fulfill the obligations proper to their state. He is to see that they have the means and the institutions for the development of their spiritual and intellectual life. He is to ensure that they are provided with adequate means of livelihood and social welfare, in accordance with the law" (Canon §384).

By way of an explanation, the law obliges a diocesan bishop to demonstrate special care and attention towards his priests. And the reason is manifestly clear: *the cooperation of all the members of the presbyterate (presbyterium) is essential to the pastoral care of the faithful in a particular church, of which the bishop is the shepherd and leader.* More specifically, a bishop has the following obligations towards his priests:

- He must defend all their rights—those accruing both from natural justice and from the law of the Church;
- He must make sure that his priests have what they need to carry out their obligations;
- He must provide whatever is necessary for their ongoing spiritual and intellectual formation, in whatever way that can best be done in the local circumstances;
- He must make sure that all his priests have "remuneration that befits their condition . . . by way of social welfare for "infirmity, sickness or old age."

Regrettably, Fr. Damien's bishop failed on all scores. Canon 1350 §1 clearly states: "In imposing penalties on a cleric, except in the case of dismissal from the clerical state, care must always be taken that he does not lack what is necessary for his worthy support." So this is a basic right that a bishop is morally bound to uphold.

The evictee deliberately fabricated a false allegation, principally to get even with the owner, Fr. Damien. No substantiating evidence had been provided. The sole aim was to settle a personal score, and in a spiteful and destructive manner. The bishop should have been a lot more judicious. Canon 1399 §1 states: "A person, who falsely denounces a confessor . . . to an ecclesiastical Superior, incurs a *latae sententiae* (automatic) interdict and, if a cleric does so he is liable to suspension."

As is clearly evident, a priest is particularly vulnerable and open to the risk of a false allegation against which he is unable to defend himself. In this particular case, the bishop committed a serious blunder in accepting the allegation as a proven fact when, in reality, it had been deliberately and spitefully fabricated so as to get even with Fr. Damien. This is canonically untenable and morally wrong.

Finally, the bishop seriously erred in not giving Fr. Damien a warning before taking the impulsive and drastic decision to suspend him, on the basis of a spurious charge. Canon 1347 §1 clearly states: "A censure cannot validly be imposed unless the offender has beforehand received at least one warning to purge the contempt, and has been allowed suitable time to do so." To begin with, there was no proven offence, and so there is no question about a conversion or repentance.

Constrained by circumstances, Fr. Damien enlisted the services of a civil lawyer, even while consulting with a reputed canon lawyer. The civil attorney wrote officially to the Apostolic Pro-Nuncio, with a copy sent to the bishop of Fr. Damien. Very plainly, the civil attorney informed the Pro-Nuncio that, if the case was not resolved within 30 days, civil action would be brought against the diocese. This pulled the rug from beneath the offending bishop. So he sent for Fr. Damien the very next day. Very wisely, the priest refused to meet the bishop without his canon and civil lawyers. Within two weeks, the case was resolved in favour of Fr. Damien.

> Come to terms quickly with your accuser while you are on the way to court with him; or your accuser may hand you over to the judge, and the judge to the guard, and you will be thrown into prison. Truly I tell you, you will never get out until you have paid the last penny.[209]

An Analysis of the Case of Fr. Errol

The bishop in this case:

- summoned the priest and apprised him of the allegation;
- gave him no specific information—the hapless priest was left in the dark;
- rashly advised the priest to undergo psychological testing without due justification;
- subtly threatened him with laicization and a complete loss of his priesthood.

Some of the aforementioned principles were blatantly violated in this case as well, such as the right to a defence. What is particularly aggravating in this case is the insistence on psychological testing. By civil law, no one can be forced to undergo psychological testing. In rare circumstances, it can be ordered by an official court order. Even the Holy See has strongly defended the right of a person to refuse psychological testing. As a matter of fact, the Congregation for the Doctrine of the Faith explicitly said in a letter that a bishop cannot force a priest to undergo psychological testing. On one occasion, a bishop issued a suspension order against a priest for

---

[209]   Matthew 5:25-26

refusing psychological testing. The latter appealed to the Holy See, and the bishop was ordered to have the decision rescinded.

Once again, Fr. Errol consulted a reputed canon lawyer and a civil attorney. He was insistently advised not to meet with his bishop on his own. The bishop was adamant; he wanted to meet with the priest without an advocate. Eventually, the former had to relent. The civil attorney ordered the bishop to furnish the evidence substantiating the allegation. The bishop refused, and agreed to withdraw the case. It was patently clear that the bishop was acting vindictively in punishing the priest and trying to settle an old score. The priest still serves in the active ministry.

In both instances, it must be emphasised that, under criminal law, a defendant has a constitutional right to legal counsel and the diocese has an obligation to provide an advocate. Some dioceses and religious communities encourage their priests to seek legal advice and agree to bear the expenses. In passing, it is advisable for a priest not to engage a canonist from his own diocese, lest there be a conflict of interests, thereby jeopardising the pursuit of truth and justice.

Finally, an instruction to observe confidentiality does not (and cannot) in any way debar a person from seeking due counsel, canonical or civil, from knowledgeable persons and close associates. And if bishops are truly eager to serve the dictates of both truth and justice in serving their priests, they should not only approve, but welcome the advocacy of a civil attorney.

To conclude, everyone, priests included, has a right to a good reputation and protection of their privacy. An accusation, as is patently clear, can irreparably harm a priest's reputation; it should not be further impaired by the wilful negligence of a bishop.

Championing the Cause of the Vulnerable Priest

Over the past two years, there has been a saturation of media coverage on cases where bishops have covered up clerical sexual abuse of minors. Under intense public pressure, the U.S. bishops passed a set of norms, which established a policy of "zero tolerance" for sexual abuse of a minor.[210] Hundreds of priests who had been accused of misconduct with a minor were removed from ministry, and their names have been publicly disseminated.

What has been usually overlooked in this whole episode is, "What happens to the accused priest?" Is he considered innocent until proven guilty? Is he afforded due process of law? Is he treated with justice and charity? All too often, unfortunately, the answer is "No." And yet, as the British weekly *The Economist* said: "No crime, not even murder, is so vilified in the western world as paedophilia. Being accused, even wrongly, of anything to do with child abuse can ruin people's lives."[211]

No one doubts that some priests have been guilty of heinous crimes and some bishops have been grossly negligent in not removing such priests from ministry. However, in an attempt to quell the public uproar, it seems that many bishops have swung to the opposite extreme. Because bishops have been accused of inappropriately protecting priests in the past, they are now reluctant to provide priests the protection of their legitimate rights. All too often, priests with outstanding reputations are being removed from ministry because of even a single nebulous, unproven charge from decades ago. Often, these are retired priests, in poor health, facing an accusation from 40 or 50 years ago.

What Should Happen

Canon law (i.e. church law) provides an imminently fair process for determining the truth of an allegation. Although the Essential Norms, passed by the U.S. bishops and approved by Rome, require that the processes of canon law are to be followed, that is rarely the case. According to canonical due process, when a plausible accusation has been made (and a lay review board can advise the bishop as to whether an accusation is plausible), the bishop is to appoint a canonical investigator, who is to be assisted by a canonical notary. Testimony is to be taken under oath and

---

[210] The Charter for the Protection of Children and Young People and the Essential Norms for Diocesan/Eparchial Policies Dealing with Allegations of Sexual Abuse of Minors by Priests, Deacons, and Other Church Personnel.

[211] *The Economist* (January 18, 2003), 10.

recorded verbatim. A formal record is to be created. The diocesan bishop is to review the record of the investigation, and determine whether there is sufficient evidence of a canonical crime (i.e. probable cause to move the case forward). He then refers the case to the Congregation for the Doctrine of the Faith.

Statute of Limitations or Prescription

Church law allows a person to bring an accusation of sexual abuse of a minor until the person is 28 years old. After that, any penal action is barred by prescription (i.e. the statute of limitations).

There are many substantive reasons for a statute of limitations. They are expressed in the United States Model Penal Code (Sec. 1.06 Comment, 1985):

> First, and foremost, is the desirability that prosecutions be based upon reasonably fresh evidence. With the passage of time memories fade, witnesses die or leave the area, and physical evidence becomes more difficult to obtain, identify, or preserve. In short, the possibility of erroneous conviction is minimized when prosecution is prompt.

> Second, if the actor refrains from further criminal activity, the likelihood increases that he has reformed, diminishing the necessity for imposition of criminal sanctions. If he has repeated his criminal behaviour, he can be prosecuted for recent offenses committed within the period of limitations. Hence, the necessity of protecting society against the perpetrator of a particular offense becomes less compelling as the years pass.

> Third, after a protracted period the retributive impulse which may have existed in the community is likely to yield to a sense of compassion aroused by the prosecution for an offense long forgotten.

Fourth, it is desirable to reduce the possibility of blackmail based on a threat to prosecute or to disclose evidence to enforcement officials.

Finally, statutes of limitations promote repose by giving security and stability to human affairs.

Repressed Memory

Some would have us believe that, in regard to this issue, there should be no statutes of limitations. They argue that many victims repress their painful memories and only find the courage to come forward decades later.

However, psychological scholarship has debunked the idea of recovered memories of sexual abuse.[212] When people have experienced a trauma like sexual abuse, they have trouble forgetting it, not trouble remembering it.[213] Studies have shown that people who are emotionally unstable are susceptible to developing false "memories" of sexual abuse.[214] This doesn't mean that they are making up stories. They may truly believe that they were abused, but it may never have happened. This is especially true in times when there is public hysteria over alleged sexual abuse.[215]

Therefore, there is all the more reason to observe the statute of limitations in regard to allegations of sexual abuse. When an allegation is made that abuse occurred decades ago, it is usually impossible to determine whether the allegation is true or false. A priest who is accused

---

[212] Terence W. Campbell, PhD, *Smoke and Mirrors: The Devastating Effect of False Sexual Abuse Claims* (New York: Insight Books, 1998); Dr. Elizabeth Loftus and Katherine Ketcham, *The Myth of Repressed Memory: False Memories and Allegations of Sexual Abuse* (New York: St. Martin's Griffin, 1994); Dorothy Rabinowitz, *No Crueller Tyrannies: Accusations, False Witness and Other Terrors of Our Times* (New York: Free Press, 2003).

[213] Richard J. McNally, *Remembering Trauma* (Cambridge, MA: Harvard University Press, 2003).

[214] Campbell, op. cit.; Loftus and Ketcham, op. cit.

[215] Philip Jenkins, *Moral Panic* (New Haven: Yale University Press 1998); Campbell op. cit.; Loftus and Ketcham, op. cit.

of such misconduct from decades ago is put in the impossible situation of proving his innocence.

In canon law, the allegation and the preliminary process are to be treated confidentially. This is to protect those who may be falsely accused, to make sure that there is not a trial-by-media, and to avoid polluting the testimony of potential witnesses.

What Does Happen

Almost every diocese now has a lay review board, which acts as investigator, prosecutor, judge and jury. Often, no written accusation is filed, so the accused does not know exactly what he is charged with. In addition, no sworn testimony is taken and no verbatim record of testimony is made. As soon as the review board advises the bishop that an accusation is plausible, without any further investigation being done, the diocese announces publicly that there is a plausible accusation of sexual abuse of a minor against the priest and he is removed from ministry. Usually, he is ordered to vacate his rectory immediately, and is given no place to live. He is given only a nominal sum to live on, and no financial support or assistance in hiring a canon lawyer or a secular lawyer. All too often, the diocese declares a priest guilty without any due process. Instead of requiring that an accusation be proven, an accused priest is considered guilty unless he can prove his innocence.

A Political Football

The issue of sexual abuse of minors has become a political football for extremists who use this as a vehicle for attacking the male, celibate priesthood and the hierarchical structure of the Church, and for arguing that the Church is finished because of moral laxity, permissiveness and a homosexual clergy.[216]

---

[216] See Philip Jenkins, *Paedophiles and Priests* (New York: Oxford University Press, 1996), chapter 6.

A Media Feeding Frenzy

The issue of clergy sexual abuse of minors has been subject to great distortion by the media. It is portrayed as a "priest" problem, despite the lack of evidence that there is any greater incidence of sexual abuse of minors among priests than there is among other clergy, teachers, scoutmasters or any group that deals with minors. It is portrayed as a "pedophile" problem, despite the evidence that there are very few reported cases of priests preying on pre-adolescent children. Characterizing the issue as one of "paedophilia," also creates the supposition that there is no hope of rehabilitation. The media also portrays this as an ongoing problem, despite the fact that there have been very few allegations made of sexual abuse occurring in the past ten years.

Often, television networks position stories on "priest paedophilia" for "Sweeps Week," when their viewer ratings are established. These viewer ratings determine the amount that stations can charge their advertisers. It is not uncommon for these programs to dredge up old file footage from years past, to give the impression that old problems have not been dealt with. Sad to say, stories of priests and the sexual abuse of minors, or illicit sexual activity with adults sell newspapers and draw viewers.[217]

A Lawyer's Dream

Of all churches, the Catholic Church is the easiest to sue, because of its centralized, hierarchical structure, and because of its extensive record keeping.[218] There is no doubt that there are true victims who deserve compensation. However, there is also the phenomenon that, after a crash of a bus holding 50 people, sometimes 100 people file claims that they were on the bus. Some "kings of torts" have used irresponsible methods to solicit thousands of claimants.[219]

These lawyers understand that most dioceses prefer to settle even a dubious claim, rather than go through the expense and the barrage of negative publicity involved in defending a lawsuit for an allegation of

---

[217] Ibid., chapter 4.

[218] Ibid., chapter 8.

[219] Daniel Lyons, "Sex, God & Greed," *Forbes* (June 9, 2003): 66-72.

sexual abuse of a minor. The Archdiocese of Chicago reported that it spent $1.2 million about ten years ago to defend one priest who was falsely accused of sexual abuse of a minor. All through the years of protracted litigation, the archdiocese was pilloried for using "aggressive legal tactics", despite the fact that Cardinal Bernardin tried to be extremely fair, and even hired a retired federal judge to study the record, and to advise him as to whether he was following the proper course. [220]

The Caiaphas Syndrome and the U.S. Catholic Bishops

Given the fact that bishops find themselves in a "no-win" situation, it is not surprising, from a human point of view, that many bishops have caved in to the pressure and decided that accused priests are expendable.[221] At the Dallas meeting of the U.S. bishops in June 2002, one American cardinal even voiced this point of view, saying, "Unfortunately, some priests have to be sacrificed for the greater good of the Church." This statement echoes—in an alarming way, for believers—that of the High Priest Caiaphas, who said to the Sanhedrin, "It is better for you that one man should die instead of the people, so that the whole nation may not perish."[222] Of course, Caiaphas has not gone down in history as a hero in the story.

A Civilized Society

The weekend after the Dallas bishops' meeting, by coincidence, newspapers also reported that Russia had joined the ranks of civilized societies, by establishing a new criminal code, which provided that a person was innocent until proven guilty, and by establishing that no one could be deprived of liberty without due process of law. Unfortunately, the Church seemed to be abandoning its great legacy of justice, by assuming the guilt

---

[220] Archdiocese of Chicago, *Ten Year Report on Clerical Sexual Abuse of Minors in the Archdiocese of Chicago*, January 1, 1993-January 16, 2003.

[221] Laurie Goodstein, "A Time to Bend: U.S. Bishops, Sure of Their Ground in the Past, Let Public Opinion Guide Them This Time," *New York Times* (June 16, 2002): 1.

[222] John 11:50.

of priests who were accused of sexual abuse of a minor, and denying them due process of law.

The Gospel of Mercy

Even more serious is that the Charter for the Protection of Children and Young People of the U.S. bishops seems to undermine the Gospel of Mercy. The charter quotes Pope John Paul II's remarks to the meeting of cardinals on April 23, 2002: "There is no place in the priesthood or religious life for those who would harm the young." But the charter fails to quote the pope's balancing statement: "At the same time . . . we cannot forget the power of Christian conversion, that radical decision to turn away from sin and back to God, which reaches to the depths of a person's soul and can work extraordinary change."

At the Dallas meeting, Cardinal George expressed the opinion that American culture is Calvinistic, and even American Catholics are tinged with Calvinism. Some theologians see the charter and Essential Norms as Calvinistic documents, expressing the total depravity of the sinner and giving short shrift to the Catholic belief in grace and redemption. The documents acknowledge that a priest can be forgiven sacramentally, but not institutionally. If a priest has ever sinned with someone under 18, no matter what the mitigating circumstances, his priestly ministry is considered forever unacceptable to the Catholic community.

Redemption

The blanket policy on exclusion from ministry ignores the reality that in some cases of sexual misconduct, a bishop, years ago, made a responsible judgment that a priest was rehabilitated and fit to return to ministry in some fashion or other. If the intervening years have shown the wisdom of that particular judgment, through a priest's exemplary ministry, by what rationale should that priest now be banished from ministry? There is no basis in canon law. It seems that the basis is simply public opinion, a poor guide to reasoned judgments.

Also, in speaking of the safety of children, it is important to remember that many ministries do not involve work with children at all: academic work, adult spiritual direction, adult retreat work, work in offices or agencies, and ministry in a retirement home or in a convent. Removing a rehabilitated priest from these ministries does not ensure the safety of children; it is reacting to hysteria.

8

Championing the Rights of Priests

Ecce quam bonum et quam iucundum habitare fratres in unum!
(How good and delightful for all to live together in fraternal harmony!)
—Ps. 133:1

Some friends play at friendship,
but a true friend sticks closer than one's nearest kin.
—Proverbs 18:24

Quite some time ago, a visiting priest from the United States was invited to address the local presbyterate in the Archdiocese of Adelaide, South Australia. The speaker was a seasoned pastor, whose priestly commitment and compassionate solicitude were as manifest as his unmistakable passion for truth and justice.

He told us that, on one occasion, he was invited to address a group some two hours away from his own parish. Around 8.00 p.m., he commenced his return journey. On the way, he felt a pressing need to use the restroom. The nearest rest stop was quite some distance away, and he just could not wait.

Suddenly, it dawned on him that he wasn't too far away from a local parish whose parish priest was known to him. So he diverted and was at the door of the presbytery within minutes. He rang the bell, and the pastor promptly responded. Brusquely pushing his host aside, the visitor excused himself saying that he needed to use the restroom urgently. The host was amused.

Minutes later, blissfully relieved, he joined the host in the dining room for a drink. As can be expected, the conversation began with the typical greeting: "So how are you?"

The host paused for a few moments before rising and going to his study. He returned with a typed letter. Placing it on the table, he sat down and said to his visitor, "I'm quitting!"

"What?" shrieked the visitor in disbelief.

"Yes," explained the host, "I'm at the end of my tether. Here is my letter of resignation to the bishop."

The visitor read it and was obviously upset. "Would you like to talk to me?" That was all the host needed—a gesture of fraternal concern and solidarity. For the next hour, the host explained the complex circumstances that had precipitated his drastic decision. The principal complaint was the recurring and utter lack of support from his bishop, in spite of repeated and unheeded communications. The poor priest was up against a wall, and had been literally pushed over the edge. His morale had sunk to its lowest and who could blame him?

Very sympathetically, the visitor assured him of his concern and support. Further, he expressed his readiness to intervene with the bishop, and to ensure that matters would be resolved to his satisfaction. That was a lifeline the distressed host needed desperately, and he speedily grabbed it. Half an hour later, he thanked the visitor, and then, to the latter's delight, he tore up the letter of resignation and jocularly remarked: "Thank you, God, for organising the timely rest stop." The ways of God are mysterious, but always marvellous![223]

The Catholic Church—a Champion of Rights and Justice

Since World War II, the Catholic Church has become a leading champion of the inviolable rights of individual human beings. Applying this principle, the bishops of the United States of America in November 2000 published *Responsibility and Rehabilitation*, a critique of the

---

[223] "Failure in communication," suggests Fr. Damian Ference, a priest of the Cleveland Diocese, "is real and endemic; further, we are running out of time to listen to the stories that will make a real difference."

American criminal justice system, in which they upheld the dignity of the accused and rejected slogans like "three strikes and you're out." Among other things, the bishops stated: "One-size-fits-all solutions are often inadequate . . . We must renew our efforts to ensure that the punishment fits the crime. Therefore, we do not support mandatory sentencing that replaces judges' assessment with rigid formulations . . . Finally, we must welcome ex-offenders back into society as full participating members, to the extent feasible."[224]

In so doing, the compassionate and courageous bishops were merely reiterating what the Supreme Shepherd, Christ Jesus, once said: "Rejoice with me, for I have found my sheep that was lost. Just so, I tell you, there will be more joy in heaven over one sinner who repents than over ninety-nine righteous persons who need no repentance."[225] (Luke 15:6-7).

A Glaring Inconsistency

Writing in the national Catholic weekly *America*, the late Avery Cardinal Dulles[226] said: "In the case of the sexual abuse crisis, the United States bishops have taken positions at odds with these high principles. Meeting at Dallas in June 2002 under the glare of adverse publicity and under intense pressure from various survivors' networks, they hastily adopted, after less than two days of debate, the so-called Dallas Charter and an accompanying set of norms that were intended, after approval by the Holy See, to be legally binding in the United States."[227]

More specifically, these are the salient points that Cardinal Dulles wished to emphasise:

- In the charter, the bishops rightly expressed the gravity of the problem that needed to be addressed. "The sexual abuse of

[224] www.archchicago.org USCCB, November 15, 2000.
[225] Luke, 15:6-7
[226] Cardinal Avery Dulles, SJ, is the Laurence J. McGinley Professor of Religion and Society at Fordham University, Bronx, New York. This article was given as a lecture to the Thomas More Society in Fort Lauderdale, Florida, on May 27, 2004.
[227] Avery Dulles, "Rights of Accused Priests," *America* (June 21, 2004), 1.

children and young people by some priests and bishops, and the ways in which we bishops addressed these crimes and sins, have caused enormous pain, anger and confusion." But in their effort to protect children, to restore public confidence in the church as an institution, and to protect the church from liability suits, the bishops opted for an extreme response.[228]

- The dominant principle of the charter was "zero tolerance." So even a single offence, committed many decades ago, no matter what the mitigating circumstances, was deemed sufficient to debar a priest for life from the exercise of his ministry.
- Having been so severely criticized for exercising poor judgement in the past, the bishops apparently wanted to avoid having to make any judgements in these cases.

Very wisely, Cardinal Dulles maintains that the Church must protect the community from harm, but it must also protect the human rights of each individual who may face an accusation.

> The supposed good of the totality must not override the rights of individual persons. Some of the measures adopted went far beyond the protection of children from abuse. The bishops adopted the very principles that they themselves had condemned in their critique of the secular judicial system. In so doing, they undermined the morale of their priests and

---

[228] The recently received co-adjutor archbishop of Los Angeles, Archbishop José H. Gomez, put it well in his remarks to priests when he said, "You are at the frontlines of this great drama of salvation. You are men of God and men of brave heart, and the bishops' first collaborators in the apostolic work of the Church. In your ministries, you are the presence of Christ, bringing God to people and people to God. You show them the compassion of the Father who seeks to carry them home—no matter how far away they might have strayed from the paths he intended for their lives"; *The Swag, Quarterly Magazine of the National Council of Priests of Australia,* 18, no.2 (Winter 2010), 3.

inflicted a serious blow to the credibility of the church as a mirror of justice.[229]

In one particular diocese, a senior, devoted and much-loved parish priest was required to stand down because of an allegation for what can *retroactively* best be described as an act of indiscretion, but by sheer force of unavoidable and harmless circumstances. Reportedly, some 25 years ago, on a group picnic, he had shared a room with a fifteen-year-old girl. On investigation, nothing offensive or conclusive could be proved, and so the case was dismissed on grounds of inadequate evidence. As can be expected, the innocent priest's reputation had been permanently and irreversibly marred.

Very dutifully, he opted to continue his priestly ministry in another diocese. Permission was willingly granted by his bishop, who was staunch in his loyalty, and firm in his support all through the investigation. It was particularly heartening to know that the bishop accompanied the priest on each and every occasion, in spite of the glare of publicity—an exemplary gesture that further endeared the courageous bishop to the members of the presbyterate and markedly boosted his own reputation and esteem among the people of his diocese. "Some friends play at friendship, but a true friend sticks closer than one's nearest kin."[230]

Some Disturbing Revelations

In June 2002, during the height of the media's focus on Catholic bishops and priests, the *Los Angeles Times* sent surveys to 5,000 Catholic priests in the United States. The respondents were contacted three more times, to increase the response rate. By October 11, 2002, 1,854 priests had responded to the survey for a completion rate of 37 percent. The survey found that 91 percent of respondents were satisfied with their life as a priest; 90 percent of respondents would choose to be a priest again if they had the opportunity; and 91 percent of respondents thought it was unlikely that they would leave the priesthood. In response to questions about their bishops, 76 percent approved of the way their bishop handled

---

[229] Ibid. 1.
[230] Proverbs 18:24

his duties and 68 percent believed that the bishops' charter (USCCB 2002) had adequately addressed child sexual abuse by priests.

Some of the more disturbing revelations are as follows:

- Bishops are unable to support their priests and, in the process, have erected a new Berlin Wall between priests and bishops. The distance between some respondents and their bishops was profound.[231]
- "I wouldn't trust my bishop or any bishop. They proved beyond all credibility that they were not interested in a prudent reaction to the revelations. Rather they were worried about church-ratings."
- "There's a rift in the priesthood, and a split between priests and bishops. These situations hurt priestly fraternity, and add lots of distrust between priests and bishops." [232]
- "I wouldn't see him (bishop) if I had a personal problem. In the ordination ceremony, the bishop talked about us being his spiritual sons. Man, that's not true!"
- "Many priests, including myself, think that their [bishops'] attitude toward priests is not very paternal. They're not acting like a father to their priests. The priests feel set-aside, shunned by their bishops."[233]
- "[The bishop] is between a rock and a hard place. He has to be immensely confidential, but at the same time, I realize that if it came down to a choice between me and the well-being of the church, I'd be out the door. What is ironic is that I felt the same even before the crisis, at least about the bishop; so maybe nothing's changed. Bishops will sacrifice anyone for themselves."

---

[231] Theoretically and even functionally, the priesthood may be the same, but the experience and perception of it is now radically different.

[232] "In fact, the healthiest priests—of whatever age—seem to embody both the "servant-leader" and "cultic" models ... Priests of different generations must learn to talk to one another about their differences instead of nursing mutual suspicions" (Damian Ference).

[233] Priests are a visible sign of the church and remind the world that God is not dead.

- "The bishops have legislated from their ivory tower. I find anything they have to say since the Charter is not to be trusted. I remember seeing a photo after the Charter where the bishops stand to applaud their priests. It made me sick. They think we're a commodity that can be bought or sold."
- "They (bishops) are worse than corporate executives. They'll do anything to keep their jobs. I like him even less than I did before, which was pretty much not at all."

Ecce Quam Bonum et Iucundum Habitare Fratres in Unum!

I am pleased to reproduce a personal communication from the president of *Opus Bono Sacerdotii*, Joe Maher:

Fr. Valladares,

Our president, Joe Maher, thought you would be interested in reading the letter below from one of the 8,000 priests that have contacted us for help in the past eight years. All of us here at *Opus Bono Sacerdotii* want to wish you a happy and blessed New Year!

Dear *Opus Bono Sacerdotii*,

I want to thank you from the bottom of my heart for what you are doing to help priests. I believe God is working through you. I am comforted in knowing that you help both those priests who, in their weakness, fell into sin and those who have been unjustly accused.

I wanted to include a letter with my enclosed donation to tell you my story.

In 2009, I was accused by an anonymous person of spending too much time with a teenager. There was no charge of sexual abuse and the family of the young person told the diocese the allegation was bogus. The anonymous person making the allegation refused to identify who they were to the diocese so there was no way to determine the sincerity of the allegation.

Nonetheless, the diocese chose to remove me from ministry as an associate pastor. Furthermore, they had a very biased psychologist evaluate me and make a false diagnosis of sexual infatuation. His bias was due to the fact that he recommended therapy in the in-house treatment program he operated. I was at a complete loss of what to do. Then I read an issue of the Knights of Columbus magazine, *Columbia Magazine*, and the article about your organization. I called and Pete Ferrara literally dropped everything he was doing to assist me. He gave me some much needed encouragement that I was not alone.

He spent hours giving me guidance and eventually directed me to two other unbiased psychologists not affiliated with in-house treatment programs for a second and third opinion. My diocese agreed to the evaluations and the results found me to be normal with no major psychological dysfunctions other than post-traumatic stress from this ordeal. The diocese accepted this evaluation and paid for counselling to work through the post-traumatic stress. I was restored to active ministry and I am blessed to say that I was recently appointed pastor of two parishes!

I cannot, nor will I ever be able thank you enough for your assistance. Without your help, I doubt I would be an active priest today. I say a Mass of thanksgiving for you and the psychologists each month. I gratefully make this donation to *Opus Bono Sacerdotii* and I will pray fervently for you. If I can do anything else to be of assistance, please let me know. May God bless you and your work and all those who support you by their prayers and sacrificial giving so that you can continue your vital work for all of us priests!

Sincerely,

"Fr. Mike"

The Pastoral Role of Bishops

Although the charter was modified as a result of consultation with Vatican officials, the revised norms are still subject to criticism. As a matter of fact, groups of priests still protest that they are not accorded the basic requirements of the process.

In the Decree on Bishops, the Fathers of the Second Vatican Council emphatically said that "in exercising his office of father and pastor, a bishop should stand in the midst of his people as one who serves. Let him be a good shepherd who knows his sheep and whose sheep know him. Let him be a true father, who excels in the spirit of love and solicitude for all and to whose divinely conferred authority all gratefully submit themselves" (#16a).

In #16c, the Fathers hasten to add: "A bishop should always welcome priests with a special love since they assume in part the bishop's duties and cares and carry the weight of them day by day so zealously. He should regard his priests as sons and friends. Thus by his readiness to listen to them and by his trusting familiarity, a bishop can work to promote the whole pastoral work of the entire diocese."

Safeguarding the Rights of Priests

With a view to upholding the rights of priests and religious, and ensuring the pursuit of truth and justice, the following procedure is highly recommended:

1. **Presumption of Innocence**—The Australian Catholic Bishops' Conference (ACBC), recognizing the problem of a baseless and damaging allegation, very rightly decreed in December 2000: "All persons are presumed innocent unless and until guilt is either admitted or determined by due process . . . Unless and until guilt has been admitted or proved, those accused should not be referred to as offenders or in any way treated as offenders."[234] It would, therefore, be unjust, imprudent and uncharitable to tell an accused priest, as some bishops have done, that he is not

---

[234] www.justiceforpriests.org/rights-of-accused-priests

101

welcome to attend gatherings of priests, including diocesan priests' convocation, the Chrism Mass or priests' retreats. And so, as per the standard practice in other sectors of society, a priest should be restored unless he is found guilty.

2. **Proportionality**—Pope John Paul II insisted on distinguishing among different degrees of gravity. In an important address given on February 6, 2004, to a plenary meeting of the Congregation for the Doctrine of the Faith (CDF), he declared: "Once a delict is proven, in each case you need to discern well both the just principle of proportionality between the offence and the penalty, and the predominant need to safeguard the people of God." So a priest who unintentionally uttered an inappropriate word or made a single imprudent gesture could not be treated the same as a serial rapist. Some observers even maintain that the penalty of laicization for each and every offence is "inconsistent with concepts of natural justice and canon law that are premised upon differentiation in penalties depending upon the gravity of the misconduct."

3. **Retroactivity**—As a general rule, neither civil nor canon law is retroactive. The Code of canon law declares that "laws regard the future, not the past, unless they expressly provide for the past."[235] It is, therefore, erroneous to apply a law drafted in 2002 to an offence that was committed long ago. *"To err is human; to forgive divine." (William Shakespeare)* In the light of this sound principle, the retroactive and baseless allegations against the parish priest referred to earlier were untenable, and certainly did not justify any investigative procedures or sanctions. Regrettably, the harm done to his personal reputation and priestly ministry was irreparable. His only option was to move to another diocese, providentially with the approval and encouragement of his solicitous bishop.

4. **Statute of Limitations (Prescription)**—In canon law, an action against a priest for crimes against a juvenile may not be brought more than 10 years after the alleged victim has reached adulthood, currently defined as beginning with one's 18th birthday. In canon and civil law, statutes of limitations or prescription, derived from

---

[235] Canon 9.

classical Roman law, have been incorporated in virtually all legal systems in the Western tradition. These limitations are established for many reasons. With the passage of time, memories fade or become distorted, witnesses die or leave the area, and physical evidence becomes more difficult to obtain. In short, with the passage of time, the possibility of erroneous conviction increases. Another reason for statutes of limitations is that, if the only accusation against a person is from the distant past, it is reasonable to conclude that the accused does not pose a present danger to society.[236]

5. **Confidentiality**—On no account should confidential files be surrendered to district attorneys and civil lawyers, especially when there are civil laws prohibiting this—statutes, for example, that protect the confidentiality of medical and psychological records. If confidential records are not protected, priests with personal problems are discouraged from turning to their bishops for help and advice. As a result, the relationship between bishops and priests is seriously ruptured. In addition, bishops become unable to minister timely help to priests who may need it.

6. **Settlements**—Not infrequently, dioceses or religious institutes enter into a financial settlement with accusers, even if the accusation is deemed false, in order to avoid the expense and negative publicity of a trial. This occurs even in cases in which the accused priest protests his innocence and requests a trial. When such settlements are reached, great care should be taken to protect the good name of the accused, so that the public does not regard the settlement as tantamount to an admission of guilt. If no guilt

---

[236] According to a distinguished canon lawyer, Fr. Ladislas Orsy, SJ, statutes of limitations and prescription are radically different in nature. Statutes of limitations merely bar actions; prescriptions create or extinguish rights or obligations. Dispensation from rights created by prescription, he says, does not make sense. Accused priests should not be denied their acquired rights.

or liability has been admitted or accepted, the announcement should make this clear.[237]

7. **Remuneration of Accused Priests**—Accused priests are in many cases very inadequately supported by their dioceses, even in cases where they have not been found guilty of any offence.[238] In effect, such priests are forced into secular employment without being accorded due process of law. In keeping with the principle expressed by the Australian bishops, accused priests should receive their full salary and benefits until there is a final resolution of their case. If they are not provided with room and board, they should be given compensation for these expenses.

8. **Access to Trial**—Although priests have a theoretical right to an ecclesiastical trial, such trials are in most cases not accessible to them, at least until years after the accusation. Part of the delay is caused by the fact that hundreds of cases have been referred to the CDF in the past two years. Many of these are cases in which there is a single accusation dating back decades. If the principle of prescription were re-established as being indispensable, many or most of these cases could be resolved early on.

9. **Laicization**—Involuntary loss of the clerical state can be imposed by a judicial sentence or by a special act of the pope (Canon 290). But such removal from the clerical state should be exceedingly rare, since it obfuscates the very meaning of ordination, which confers an indelible character and consecration. It reinforces the

---

[237] "The cross that Jesus was made to carry, a sign of profound embarrassment and shame was in his case, TOTALLY undeserved. He was called to carry it and to die on it with pain and derision and with patience, submission and forgiving love. The experience, like it or not (and, surely, we don't like it) is at the heart of the following and being one with Jesus, it is the only path to resurrection and new life; for every ordained priest and for the Church," Hal Ranger, editor, *The Swag, Quarterly Magazine of the National Council of Priests,* 18, no.2 (Winter 2010), 4.

[238] The "Essential Norms" say nothing about the support of priests who have been removed from ministry, and as a result, some bishops seem to be failing to give the decent remuneration required by Canon 281 and 1350 §1.

false impression that priesthood is a job dependent on contract, rather than a sacrament conferred by Christ Jesus.[239]

10. **Prospect of Reinstatement**—When addressing the American cardinals, Pope John Paul II said: "There is no place in the priesthood or religious life for those who would harm the young."[240] However, the Sovereign Pontiff was quick to add a balancing statement: "At the same time . . . we cannot forget the power of Christian conversion, that radical decision to turn away from sin and back to God, which reaches to the depths of a person's soul and can work extraordinary change."[241]

11. **Equitable Treatment**—It is hoped that there will be a more equitable treatment accorded to accused priests, especially those who may be presumed innocent. "Zero tolerance" may be appropriate in cases where a serious crime is known to have

---

[239] Upon being ordained, a priest gains the right to exercise the ministry corresponding to his order. After a formal ecclesiastical process has been initiated, the bishop may for prudential reasons forbid a priest to exercise public ministry for a period of time (Canon 1722), but removal from public ministry without a canonical trial or special action by the Roman Pontiff should never be permanent or excessively prolonged, since for practical purposes, such removal amounts to the very harsh penalty of forced laicization.

[240] April 23, 2002.

[241] Forgiveness and reinstatement are appropriate when the sinner has repented and made a firm resolve of amendment and when there is no reasonable likelihood of a relapse. The *John Jay Report*, published in February 2004, makes it clear that the majority of accused priests have only a single accusation against them. There is no reason to think that the protection of young people requires the removal from the ministry of elderly or mature priests who may have committed an offence in their youth but have performed many decades of exemplary service. Such action seems to reflect an attitude of vindictiveness to which the church should not yield. The policy of the Canadian bishops, in stark contrast to the U.S. "Essential Norms" contains provisions even for the possibility of reintegrating an offending priest into public ministry after being released from prison.

been committed, and as long as there is a palpable risk of its being repeated. After doing everything necessary to create a safe environment for children, the bishops should strive to do what they can to see that innocent priests are not treated as though they were guilty and that all priests are treated with justice and Christian charity.[242]

Conclusion

Priests, like others, should be given due process of law. Even when it is clear that an offence has been committed, the church should not, by her policies, send the message that she does not care about the clerical sex offender or that she believes him to be beyond redemption. After correction, offenders should be welcomed back into their dioceses or order "as full participating members, to the extent feasible."[243]

---

[242] As the U.S. bishops themselves declared less than five years ago in *Responsibility and Rehabilitation,* "One-size-fits-all solutions are often inadequate." They appealed to the teachings of Jesus in the Gospels: "The Parable of the Prodigal Son (Luke 15) shows God's love for us and models how we are to love one another. In spite of his younger son's reckless life and squandering of his inheritance, the father celebrates his return home, recognizing that his son has shown contrition and has changed his life. The lost who have been found are to be welcomed and celebrated, not resented or rejected."

[243] "The various crises in the Church—and there are certainly many more than just the obvious one—can be an opportunity for us to go on trying rather than feel defeated. This is the moment that Stephen Rosetti calls a tragic grace—tragic in the harmful impact on the lives of so many innocent people but a graced moment in offering the possibilities for a better future. But I would suggest that what is needed most in building that future is expansive imagination and engagement in pastoral ministry, rather than a retreat behind a barricade to what can seem like a safe and secure place. Our focus in ministry needs to be outreaching rather than retreating, even if in the end we ministers of this age simply serve to nourish the life of significant soil. St. Paul recognised that the work of God is in the ministry, not so much in the result," Roy J. O'Neill,

9

Strike the Shepherd

Then Jesus said to them,
"You will all become deserters because of me this night;
for it is written, 'I will strike the shepherd,
and the sheep of the flock will be scattered.'"
—John 26:31

Like a Lamb that Is Led to the Slaughter

Fr. Michael Sullivan of Minneapolis-St. Paul, Minnesota, is a canon lawyer, who earlier had served as the judicial vicar in the Diocese of Crookston, Minnesota. He reports that, some four years ago, an adult woman informed her local diocese that a young priest had groped her. No criminal or civil charges were filed, and the initial investigation showed that the accusation was plausible, that it could have happened. And so, a diocesan review board was set up. It was eventually proved that the charges were trumped up by the woman as a personal vendetta. The priest had "spurned her affection" by informing her that "I'm a celibate and we're not going there."[244] That was her spiteful way of getting even with the

---

MSC, *The Swag, Quarterly Magazine of the National Council of Priests of Australia*, 18, no.2 (Winter 2010), 14-16.

[244] There are thousands of priests, completely happy with their ministry and with the Church, who quite simply fall in love. And some do marry.

hapless and innocent priest. In the poignant words of William Congreve (1670-1729): "Heaven has no rage, like love to hatred turned, nor hell a fury, like a woman scorned."[245]

Regrettably, said Fr. Sullivan, the bishop did not accept the review board's fair, honest, and substantive judgement, nor did he allow the young priest to return to the pastoral ministry.[246] "The priest has appealed the bishop's ruling, but the case is swallowed up in Rome," added Fr. Sullivan. The priest currently receives no pay or medical benefits from the diocese. "The details differ from case to case, but it's a story I have heard countless times. Due process for priests accused of abuse is a sham."[247]

"Nearly five years after the U.S. bishops approved national policies to remove sexually abusive priests from public ministry, critics of the process

---

Maryknoll missionary, Fr. Dan McLaughlin, himself a lifelong celibate, described it to David Rice with compassion: "It could well be that a man makes a vow and lives it. And then meets a woman. There is an attraction, but deeper than that, there's a goodness in the person that draws out a goodness in the man. The man says, God wants me to spend my life with her. So I have a right to deny God's action? I could once have said in all sincerity, I want to make this vow for life. But none of us has power to see down the line. Grace happens not just the day I was born: God acts on us every day of our life. And God could choose to give me the grace to continue in celibacy, or the grace to react to love" (David Rice, *Shattered Vows: Priests Who Leave*), 36.

[245] William Congreve, *The Morning Bride*, act 3, scene 8.

[246] Father John X came from an Irish county village and was a curate in Dublin, Ireland. He decided to leave the ministry, sending word of this to his family down in the country, but stayed on in the parish for a few weeks until a replacement came. A colleague tells the rest: "A few nights later the priest was set upon outside his presbytery and beaten up most viciously by members of his own family who had travelled to Dublin for the purpose. They were cousins and relatives from the country—presumably they were doing it for God's sake. I remember thinking, such violence comes out of great fear" (David Rice, *Shattered Vows: Priests Who Leave*), 42.

[247] Joe Feuerherd, "Clergy Witch Hunt? Due Process for Accused Priests Is a Sham, Critics Say," *National Catholic Reporter* (April 25, 2007).

say the system is broken—shielding some abusers from the consequences of their actions while simultaneously failing to ensure the rights of the accused, who are presumed innocent under both church and criminal law."[248]

Fr. Sullivan candidly maintains that the standard of judging credibility is deplorably low. And he knows exactly what he is saying because he chairs the Board of Justice for Priests and Deacons, a ten-year-old organization, whose 90 affiliated canon lawyers have assisted approximately 540 priests and deacons, the vast majority of whom face allegations of sexual abuse.[249]

Like a Sheep that before Its Shearers Is Silent

In 1984, Fr. Rick Boyd, then an associate pastor in the Diocese of Crookston, Minnesota, was arrested and convicted of possessing child pornography received through the mail. He served no prison time but instead received six months of treatment at a counselling centre for priests. For nearly two decades following his release from the centre, Boyd served as pastor of three parishes in Crookston, thinking, he told *National Catholic Reporter*, that the episode was behind him.

No additional charges were ever made against him. And the counselling helped him confront his behaviour, said Boyd, which he explained resulted from the sexual abuse he had suffered as a child. "I was a happy priest," he said.

And he would remain so until 2003 when, near the height of the national clergy sexual abuse scandal, a group of parishioners familiar with Boyd's 1984 conviction demanded that Bishop Victor Balke remove him from ministry.

Boyd, 57, then left the diocese and spent part of the next two years studying canon law at the Catholic University of America and received additional counselling. During that time, Boyd said, he was unaware that the diocesan review board was investigating his case. His advocate, canon lawyer Fr. Virgil Helmin, was kept in the dark about his case, Boyd added. He was subsequently laicized.

---

[248] Feuerherd, Ibid.
[249] Feuerherd, Ibid.

Undeterred, Boyd appealed his dismissal. "Procedurally, neither Rev. Helmin nor I was informed of any of the precise allegations against me; I received no formal citation," Boyd told a Vatican official in a July 2006 letter. "Neither Rev. Helmin nor I was ever given an opportunity to give any canonical input or even a personal comment. Rev. Helmin was denied permission to view any documents. It appears that Rev. Helmin was advocate in name only, and he was never able to exercise his office."[250] Concluded Boyd, "I was never given an opportunity for a right of defence and there was no actual due process given to me." Constrained by circumstances totally beyond his control, Boyd currently lives with friends in Minnesota, still hoping to get a response from the Vatican.

A Devious Ploy

David Clohessy is the national director of SNAP—Survivors' Network of those Abused by Priests. This is what he maintains: "I think the overwhelming majority of suspended priests are still priests and that is very advantageous to bishops. What many bishops fear most is a defrocked predator who sings, who discloses how much bishops knew and how little bishops did about abuse."[251]

What is particularly disturbing in these instances is the total lack of compassion, a sensitive understanding and unconditional forgiveness as clearly prescribed by our Lord and Saviour. Said Jesus: "I tell you, there will be more joy in heaven over one sinner who repents than over ninety-nine righteous persons who need no repentance."[252]

---

[250] Feuerherd, Ibid.

[251] Feuerherd, Ibid.

[252] Luke 15:7. "In fact leaving the ministry is rather like a divorce—where the parish is the spouse and the people are the offspring. There is, however, one way in which it can be harder than a divorce. If a doctor divorces, he remains a doctor. If he marries, he still keeps his role. A priest does not. But he loses something far more than a role—he loses his very identity. For a priest is so trained that his person and his ministry are one and the same. So he almost ceases to exist as a person and must try to build a totally new personality. It takes years and it takes tears" (David Rice, *Shattered Vows: Priests Who Leave*), 43.

On another occasion, Jesus openly rebuked the self-righteous guests at a meal and warmly commended a courageous intruder and sincerely repentant woman—a public sinner: "Therefore, I tell you, her sins, which were many, have been forgiven; hence she has shown great love. But the one to whom little is forgiven, loves little."[253]

On a third occasion, Jesus launched a scathing attack on those who presumptuously prided themselves on their assumed superiority: "But woe to you, scribes and Pharisees, hypocrites! For you lock people out of the kingdom of heaven . . . How blind you are! For which is greater, the gift or the altar that makes the gift sacred? . . . For you clean the outside of the cup and of the plate, but inside you are full of greed and self-indulgence. You blind Pharisee! First clean the inside of the cup, so that the outside also may become clean" (Matthew 23:13-36).

The man waiting inside (his presbytery) to be evicted wore a black suit and a Roman collar, and the landlord who had called in the sheriff to evict him was His Grace, Most Reverend Dermot Ryan, archbishop of Dublin and primate of Ireland.

The priest was Mayo-born Fr. Michael Keane, and he was being evicted from his rectory because the archbishop had suspended him and ordered him out. A Dublin diocesan spokesman told me (David Rice) that the archbishop "had agonized an awful lot before taking the decision to evict" and had waited four years before doing so. However, what shocked the people of Ireland was that an archbishop would evict a priest under any circumstances; that Mother Church would do that to one of her children, one of her priests, for any reason whatsoever."

As another active priest, Brendan Hoban, wrote in the *Western People* newspaper: "What about all the theory we hear about community and love and brotherhood? What about all the sermons we hear on forgiveness and Christian reconciliation? What about the scripture quotation about turning the other cheek, going the extra mile, giving your cloak as well as your coat? Or is the preaching (people ask) not for the preachers, too? Is keeping the clergy in line such a priority in our church that our leaders

---

[253] Luke 7:47

prefer to place their faith in a civil court before the Gospel of love that Christ Jesus preached?"[254]

And on a fourth occasion, Christ Jesus urged one and all: "Do not judge, and you will not be judged; do not condemn, and you will not be condemned. Forgive, and you will be forgiven; give, and it will be given to you."[255] And again, "For if you forgive others their trespasses, your heavenly Father will also forgive you; but if you do not forgive others, neither will your Father forgive your trespasses."[256]

John Dubay, a married priest and family psychotherapist in Binghamton, New York, has worked for years with priests leaving the ministry. He speaks of his concern "for those men who were honest or attempted honesty in their resignation from the active priesthood and were treated in a monstrous, unchristian, and inhuman manner by fellow clerics."

"The range of stories approaches the absurd," Dubay writes, "when we learn of the devices of evil that were brought against them by men of God. Men have spoken of phone calls from the diocesan office at 2.00 a.m. to their family residence. Others have spoken of pressure on prospective employers, possibly with the hope that if unsuccessful at work, they would return to the active priesthood."[257]

"A common outcome," said a canon lawyer, "is what amounts to a settlement. I think there are a number of priests who have felt that things have come to one person's word against another's, that they don't have the emotional, psychological, or spiritual energy or financial resources to fight the charges that have been brought against them."[258]

---

[254] David Rice, *Shattered Vows: Priests Who Leave* (William Morrow & Co. Inc., 1990), 59.

[255] Luke 6:37

[256] Matthew 6:14-15

[257] David Rice, *Shattered Vows: Priest Who Leave* (William Morrow & Co. Inc., 1990), 63-64.

[258] John Dubay, a married priest of Binghamton, New York, describes it: "It is a journey that has no historical precedent ... It is indeed dark night, since our journey has so few handholds or footholds to guide and direct our way. This sense of having no reference in reality by way of history, legacy, legend, experience, or knowledge, adds to the dark night." In a

In its human dimension, says David Rice, the Church is a group like any other. But there is more to the Church than the merely human dimension. It happens to be a community that derives from Jesus Christ, He who taught that the Sabbath was made for people, not people for the Sabbath. *The Church's real crisis lies in ignoring that very injunction.*[259]

The great Trappist monk, Thomas Merton, speaks of "the crisis of authority brought on by the fact that the Church, as institution and organization, has in fact usurped the place of Church as a community of persons united in love and in Christ. Love is equated with obedience and conformity within the framework of an impersonal corporation. The Church is preached as a communion, but is run in fact as a collectivity, and even as a totalitarian collectivity."[260]

"We speak of *ecclesia semper reformanda (the Church is always in need of reform)*, Jesus taught that 'by this shall all people know that you are my disciples, that you love one another.' That love is already richly alive among Church members as individuals, at whatever level they are found, and there are many moving instances of it. But that same love now needs to percolate upward through the structures, transforming them to the words of Christ Jesus: 'Do not lord it over them as the Gentiles do.' So far it has signally failed to do so."[261]

The Best Practice for the Prevention of and Response to Sexual Abuse

On August 5, 2010, Dr. Monica Applewhite, who holds a master's degree in the science of social work and a PhD in clinical social work, addressed approximately 50 priests and religious men in Adelaide, South Australia, on "The Impact of Abuse in the Church on Priests and Religious

---

sense, a Catholic priest who leaves takes with him neither a future nor a past. He has nothing—except his own strength of character, his personal qualities, and the grace of God. Yet these turn out to be enough (David Rice, *Shattered Vows: Priests Who Leave*, 43-44).

[259] David Rice, *Shattered Vows: Priests Who Leave* (William Morrow & Co. Inc., 1990), 72.

[260] Ibid. 73, quoting Thomas Merton.

[261] Ibid., 73.

Men: Understanding the Past, Living in the Present, and Preparing a Future of Safe Environments." She had spent the past seventeen years in conducting research and root-cause analysis in the area of sexual abuse and assisting organizations in developing the best practices for both prevention and response. Beginning in 2002, Dr. Applewhite was instrumental in developing an education and accreditation program for religious orders and congregations within the Catholic Church called *Instruments of Hope and Healing*, which was designed to hold Catholic religious men to the highest standards of child protection and response. This program has been adopted by the vast majority of religious institutes of men, constituting more than 15,000 Catholic priests and religious.

"It is an urgent priority to promote a safer and more wholesome environment, especially for young people," so said Pope Benedict XVI in St. Mary's Cathedral, Sydney, New South Wales. Basing her work on that clear and definite objective, Dr. Applewhite truly left no stone unturned in emphasising the paramount need for one and all to be extremely cautious and judiciously prudent in interpersonal communication with people in general, but minors and children in particular. Looking back over the sexual abuse scandal that rocked the entire Catholic Church and the secular world, Dr. Applewhite asked: "What was a strangely surprising but particularly unfortunate failure in the honest resolution of the problem? A blatant disregard of Canon Law, civil law and, I add, divine law!"

Very sincerely and gratefully commending the admirable work of all who worked for the revised Code of Canon Law, Pope John Paul II wrote: "Over the course of time, the Catholic Church has been wont to revise and renew the laws of its sacred discipline so that, maintaining always fidelity to the Divine Founder, these laws may be truly in accord with the salvific mission entrusted to the Church."[262] And what is the Code? "For an accurate answer to this question, it is necessary to remind ourselves of that distant heritage of law contained in the books of the Old and New Testaments. It is from this, as from its first source, that the whole juridical and legislative tradition of the Church derives."[263]

A Code of Canon Law is absolutely necessary for the Church. Since the Church is established in the form of a social and visible unit, it needs

---

[262] John Paul II, Apostolic Constitution (January 25, 1983).
[263] John Paul II, ibid.

rules, so that its hierarchical and organic structure may be visible; that its exercise of the functions divinely entrusted to it, particularly of sacred power and of the administration of the sacraments, is property ordered; that the mutual relationships of Christ's faithful are reconciled in justice based on charity, with the rights of each safeguarded and defined; and lastly, that the common initiatives which are undertaken so that Christian life may be ever more perfectly carried out, are supported, strengthened, and promoted by canonical laws.

A civil attorney in California, who has defended four priests charged with alleged sexual abuse, said that three faced allegations that had little or no basis. "For these men who are wrongfully accused and where the claim itself is found to be without basis, there needs to be an expedited process. The diocese should pay for a quick review because these men do not have the financial resources to wait years and it is unfair to expect someone who lives on $1000 a month to have a legal defence fund—that's basically what they are asking these priests to have."[264]

When a not-so-curious lawyer once asked Jesus, "Teacher, what must I do to inherit eternal life?", Jesus promptly threw the ball back at him, "What is written in the law? What do you read there?" So the answer was well known to him but he wanted to test Jesus. Being a knowledgeable man, he could not conceal the truth: "You shall love the Lord your God with all your heart, and with all your mind and all your soul, and with all your mind."[265] Without even pausing to take a breath, the inquirer instantly and truthfully added, "and your neighbour as yourself."

Commending him for his candour, Jesus said to him, "You have given the right answer; do this, and you will live."[266] This is indeed a sacrosanct obligation that is incumbent on one and all without exception, and the reward is absolutely guaranteed—happiness in this life and eternal happiness hereafter. All the wealth in the entire world could never buy that!

On another occasion, listed in the Gospel according to Matthew, we are told that one of the Pharisees asked Jesus a question in order to test him: "Teacher, which commandment in the law is the greatest?" Without batting an eyelid, Jesus both consistently and candidly answered: "You

---

[264] Joe Feuerherd.
[265] Mark 12:30
[266] Luke 10:25-28.

shall love the Lord your God with all your heart, and with all your soul, and with all your mind. This is the greatest and first commandment. And the second is like it: You shall love your neighbour as yourself. On these two commandments hang all the law and the prophets[267] "(Matthew 23:34-40). In a word, the love of God is best proved in the love and service of people, and this is a duty that is incumbent on one and all without exception.

Strike the Shepherd

"Strike the shepherd" is a capital crime that isn't new. Deploring this age-old and recurring problem, Christ Jesus openly and unequivocally denounced it saying: "Jerusalem, Jerusalem, the city that kills the prophets and stones them who are sent to it! How often have I desired to gather your children together as a hen gathers her brood under her wings, and you were not willing! See, your house is left desolate."

This is a poignant tragedy of rejected love. And Christ Jesus here speaks not so much as a stern and punitive judge but as an ardent lover of those entrusted to the care of the constituted shepherds—priests and religious. More specifically, this passage reveals four great truths.

First, it shows the patience of God. In spite of the fact that Jerusalem has brutally and unashamedly killed the prophets and stoned the messengers, God did not retract his unchangeable love nor cease his compassionate care in and through his visible representatives. There is a limitless patience in the love of God, which bears with human ingratitude and malice. True to his name, God is "I am who I am."

Second, it shows the appeal of God. Jesus speaks as a spurned but persistent lover, who has nothing but the best interests of his beloved at heart. He is no gate-crasher and will never force an entry—the only weapon he can and will use is the appeal of his love. God waits with outstretched arms as is so vividly manifested in the classical parable of the prodigal son. Humans now have the awesome responsibility of being able to either accept or to refuse.

Third, it shows the deliberation of the sin of man. In spite of repeated rejection, God did not desist in appealing for the willing response of his

---

267   Matthew 23:37-39.

people. Eventually, God sent his only-begotten Son with the hope that humans would relent and repent. Oddly, in spite of all that Christ Jesus did and said, people rejected him, thereby evoking a heartbreaking lament: "Truly I tell you, no prophet is accepted in his hometown."[268] The door to the human heart opens only from the inside, and sin is the deliberate refusal of the appeal of God in Christ Jesus.

Fourth, it shows the consequences of rejecting Christ Jesus. Just forty years after that incident, in AD 70 to be precise, Jerusalem was nothing but a pile of ruins. That disaster was the direct consequence of the wilful rejection of Christ Jesus. Had the Jews accepted the way of love and abandoned the way of power politics, Rome would never have descended on them its avenging and ruinous might. In a word, it is a fact of history that the nation that rejects God is doomed to disaster.

Making a Mountain out of a Mole Hill

In his New Year's message (2011), Fr. Gordon MacRae very truthfully states: "Trusting too much can harm your reputation. Not trusting enough can harm your soul." And this is how he corroborates that candid assertion.

I arrived at St. Bernard Parish in Keene, New Hampshire, on June 15, 1983. I was told by our diocesan personnel director at the time that I was going to a positive and worry-free assignment after a difficult year in a very troubled parish. But as was typical for my diocese then—and perhaps for many others—there seemed to be no limit to how out-of-touch the Chancery Office could be.

I arrived to learn that the pastor had been charged with driving while intoxicated and was awaiting my arrival so he could leave for his third attempt at residential treatment for alcoholism. My heart went out to this man who struggled so much with his fragile humanity while his superiors seemed oblivious to it. I was there to replace another priest who was bitterly leaving the priesthood after three years at that parish, but stayed on to help me until the pastor returned. He was angry and disillusioned, and not exactly a fraternal support.

---

[268]   Luke 4:24

The parish was immense, for New Hampshire, at least. It had over 2000 families, provided round-the-clock pastoral care for a regional hospital and trauma unit, three nursing homes, a college campus, a regional Catholic school, and a mission church about fifteen miles away—and I arrived to learn that I was essentially alone. You can read about some of this tumultuous time in "Case History Part I: Origins of the Case."

In that summer of 1983, there was a lot going on in my own life, too. Just a month earlier, my father died suddenly at the age of 52. I had literally gone from presiding over his funeral Mass, and caring for my family, to packing and moving to a new rectory and parish 100 miles away.

A few weeks after I arrived and got settled, my sister and her family drove up from the Boston area to visit me. We still had some unfinished details over the death of our father, and two months earlier my sister gave birth to her second child. I had the privilege of baptizing her in my new parish. While my brother-in-law unpacked my boxes of books, my sister and I took my two nieces for a stroll down Keene, New Hampshire's picturesque Main Street. It was a beautiful summer day, and we had lots to discuss while we pushed the stroller down the busy street.

By the middle of the following week, the rectory phone started ringing. First, it was a priest in a neighbouring parish. "I just wanted to give you a heads-up," he said. "I've heard from two people that you have a secret wife and kids." I laughed, at first, but by the end of that week I wasn't laughing anymore. Then the parish council president called. "We don't need another scandal," he said. "People are calling me with a rumour that you've fathered two children." By then, I was furious.

We were able to backtrack who said what to whom and when, and learned that the ugly rumor began with that innocent Sunday afternoon walk with my sister and nieces. And ground zero of the rumor was one parishioner, Geraldine (long since forgiven, no longer with us, and not her real name!), who also happened to be out on Main Street that afternoon. Geraldine jumped to a conclusion—a rather strange one, I think—then jumped on the telephone. It was like a virus that spread from person to person, growing and mutating along the way. Poor Geraldine had no intention that her bit of gossip would spread like a wildfire, but it did. It spread everywhere.

I waited for a time when I was a little calmer to call Geraldine, but she didn't make it easy. At first she was embarrassed that I had traced the story back to her, but she was far more embarrassed to learn that my sordid stroll down Main Street that day was with my sister and two nieces who had come to visit to discuss the death of our father. "Well, never mind!" Geraldine said, "But we do have a right to know what our priests are up to!"

Yes, priests are public people, and perhaps there have been too many times when the Church didn't know enough about what they were all up to. But what was missing from this story was any sense of trust and human respect—not to mention any benefit of doubt. A simple, "Who were those people you were with?" would have produced an explanation and saved a lot of grief.[269]

Malice, like Beauty, Is in the Eye of the Beholder

Here is yet another sad story candidly shared by Fr. Gordon MacRae in his blog dated December 20, 2010.

> "It happens so easily and sometimes even innocently. Very few of us are exempt from being both the victims and the proponents of gossip. As I wrote in **"The Mirror of Justice Cracked,"** the first of a three-part post in October, I was once Director of Admissions for a treatment and spiritual renewal center for priests. I had been on staff there only a month when asked one day to give a tour to a visiting bishop. In the main corridor, we stopped to look at a display of Native American art from a local Pueblo. As the bishop backed up to view the display, he backed right into the lady's room door just as it opened and a secretary emerged. It was an awkward moment.
>
> I reached out to steady them both as they collided, and to lighten the startled secretary's embarrassment I said, "It's not a vision; it's just us." The next morning I was summoned to the facility director's office. The secretary had filed a complaint alleging that on the previous day I approached her as she emerged from the lady's room and said, "Oh, it's my vision of lust!"

.

Fr. Gordon MacRae, *These Stone Walls* (December 20, 2010).

When I told the director what really happened, he inquired with the visiting bishop who corroborated my account exactly, but not before the secretary passed along her version to the rest of the office staff. I was new there, and for weeks afterward I had a creepy feeling that I was the subject of a lot of office gossip. Over time, once the staff got to know me better and a trust level developed, the incident just evaporated. Eventually even the offended secretary just brushed it aside with a casually mumbled, "I might have heard wrong."

There was a time when women were subjected to real and egregious affronts and harassment in the work place, and there was little they could do about it because of an inherent imbalance of power. I would never want to see a return to the bad old days of grotesquely unjust harassment and abuse. But the problem with the story above wasn't what the secretary thought she heard versus what really happened. It was with the fact that the truth had a steep uphill climb once everyone else was told only one side of the story. Once such a thing takes root, it spreads and forms a life of its own. An untrue rumor can be repeated so much, and spread so far, that the truth doesn't stand a chance.

Actually, this is exactly what has happened in the sexual abuse crisis in the Church. The media spread one story with such ferocity that the truth is just swatted like a pesky fly. To see just how this happened, have another look at my *Catalyst* article, "**Due Process for Accused Priests.**"[270]

Conclusion

In his homily at the Chrism Mass on April 13, 2006, Pope Benedict said to the priests present: "The mystery of the priesthood of the Church lies in the fact that we, miserable human beings, by virtue of the Sacrament

---

[270] Fr. Gordon MacRae, *These Stone Walls*, (December 20, 2010).

of Holy Orders, can speak with [the] "I" [of Jesus] *in persona Christi*. He wishes to exercise *his* priesthood through us."[271]

And then, with all the love of a fatherly heart, the Holy Father said:

> Dear priests, the quality of your lives and your pastoral service seem to indicate that in this Diocese (Rome), as in many others of the world, we have now left behind us that period of identity crisis that troubled so many priests. However, still present are the causes of the "spiritual wilderness" that afflict humanity in our day and consequently also undermine the Church, which dwells among humankind. How can we not fear that they may also ensnare the lives of priests? It is indispensable, therefore, to return ever anew to the solid root of our priesthood. This root, as we will know, is one: Jesus Christ our Lord.[272]

---

[271] Pope Benedict XVI (homily at Chrism Mass, Holy Thursday, April 13, 2006).

[272] Pope Benedict XVI (address to the Clergy of the Diocese of Rome, May 13, 2005).

The Beautiful Hands of a Priest

We need them in life's early morning,
we need them again at the close;
we need their warm clasp of true friendship,
we seek them when tasting life's woes.

At the altar each day we behold them,
and the hands of a king on his throne;
are not equal to them in their greatness—
their dignity stands all alone.

And when we are tempted and wander,
to pathways of shame and of sin;
it's the hand of a priest that will absolve us—
not once, but again and again.

And when we are taking life's partner,
other hands may prepare us a feast;
but the hand that will bless and unite us
is the beautiful hand of a priest.

God bless them and keep them all holy,
for the Host which their fingers caress;
when can a poor sinner do better than
to ask Him to guide thee and bless?

When the hour of death comes upon us,
may our courage and strength be increased;
by seeing raised over us in blessing,
the beautiful hands of a priest!

—Henri Lacordaire, the great French Dominican

10

Base, Baser, Basest

"In the light of my investigations in the Clergy Cases referred to me,
about ONE-HALF of the claims made were either false
or so greatly exaggerated
that the truth would not have supported
a prosecutable claim for childhood sexual abuse."
—A retired FBI Agent

In 1692, Cotton Mather wrote an essay entitled "The Wonders of the Invisible World."[273] In it, he defended the "justice" of the Salem Witch Trials. Among other "proofs" utilized was a practice of binding a suspected witch's hands and feet, then tying a heavy stone around her neck, and throwing her into a pond. If she somehow managed to free herself, it would serve as evidence that she was guilty of witchcraft and she was summarily hanged. If, on the other hand, the accused sank to the bottom and drowned, then the blithe assumption was that she was innocent after all. "Damned if I do, and damned if I don't." That was the state of the juridical process in 1692 Puritan America.

Base

In November 2009, Representative Tom Murt filed legislation in Pennsylvania that would increase penalties for knowingly

---

[273]   Etext.virginia.edu.

filing a false police report about a crime. The legislation was inspired by a shameful incident that had occurred a decade earlier to a highly respected and now retired Abington, Pennsylvania, public school teacher, Michael Gallagher.

For ten years, Michael lived through a dedicated teacher's worst nightmare. After serving for 26 years as a conscientious and highly respected teacher, the police arrested him on January 22, 1998. A former student had claimed that Michael had repeatedly raped her a dozen years earlier in the 1985-1986 school year. Michael was arrested, booked, and finally released when he and his wife put up their house to secure a $150,000 bail requirement. Said the innocent husband, father and teacher: "I was thrown into jail . . . and then paraded in handcuffs to the District Justice's office with every major news channel there."[274]

Michael was then suspended without pay from the teaching position that he had held with professional integrity and respect for 26 years. The 23-year-old former student claimed that Michael had raped her more than 20 times. Michael's face was plastered on newspapers and in the evening news through the region, a tactic often employed by prosecutors and contingency lawyers to generate more claims against the accused. For ten agonising months, Michael, his wife Betty and their three sons aged 18, 24 and 30, braced for a high-profile trial. Of course, trial by media and innuendo was already well underway. *A claim of sexual abuse is far more devastating for the innocent than for the guilty.*

As can be expected, Michael and Betty wondered how they would cope when the money ran out. In addition to the suspension without pay, the Gallaghers faced $45,000 in legal fees to defend Michael. Providentially, his family and friends stood by him loyally and courageously. Perhaps the

---

[274] Michael Gallagher, in Gordon MacRae, Op.Cit., 13 January 2010.

most telling statement came from his devoted and loving wife, Betty: "I think I know my husband best after 32 years of marriage. I have no doubt whatsoever."

On October 20, 1998, Michael realized that his criminal trial was but a month away and that a group of 12 strangers would determine his guilt or innocence. If found guilty, the 60-year-old teacher would face a long prison sentence. "That was the worst day," confessed Michael.

The very next day, October 21, 1998, Michael's lawyer showed up at his door. He told Michael to pick a date for a celebration. The charges had been dropped, because the prosecutors somehow learned that the 23-year-old accuser had fabricated the entire story. It was over, but not before Michael had to pay again to have his record cleared after he was exonerated. Ironically, his accuser simply walked away from the case, with no accountability whatsoever.

Baser

In May 2010, a 43-year-old man walked into the Jesuits' Sacred Heart Retirement Home in Los Gatos and lured a 65-year-old priest to the lobby. He began rather civilly by inquiring if the priest did recognise him. The cleric did honestly try to jog his memory but was unable to identify the visitor. At this, the latter flew into a violent rage and attacked the unsuspecting cleric beating him mercilessly in front of horrified witnesses.[275]

The assailant, Will Lynch, alleges that Rev. Jerold Lindner had sexually abused him and his younger brother during a camping trip in May 1975. Lindner has repeatedly denied abusing anyone, and has never been criminally charged. In a deposition in the late 1990s, Lindner said that he didn't recall either Lynch or his brother. The consequences were as follows:

---

[275] TheMediaReport.com, "Examining Anti-Catholicism and Bias in the Media" (November 2010).

- The Lynch brothers received a financial settlement from the Jesuits in 1998—$625,000.00!
- Lindner's younger sister and several nieces and nephews have accused Lindner of abuse, as have several women whose families were friendly with him when they were children.
- The Archdiocese of Los Angeles also settled two cases involving Lindner in its record-breaking $660 million payout in 2007. Ironically, the LA settlement does not in itself acknowledge that the alleged abuse did actually occur.
- "Hundreds" of "clergy abuse victims" are publicly supporting the alleged attacker and "want to contribute to a legal defence fund" for Lynch.
- Lynch plans to use his criminal trial as a way to "heighten awareness of clergy sex abuse."[276]
- In August 2003, a cleric, John Geoghan, imprisoned for abuse, was murdered. This was the statement issued by SNAP (The Survivors' Network of those Abused by Priests): "Violence does not solve the problem of clerical sexual abuse or promote healing among victims. It can never be condoned."

Basest

In 1974, 19-year-old James "Jamie" Bain was sentenced to life in prison in a Florida courtroom for kidnapping and raping a nine-year-old boy. A heinous crime deserved heinous treatment, which the prison inmates did not hesitate to heap upon the supposedly guilty culprit.

Thirty-five years later, a week before Christmas (2009), Jamie walked out of a Florida courtroom a free man after it was proven that he had no connection whatsoever to the crime for which he had been wrongly incarcerated for 35 years. He was 19 when he entered prison; he left at the age of 54.

DNA evidence preserved from the crime scene satisfactorily and conclusively excluded Jamie Bain as a suspect. In other words, for 35 years,

---

[276] In the light of the never-ending *tsunami* of media coverage on this issue for the past two to three decades, is there anyone left on the planet who is not aware of the crimes committed by priests?

the real criminal roamed freely while Jamie suffered decades of infamy and torture for being a child rapist. On the steps of the courthouse after his shackles were removed, he faced a small group of family and reporters. All he asked for was to be taken home to his dear 77-year-old mother—she was 42 when her son was falsely accused and unjustly slapped with a life sentence.

Across the United States, 247 wrongly convicted prisoners have been released after preserved DNA evidence proved conclusively that the wrong person was serving a prison sentence. Most were convicted of sexual assault, and many served 20 years or more in prison before being exonerated.

In Jamie's case, the sole witness was the traumatized nine-year-old victim, who identified his attacker as "one with bushy sideburns." Hastily, but rashly, the boy's uncle, who was a high school principal at the time, said, "That sounds like Jamie Bain." When a photo lineup was placed before the victim, he picked out Jamie Bain on the basis of his recollection of "one with bushy sideburns."

The most sordid aspect of this story is the inflexible behaviour of the prosecutors long after the trial. Repeated and multiple petitions to have the DNA evidence examined were not only callously rejected but vehemently opposed. It was only when the Innocence Project got involved with their own attorneys that the DNA was finally tested and Jamie Bain was acquitted. "I'm not angry," said Jamie on the courthouse steps. "I've got God!"

Commenting on this heartbreaking story, this is what Fr. Gordon MacRae rightly said: "God's got Jamie Bain. What else could have preserved his soul and his mind for 35 years of mistreatment in prison?"[277]

Equally heart-rending is the story of Bernard Baran. Reportedly 247 men were exonerated when retested for DNA evidence. By the same token, there have been other exonerations when it was conclusively proved that no crime was actually committed. For instance, in June 2009, a Berkshire Country, Massachusetts, judge announced that all charges were being dropped against Bernard Baran, who was wrongly convicted of child rape when he was 19. Twenty-four years later, at the age of 44, he was released and for an imagined crime—one that never did occur at all. The judge

---

[277] Gordon MacRae. Op.Cit.

who released him declared that Bernard's lawyer at trial was incompetent and prosecutors withheld crucial evidence of Bernard's innocence.

That evidence consisted of videotapes of interviews with the child "victims." The tapes showed them insisting that no sexual assaults ever took place while interrogators kept asking the same questions over and over again until the children changed their story. All the children's denials were edited out of the tapes before they were presented to Bernard's defence lawyer—and to the jury.

Sadly, Bernard Baran was himself raped and beaten during his more than two decades of wrongful imprisonment. The National Center for Reason and Justice (www.ncrj.org) sponsored Bernard Baran's new appeals and helped win his release. The NCRJ is also sponsoring the defence of Fr. Gordon MacRae, who has been unjustly imprisoned for a crime that he did not commit and, for as long as 35 years, only because he is firm on pleading his innocence, and uncompromising in his rejection of a plea bargain that could see a long term in jail reduced to a minimum three-year stint. For this, Fr. MacRae is most grateful.

Commenting on this woeful miscarriage of justice, this is what Fr. MacRae said:

> Sometimes the prosecutorial misconduct in sexual cases is just a subtle form of "spin." In one now thoroughly discredited sexual abuse case that has been widely written about—the Massachusetts case against the Amirault family—the spectre of child pornography rose to the surface. When not a shred of evidence for it was found, the prosecutor said to the news media, "The fact that child pornography wasn't found doesn't mean it never existed." So, the absence of evidence is evidence of evidence![278]

---

[278] Fr. Gordon MacRae, "The Eighth Commandment" (January 13, 2010).

"Thou Shalt Not Bear False Witness against Thy Neighbour"

The Eighth Commandment expressly says: "Thou shalt not bear false witness against thy neighbour."[279] It is forbidden, under pain of grievous sin, to give false testimony in a juridical proceeding that could result in serious and irreparable harm to an innocent person. This is all the more crucial in a system in which one person's word could condemn another, with no possibility of a reprieve.

The book of Deuteronomy is even more direct and explicit:

> A single witness shall not prevail against a man for any crime or for any wrong in connection with any offence . . . Only on the evidence of two witnesses, or of three witnesses, shall a charge be sustained. If a malicious witness rises against any man . . . and if the witness is a false witness and had accused his brother falsely, then you shall do to him as he meant to do to his brother; you shall purge the evil from the midst of you.[280]

In the light of this unambiguous and incontestable injunction, Fr. Gordon MacRae rightly asks: "How is it, then, that priests accused from twenty, thirty, or forty years ago—with no evidence whatsoever beyond the word of someone who stands to gain hundreds of thousands dollars—are presumed by so many to be guilty?"[281]

On hearing of his heart-rending plight, a reader of Fr. MacRae's three-part case history on his widely publicized blog, *These Stone Walls*, wrote him a very sympathetic letter in which, among other things, he said: "I don't know why you haven't lost your faith. And I don't know why you haven't lost your mind." Adds the noble and brave priest: "I wonder which would be the first to go. There are lots of people around me here with a tentative grasp on both."[282]

---

[279] Exodus 20:16.
[280] Deuteronomy 19:15-19.
[281] Ibid.
[282] Ibid.

A Bombshell

TheMediaReport.com "Examining Anti-Catholicism and Bias in the Media" published a bombshell on January 2, 2011, entitled: "Special Report—Los Angeles Attorney Declares Rampant Fraud—Many Abuse Claims against Catholic Priests are 'Entirely False.'"

> In a stunning ten-page declaration recently submitted to the Los Angeles County Superior Court, veteran attorney, Donald H. Steier, stated that his investigations into claims of sexual abuse by Catholic priests have uncovered vast fraud and that his probes have revealed that many accusations are completely false.

> Counsellor Steier informs us that he has played a role in one hundred investigations involving Catholic clergy in Los Angeles. This is what one retired FBI agent, who worked with him in the investigation of many claims in the clergy cases had to say: "ONE-HALF of the claims made were either entirely false or so greatly exaggerated that the truth would not have supported a prosecutable claim for childhood sexual abuse. In several cases, the objective information was not consonant with the subjective allegations. That is to say, in many cases the objective facts showed that the accusations made were false."[283]

> More specifically, herewith is the gist of some of his observations:

> • Accused priests were required to take a polygraph examination by very experienced former law enforcement experts, including the LAPD, the sheriff's department, and the FBI. In many cases, it was established beyond doubt that the denial of wrong-doing was "truthful."

---

[283] The capitalization is his.

- Accusers were similarly asked to undergo a polygraph examination at their personal expense. In every case, the accuser refused to have his veracity tested by that investigative tool.

- Several plaintiffs testified that they realized that they had been abused only after learning that some other person—sometimes a relative—had received a financial settlement from the archdiocese or another Catholic institution.

- The stories of some accusers changed significantly over time, sometimes altering years, locations, and what was actually alleged so as to exact claims against innocent clients.

- False memories were planted or created by various psychological processes and by therapists who might be characterized as "sexual victim advocates," if not outright charlatans.

- In the State of California, a certificate of merit from a licensed mental health practitioner is required before filing an abuse lawsuit.[284] Most of the approximately seven hundred psychiatric certificates of merit filed in these clergy cases *were signed by the same therapist!*

- These startling and disturbing revelations aroused the ire of SNAP (Survivors' Network of those Abused by Priests). Reportedly, SNAP maintains an interactive website with a user forum and message board, among other features, where people can share detailed information between alleged victims pertaining to the identity of specific alleged perpetrators, their alleged "modus operandi," and other details of alleged molestation. As a consequence, a person who wanted to make a false claim of sexual abuse by a priest could go to that website and find a "blueprint" of factual allegations, and make one that would coincide with allegations made by other people. Law enforcement also uses the SNAP website to attempt to locate new victims and allegations against Catholic priests.

- In a frantic retort, SNAP issued a press statement dated December 13, 2010, deriding Steier's declaration as a "legal manoeuvre" that was "among the most outrageous and hurtful ever made by a church defence lawyer."

---

[284] California Code of Civil Procedure §340.1

- Threatening to file a complaint with the California Bar Association, SNAP demanded that Los Angeles Cardinal Roger Mahony "denounce Steier's claims and disclose how much archdiocesan money has been paid to Steier." Adds the veteran attorney, "The last time I checked, SNAP steadfastly refused to divulge how much of its income is derived from the number of lawyers with whom it closely collaborates."

- Ironically, in its statement, SNAP does not refute or deny any of the specific claims made by Steier. It simply labels them as "outrageous and hurtful." *Truth is beginning to prevail.*

- Yes, admits Steier candidly and unequivocally, Catholic priests terribly abused minors, and bishops failed to stop the harm. That's an undeniable truth. There are few crimes that revolt more than sexual abuse. The abuse of minors is a dark episode, Steier frankly concedes, that the Church will forever have to live with.[285]

- This is how best-selling author and *Wall Street Journal* writer Dorothy Rabinowitz, summarises the highly suspect plethora of false allegations: "People have come to understand that there is a large scam going on with personal injury attorneys, and what began as a serious effort has now expanded to become a huge money-making proposition."[286]

- Vincent Carroll, writing in the *Denver Post*, is a rare voice of acknowledgement: "Fraudulent or highly dubious accusations are more common than is acknowledged in coverage of the church scandals—although they should not be surprising, given the monumental settlements various dioceses have paid out over the years."[287]

---

[285] TheMediaReport.com, "Examining Anti-Catholicism and Bias in the Media" (January 2, 2011).

[286] Ibid., Ms Rabinowitz made this remark in 2005. Since then, the Church has doled out an additional $1 billion in settlements.

[287] Vincent Carrol, *The Denver Post* (October 10, 2010).

The High Cost of Innocence

Well aware of the media reports on scores of innocent men wrongly imprisoned, a California lawyer's study shows that up to half the claims against Catholic priests are false. "If you let 'em get away with this, you give 'em the eternal right to do the same damn thing to any one of you!" That poignant and memorable line was delivered with blunt force by actor Joe Don Baker portraying the famous anti-corruption sheriff, Buford Pusser, in the 1973 film, *Walking Tall.* Buford stood shirtless before a packed courthouse, the lacerations of his brutal scourging by local thugs still glistening with blood, while a corrupted judge pounded his gavel charging Buford with contempt. The entire courtroom and the viewing audience gasped with contempt, but their contempt was not for Buford Pusser, but for a system that rashly and unjustly sets a high price on innocence.

In 1979, 20-year-old Cornelius Dupree was arrested for a sex crime that he had nothing to do with. He was sentenced to 75 years in prison. In 2004, he was set to be released on parole. Dupree refused because he was required to submit to a sex offender treatment program, which would be tantamount to an admission of guilt. This happened twice and Dupree was implacable in protesting his innocence. Thirty-one years after his imprisonment, the innocent Dupree was exonerated and released.

As he stood before cameras in front of the Dallas courthouse with Innocence Project Founder, Attorney Barry Scheck, Cornelius Dupree could have said something similar to Buford Pusser's declaration: "If you let 'em get away with this, you give 'em the eternal right to do the same damn thing to any one of you!" Dupree served time for a crime he didn't commit. He was no less innocent than the 41 wrongfully convicted and exonerated prisoners in Texas since 2001.

Says Fr. Gordon MacRae in words that will tug at the heartstrings of any right-thinking and truth-embracing individual:

> Well, Buford Pusser provided THAT answer. I woke up one night in prison muttering his very same words. I think the court I was standing before was the court of public opinion,

and it wasn't my body that was lacerated, but my name and my priesthood and the entire Church.[288]

Such is the high cost of innocence!

Vengeance Is a Double-Edged Sword

With a heart overflowing with genuine pastoral solicitude, St. Paul cautions the members of his community with these wise words: "Indeed, the word of God is living and active, sharper than any two-edged sword, piercing until it divides soul from spirit, joints from marrow; it is able to judge the thoughts and intentions of the heart. And before him no creature is hidden, but all are naked and laid bare to the eyes of the one to whom we must render an account."[289]

In the recent past, for instance, the National Center for Reason and Justice[290] steadfastly expressed its full support of Nancy Smith and Joseph Allen, just days after the Ohio Supreme Court overturned Lorain County Common Pleas Court Judge James Burge's 2009 acquittal of the pair.[291]

During the 1994 trial, prosecutors contended that Smith would take 4—and 5-year old children from her Head Start bus route to Allen's home, where the children would be sexually abused. Both strenuously maintained their innocence. Even more, they vigorously insisted that they didn't even know each other until they were charged in the case. Regrettably, Smith and Allen were found guilty. Smith was sentenced to 30 to 90 years in prison, and Allen was sentenced to five consecutive life sentences.

After a paperwork error[292] sent the pair to Judge James Burge's courtroom in 2009, rather than correct the entry, Burge acquitted them, stating he believed Smith and Allen were innocent.

---

[288] Fr. Gordon MacRae, "Walking Tall: the Truth behind the Eighth Commandment."

[289] Hebrews 4:12

[290] The National Center for Reason and Justice (NCRJ) is a legal advisory group for the falsely accused and wrongfully acquitted.

[291] Published Monday, January 31, 2011.

[292] The original entries failed to note that Smith and Allen had been convicted by a jury, language that is necessary to have a final appealable order.

The Ohio Supreme Court issued a decision stating Burge lacked jurisdiction to make such an order and directed Judge James Burge to set aside his 2009 acquittal of Nancy Smith in the controversial Head Start child molestation case. So Burge's jurisdiction was at issue. Said a very disappointed judge, "I never thought I would witness anything quite so tragic in the criminal justice system, much less be any part of it."[293]

Jack Bradley, Smith's lawyer, and K. Ronald Bailey, who represented Allen, said they too were horrified by the implications of the decision but promised to continue their efforts to keep their clients from returning to prison. "I'm going to keep fighting this until I'm dead," Bailey said.

Robert B. Chatelle, executive director of the National Center for Reason and Justice, acknowledged that the Ohio Supreme Court judges' move sparked outrage among supporters of Smith and Allen.[294]

Chatelle also made mention of other victims of nationally known "child sex abuse panic," such as the McMartins, Kelly Michaels, and Bernard Baran, who were acquitted or free years later and compared the hysteria to that which surrounded the case of Smith and Allen.

Even more, Chatelle wrote the NCRJ has never heard of another like the Head Start case, as this case has become known. "We know of no other instance in American law where a court has attempted to imprison the acquitted—a blatant infringement of Constitutional protection against double jeopardy, as well as the constitutional principle of due process of law," Chatelle said.[295]

One of the responses to "High Court Overturns Judge's Acquittals in Head Start Case" reads as follows:

---

[293] After he ordered Smith and Allen freed on bond, Burge reviewed the case file and the trial transcript before acquitting the pair. At the time, Burge said he didn't believe the pair had committed the crimes they were convicted of during the trial. "I have absolutely no confidence that these verdicts are correct," Burge said in 2009.

[294] Ibid.

[295] "The NCRJ has sponsored Nancy Smith's and Joseph Allen's cases for years, and we firmly believe in their innocence. They will continue to have our full support. We will fight for them until justice is achieved."

135

Isn't the goal of justice to get it right? I remember reading this story as it unfolded back in the 90's and the whole thing never quite added up! Can someone post where you can write as a tax payer to have the case re-opened and vacate this gross miscarriage of justice? I don't know either of these individuals and have raised three children while living in Lorain during that period of time. If I thought for one moment they were guilty, I'd be the first to shout "Hang-um!" However, everything I've read and heard since the case was brought has strengthened my conviction that two innocent people may spend the rest of their lives in prison because of the almighty dollar! And that to me is ATROCIOUS![296]

This is a second response:

I worked for the attorney who filed the first appeal for Joseph Allen and read the ENTIRE transcript of the trial, logging all the inaccuracies of testimony. There were so many contradicting pieces of "evidence" that I could never figure out how a jury could convict these people. I have always believed whole-heartedly that they are innocent and hope that someday justice is served.[297]

A third response comes from James Bohannon: "Maybe someone needs to go to our Ohio Supreme Court and state the law was created to protect people not to entrap them. A case so obviously wrong should have a simple means of correcting it."[298]

Finally, this was the response of Tazz:

---

[296] DaddyOh (January 28, 2011, at 8.05 a.m).
narj.org/nancy-smith-joseph-allen
[297] Lookin4thesun (January 28, 2011, at 8:51 a.m.).
[298] James Bohannon (January 28, 2011, at 11:27 a.m.).

This has been a true miscarriage of justice. The children in question speak of coaching from parents and the office of the prosecutor. This was a high profile case and should have been moved out of Lorain at the very least. Murderers don't get this harsh a sentence. Something is definitely wrong here. These people have been offered parole if only they would admit guilt and to this day they claim innocence of this crime. They could have already been free or paroled, but will not admit to a crime neither one committed. That in itself should show proof of innocence. It certainly does to me.[299]

---

[299] Tazz (January 28, 2011, at 12.23 p.m.).

11

A Stitch in Time Saves Nine

If you want peace, work for justice.
—Pope Paul VI

The Universal Declaration of Human Rights

A little over fifty years ago, the United Nations promulgated the Universal Declaration of Human Rights. Generally hailed as "the people's document," it consists of 30 articles that are both easily legible and intelligible to each and every human being in our global family. The principal aim is fourfold: first, to emphasize the dignity of a human being; second, to uphold a person's civil and political rights; third, to ensure the economic and social rights of one and all; and fourth, to guarantee every human being the wherewithal to live with dignity and in peace.

The Preamble clearly, unequivocally and definitively states:

> *Whereas recognition of the inherent dignity and of the equal and inalienable rights of all members of the human family is the foundation of freedom, justice and peace in the world,*
>
> *Whereas disregard and contempt for human rights have resulted in barbarous acts which have outraged the conscience of mankind, and the advent of a world in which human beings shall enjoy freedom of speech and belief and freedom from fear*

and want has been proclaimed as the highest aspiration of the common people . . .

Now, therefore, the General Assembly proclaims this Universal Declaration of Human Rights . . .

(1) Everyone charged with a penal offence has the right to be presumed innocent until proved guilty according to law in a public trial at which he has had all the guarantees necessary for his defence.
(2) No one shall be held guilty of any penal offence on account of any act or omission which did not constitute a penal offence, under national or international law, at the time when it was committed. Nor shall a heavier penalty be imposed than the one that was applicable at the time the penal offence was committed. (Article 11)

This was one of the 30 articles that were deemed sacrosanct, inalienable, and inviolable by the United Nations General Assembly on December 10, 1948, and with not a single dissenting vote. It was unanimous, unqualified and unconditional, so much so that Eleanor Roosevelt, the chair of the Drafting Commission, referred to it as a new Magna Carta for humanity. World leaders, such as Pope John Paul II, called it a "milestone in the long and difficult struggle of the human race."[300]

Today, the Declaration of Human Rights has assumed burgeoning global significance and is increasingly referred to *as customary international law* by human rights scholars and even federal judges. For instance, in 1980, a United States court ruled against Pena, a military commander (*Filartiga v. Pena*) for torturing and murdering a 17-year-old high school student, Joelita Filartiga, in Paraguay. After the torture, Joelita's father and Pena had moved to the United States. Upon learning of Pena's whereabouts, Dr. Filartiga filed a suit. The ruling came after extremely long litigation. Federal Judges Kaufman, Kearse, and Feinberg of the Second Circuit reached the following conclusion, resulting in what has come to be known as "the Filartiga principle":

---

[300] John Paul II. Quoted in Catholic Bishops of Australia's "A Milestone for the Human Family". www.catholicculture.org.

> Official torture is now prohibited by the law of the nations.
> This prohibition is clear and unambiguous and admits no
> distinction between treatment of aliens and citizens . . . This
> prohibition has become part of customary international law,
> as evidenced and defined by the Universal Declaration of
> Human Rights.[301]

Similarly, a Massachusetts court ruled against General Hector
Gramajo, a former minister of defence in Guatemala, who ordered, among
other things, the disembowelment of children in front of their parents.[302]
As a consequence, jurists around the world argued that, in addition to
the prohibition against torture, other rights contained in the Universal
Declaration of the United Nations should be considered part of *customary
international law*. So the dictates of Article 11—the presumption of
innocence until proven guilty—is a sacrosanct, inalienable, and inviolable
right of each and every human being, priests included.

"If You Want Peace, Work for Justice"

In his letter to the priests of the world on the occasion of the 150th
Anniversary of the *Dies Natalis* of St. John Vianney (the Curé of Ars),
Pope Benedict XVI (2009) very realistically and rightly said: "In today's
world, as in the troubled times of the Curé of Ars, the lives and activity
of priests need to be distinguished by a forceful witness to the Gospel.
As Pope Paul VI rightly noted, 'modern man listens more willingly to
witnesses than to teachers, and if he does listen to teachers, it is because
they are witnesses.'"[303]

In his time, the Curé of Ars was able to transform the hearts and the
lives of so many people because he enabled them to experience the Lord's
merciful love. And so our Holy Father reminds priests of the urgency of a
similar proclamation and witness to the truth of Love: *Deus caritas est.*[304]

---

[301]   Joseph Wronka, *Human Rights and Social Policy in the 21st Century*
(1998), 3.

[302]   Ibid., 4.

[303]   *Evangelii nuntiandi*, no. 41.

[304]   1 John 4:8

Thanks to the word and the sacraments of Jesus, John Mary Vianney built up his flock, although he often trembled from a conviction of his personal inadequacy and desired more than once to withdraw from the responsibilities of the parish ministry out of a sense of his unworthiness. Nonetheless, with exemplary obedience, he never abandoned his post, consumed as he was by apostolic zeal for the salvation of souls. "A priest's existence must be wholly dedicated to God and to others; he must become a sacrificial gift."[305]

"It Is Better to Light a Candle, than to Curse the Darkness"[306]

In his pastoral letter to the People of Ireland, Pope Benedict XVI humbly and candidly acknowledged:

> All of us are suffering as a result of the sins of our confreres who betrayed a sacred trust or failed to deal justly and responsibly with allegations of abuse. In view of the outrage and indignation which this has provoked, not only among the lay faithful but among yourselves and your religious communities, many of you feel personally discouraged, even abandoned.[307] I am also aware that in some people's eyes you are tainted by association, and viewed as if you

---

[305] Cardinal Sean O'Malley, Archbishop of Boston (July 2009).

[306] Motto of the American Christopher Society (founded 1945). Oxford Dictionary of Quotations, Oxford Uni Press, 2009.

[307] Professor Richard Schoenherr, a sociologist at the University of Wisconsin at Madison, presents some daunting figures for the United States: "By the tenth anniversary after ordination, on the average, 20 percent of the priests have resigned from the active ministry. By their fifteenth anniversary, an additional 15 percent resign. So that by the time they reach their twenty-fifth anniversary, 42 percent of each ordination class has resigned from the active ministry ... In three or four years there are going to be more resigned priests alive in the United States than active priests" (Richard Schoenherr, "Trends in Ministry: Patterns in Decline and Growth," lecture).

were somehow responsible for the misdeeds of others. At this painful time, I want to acknowledge the dedication of your priestly and religious lives and apostolates, and I invite you to reaffirm your faith in Christ, your love of his Church and your confidence in the Gospel's promise of redemption, forgiveness and interior renewal. In this way, you will demonstrate for all to see that where sin abounds, grace abounds all the more. (cf. *Rom* 5:20).[308]

The following respondents strikingly indicate the positive attitude that imbues a sizeable majority of priests, who very wisely distinguish between their diocesan status and their membership in the larger ecclesial community, often referring to their membership in and service to "God's Church":

- "I felt shocked, hurt, scandalized. But in the long run I still feel as ardent about my vocation."
- "It's a challenge to be a priest but I feel firm in my vocation; as firm as ever before."
- "I was distraught by the events. I couldn't believe the abuse was so wide-spread. As time went on, however, my reaction was tempered. Most of the time, I like being a priest."

These responses must be truthfully balanced by others that were not so positive, but sincerely hopeful:

- "When I went to the Seminary, perhaps naively, I saw the bishop as being a father and friend to his priests. This is not the case, and has made me reflect whether this is what I want to do for the rest of my life. At the drop of a hat, he might throw me out." This respondent very seriously considered quitting the active ministry.
- "Overall, however, it (the sexual abuse scandal) has affected my thinking about the priesthood and my ability to minister. I must now add great caution to my ministry, which prohibits some

---

[308] Pastoral letter to the People of Ireland, 2010. www.vatican.va/holy-father/benedict_xvi

kinds of ministry. And it prohibits joy. You can't even hug people any longer."

- "I prefer not to be around kids. I'm afraid of kids. I don't want to be in any position that casts me in a suspicious light of being improper. I don't touch kids. I won't even shake their hands. I don't show up at the catechetical lessons that are provided on church grounds. It's made my ministry harder because the priest can't be seen as a loving father, but rather a prospective paedophile or pervert."

The third category of responses indicates the woeful erosion of trust between laity and priests, thereby compounding an already complex and disturbing problem:

- "As for trust, some [members of the laity] do, others don't. More loyal parishioners do, but those on the periphery do not. Strangely loyal people are more trusting of priests than are the bishops. A sizeable majority think that we all are perverts."
- "At one time we priests were placed on a pedestal. People looked up to us with respect and trust. That has changed dramatically. It too will pass."
- "The laity do not trust priests like they used to—no, and rightly so. Bishops and priests get the respect they deserve by their shepherding, not by virtue of their ordination. This is part and parcel of their ministry, and wearing a collar doesn't give infallibility."

Not to Learn from History Is to Repeat It

Between 1850 and 1900, Rome was inundated with appeals from priests in the United States of America, alleging violations of rights and asking for the protection of canon law. As Robert Trisco has observed, there were a number of bishops who ruled their dioceses with a certain arrogance. "As far as the bishops were concerned, it is clear that some of them frequently, even habitually, treated their priests in an arbitrary manner and—what was worse—that the legal system permitted such treatment."[309] Many bishops seemed to be almost needlessly distrustful of their priests and quite unwilling to listen to advice or any counsel beyond a select few of their advisors. Said Henry Ford: "Coming together is a beginning; keeping together is progress; working together is success." The *de facto* situation then was very far from this ideal.

A Plea for Canon Law in the United States

William Mahoney, a priest ordained for the Archdiocese of Baltimore, and later deprived of his faculties, sought to plead the cause of oppressed priests by the anonymous publication of his book in 1883, *Jura Sacerdotum Vindicata: The Rights of Clergy Vindicated; or A Plea for Canon Law in the United States.*[310]

This book is a stinging condemnation of what the author would consider the abuse of power on the part of bishops, to the severe detriment of the clergy. Such chapters as "The Evil of Dismissing Uneconomically Any Clergyman from His Diocese," "Charity and Justice Forbid the Uncanonical Dismissal of a Clergyman from His Diocese," and "To Dismiss Uncanonically a Clergyman from His Diocese is to Reduce Him, as a Rule, to Beggary, or to Oblige Him to Engage in Secular Pursuits to Gain a Livelihood, Both of Which are Positively Forbidden by the Church,"[311] clearly indicate the thrust of Mahoney's argumentation in the protection of clergy rights.

With a rapid increase in the numbers of the Catholic Church in the United States, Mahoney considered it imperative that there be a centralizing process for uniformity in matters of faith across the country, *including* disciplinary matters.

> We must have the same Catholic Church in the West as in the East, in the South as in the North, not only in

---

[309] Robert Trisco, "Bishops and their Priests in the United States," in *The Catholic Priest in the United States: Historical Investigations*, ed. John Tracy Ellis (Collegeville, MN: St. John's University Press, 1971), 270.

[310] William Mahoney, *The Rights of Clergy Vindicated: Or, a Plea for Canon Law in the United States* (New York: James Shedhy, 1883).

[311] Ibid., 383-384.

matters of faith, but in matters of discipline, likewise; one homogeneous Catholic Church, united in indissoluble bonds to Rome, the centre of unity; the faith, obedient to their pastors, these latter obedient to their bishops, and the bishops themselves obedient to the voice of Peter, to the voice of Rome; all kept in unity and harmony, not only by the charity of Jesus Christ, but by wise and uniform laws, strictly and conscientiously observed by all.[312]

He then adds, "Plainly, then, we can look only to Rome . . . that will put new life and vigour into the church in these United States, who will bring law and order out of the chaos that now exists, who will govern the church of these provinces with a just, yet mild and paternal hand for a few years, until ecclesiastical discipline has been firmly and securely established."[313] As a matter of fact, there had been too much legislation and not enough implementation: "Words to the heat of deeds, too cool breath gives," said that immortal genius William Shakespeare. And said Mahoney, "The clergy are heartily sick and tired of the arbitrary and uncanonical manner in which, as a rule, they have been treated. They cry out for a representative of the Holy See in the United States."[314]

Another pressing need, way back then—as even now—was ensuring the authentic mission of Catholic Schools:

No Catholic bishop, at the peril of his immortal soul, can be indifferent now-a-days to Catholic education. Let the cathedral wait, let the grand church wait, let all the other improvements of his diocese wait, he has need only of the school-house—the school-house or seminary to educate his priests and the school-house to educate the children of his people. His cathedral, and the ample parish church, and all else for the glory of God will follow of necessity.[315]

---

[312] Ibid., 341-342.

[313] Ibid., 344.

[314] Ibid., 347.

[315] Ibid., 353.

James Valladares, PhD

Finally, for the outspoken and daring cleric, there was yet one urgent necessity that remained to be addressed: *trusteeism*. This meant that the laity had complete control over the ecclesiastical goods and assets of a parish, immune to any interference by bishop or pastor. And this is what Mahoney said: "In some places Committeeism or Trusteeism is a veritable curse, undermining the authority of the priest and consequently of the Bishop, and accompanied with many other fruits of evil, of which every priest is cognizant, and I suppose every bishop in the dioceses where this system, foreign to the constitutions of the church, exists."[316]

By way of a positive recommendation, Mahoney strongly insisted on the presence of an apostolic delegate in the United States. In his personal opinion, such an authoritative papal representative would not only be useful in resolving the recurring conflicts between priests and bishops in the United States but also in the bishops working together in closer collaboration for the good of the entire American Church. *"United we stand, divided we fall."*

In 1853/1854, Archbishop Gaetano Bedini was sent by Pius IX to the United States on an official visit. Among other things, he included his observation about the strained relationship between bishops and their priests.

> It seems that the priests during their ministry do not have the full guarantee of security which Canon Law gives them, and their positions may be changed from one moment to the next. There are no parishes but missions, and so, the priests assigned to them find themselves in such a precarious position that they always fear an immediate change."[317]

In a word, it is virtually impossible for a priest to function effectively and happily if he can be suddenly removed by the unexpected whim of the bishop.

---

[316] Ibid., 354.

[317] James Connelly, *The Visit of Archbishop Gaetano Bedini to the United States of America, June 1853-February 1854* (Rome: Gregorian Company, 1960).

146

In 1878, there was yet another visitor from Rome—Bishop George Conroy of Arlagh, Ireland. In his report, he quoted from a priest's letter that he had earlier received: "We shall not have peace in this country until the relations between bishops and priests shall be established and made clear according to the norms of the provisions of canon law, which is desired so much by all of us." The letter went on to conclude, "Today, priests have no rights at all; they can be chased from their posts at whim while the bishops exercise a veritable tyranny over them."[318]

Conclusion

The bishops largely refused to acknowledge the possibility of some structural problems in their handling of clergy issues, preferring instead to blame the perverseness of certain priests. Unfortunately for the priests, the bishops never communicated adequately to them some of the rationale that prompted their decision making and behaviour. In the precise words of Fr. Kevin McKenna: "The Code of Canon Law promulgated in 1917 by Pope Benedict XV, although not granting priests participation in the selection of their bishops, would seek to ensure that pastors could not be removed frivolously or capriciously. And for this many priests would be grateful for a little more hospitality in the household."[319]

---

[318] Robert Trisco, "Bishops and Their Priests in the United States," in *The Catholic Priest in the United States: Historical Investigations*, ed. John Tracy Ellis (Collegeville, MN: St. John's University Press, 1971), 270.

[319] Kevin E. McKenna, *The Battle for Rights in the United States Catholic Church* (Mahwah, NJ: Paulist Press, 2007), 168.

12

Friend or Foe?

*A bishop should always welcome priests with a special love
since they assume in part the bishop's duties and cares
and carry the weight of them day by day so zealously.
He should regard his priests as sons and friends.*
—Decree on Bishops, Vatican II, #16c

*With sympathetic understanding and principal help,
the bishops should take care of priests
who are in danger of any kind,
or who have failed in some way.*
—Decree on Bishops, Vatican II, #16d

A Paternal Understanding

Fr. Abe is a committed and hardworking priest in the pastoral ministry. With regret, he realised that before he commenced his seminary studies he had violated a teenage girl, who was just 14. Fearing for his future, the contrite priest made a clean breast of his wrong-doing to his bishop, who was both sympathetic and understanding. In accordance with the law, a due investigation was made and the offending priest was constrained to comply with all the dictates of retributive justice.

Thereafter, Fr. Abe expressed his desire to return to the pastoral ministry. As is obvious, he could not return to his parish or diocese. And so, through his bishop, Fr. Abe made an application to another, who was equally compassionate and supportive. After a due process and a clear stipulation of the parameters within which he could licitly serve in the pastoral ministry, the other bishop had him come across to his diocese. And as a special sign of his paternal affection, the new bishop gave Fr. Abe a desk within his own office and clearly assigned him his special duties. Being a diligent priest, he served most efficiently and satisfactorily, and for this he was warmly and publicly commended by the bishop in the diocesan newspaper. "Be merciful, just as your Father is merciful."[320] "For judgement will be without mercy to anyone who has shown no mercy; mercy triumphs over judgement.[321]"

A Fatherly Concern

Fr. Bede was a very dutiful and industrious parish priest, who was respected and loved by all his parishioners and others in the wider community. When the children of the local parish school were presented for the Sacraments, Fr. Bede realised that they were not adequately prepared. So he spoke to the religious education coordinator (REC), who was not impressed, and so referred the matter to the school principal.

Thereafter, both the parish priest and the school principal did meet but were unable to come to a reasonable and amicable resolution.

So the school principal relayed her displeasure to the director of Catholic education. He, in turn, referred the matter to the local bishop, who did not hesitate in writing to the parish priest with a formal directive that he leave the parish. The priest remonstrated with the bishop, but to no avail. The parishioners were up in arms and protested, even to the extent of organising a demonstration outside the bishop's residence; the protesters peacefully disbanded when requested by the local police. From there, the crisis escalated with every passing day, so that the entire parish and even the diocese were polarised into rival factions—some for the priest, others for the bishop.

As Fr. Bede felt that he was being done a severe injustice, he wrote officially to the Congregation for Clergy in Rome. There was a protracted inquiry, and on the basis of the outcome, the bishop was expressly

---

[320]   Luke 6:36
[321]   James 2:13

instructed to reinstate Fr. Bede as the parish priest. The bishop obstinately refused.

The matter was once again referred to the Congregation of Clergy and, once more, the bishop was formally instructed to reinstate the priest, as he was blameless and, therefore, undeserving of the disciplinary action. The bishop was adamant and expressly said to Fr. Bede that he was welcome to leave the diocese. And so, the hapless priest had no alternative but to appeal to a compassionate and understanding bishop.

Providentially, he did meet with one, who encouraged Fr. Bede to come over and had no hesitation in assigning him as a parish priest. Reportedly, the people of his new parish are overjoyed. The attendance at all services has markedly increased, the spirit all around is very positive, and the parishioners are truly delighted to enjoy the committed ministry of a very pastoral priest. "Blessed are the merciful, for they will receive mercy."[322] "And have mercy on some who are wavering; save others by snatching them out of the fire; and have mercy on still others with fear . . ."[323].

"A bishop should always welcome priests with a special love since they assume in part the bishop's duties and cares and carry the weight of them day by day so zealously. He should regard his priests as sons and friends."[324]

It is reported that the late Basil Cardinal Hume of the Westminster Archdiocese in England was so solicitous about his priests that he had a special telephone installed in his office, apartment and bedroom. The number was known solely to his priests, and they were encouraged to call him whenever they needed his personal and urgent attention, whatever the crisis or the time of day or night. Indeed, every bishop "should regard his priests as sons and friends."

Regrettable but True

Fr. Cecil was a newly appointed parish priest. On his arrival, he made two very distressing observations: first, the community had been torn by acrimonious rifts and rival factions; and second, the financial status of the

---

[322] Matthew 5:7

[323] Jude 1:33

[324] Decree on Bishops, Vatican II #16c.

parish was grim, principally because of inefficient administration, reckless spending and no accountability. With steadfast dedication and painstaking reorganisation, Fr. Cecil worked assiduously in order to revive the overall tone in the parish. Within months, the morale was higher, confidence was stronger, and people, especially the alienated, began to return with the hope of making a new start. In a word, there was a manifest change for the better. Fr. Cecil was indeed a welcome breath of fresh air.

At one stage, the church organist suggested that the parish buy a new organ. The matter was discussed by the Parish Pastoral Council and approved. It was referred to the Parish Finance Committee, who suggested a drive in order to raise the desired money. Thanks to the generosity of some affluent parishioners, the parish was able to raise a little over $6,000.00 and within just a couple of months.

Negotiations were made with two musical companies. One offered the parish a brand-new electronic organ for $6,000.00. Another company offered a more expensive and larger organ for $13,000.00. The latter was approached by the church organist herself. Both companies agreed to have the organs delivered for a month's trial with no strings attached.

After a month, there was a consultation with the entire parish, via a secret ballot that was openly and fairly conducted at all the Masses on a weekend. An overwhelming majority opted for the former. And so, *both the Parish Pastoral Council and the Finance Committee, with the expressed approval of Fr. Cecil, decided to purchase it.* This decision did not please the church organist. She wanted the more expensive one, and lobbied her friends to vote for it. However, the majority did opt for the other. In frustration and, as a form of protest, the church organist resigned and said that she would not be returning. Fr. Cecil wrote her a sincere letter of appreciation. "Heaven has no rage, like love to hatred turned; nor hell a fury, like a woman scorned."[325]

The disgruntled and vengeful church organist felt the need to retaliate, and so chose the easiest and most vulnerable target. She used her personal connections to slander Fr. Cecil with the bishop, labelling him "autocratic" and on the grounds that "he takes decisions unilaterally without due consultation." The die had been cast—the parish priest was guilty until proven innocent. He was removed shortly thereafter. "I find

---

[325] *The Mourning Bride* (1697), act 3, scene 8.

no case against him. But you have a custom that I release someone for you . . . Then Pilate took Jesus and had him flogged."[326]

Said Pope Benedict XVI: "If you (bishops) yourselves live in a manner closely configured to Christ, the Good Shepherd, who laid down his life for his sheep, you will inspire your brother priests to re-dedicate themselves to the service of their flocks with Christ-like generosity. Indeed a clearer focus upon the imitation of Christ in holiness of life is exactly what is needed in order for us to move forward."[327]

A Priest Is an Immense Gift

When St. John Vianney was assigned to Ars, a village of just 230 souls, the bishop cautioned him that he would find religious practice in a sorry state: "There is little love of God in that parish; you will be the one to put it there." Undeterred, the zealous pastor did go to his new assignment deeply aware that he needed to embody the presence of Christ Jesus and to bear witness to his saving mercy. With fervour, he would pray ceaselessly: "Lord, grant me the conversion of my parish; I am willing to suffer whatever you wish, for my entire life." And, as the saying goes, "The rest is history!" In the precise words of the saintly Cure, "A good shepherd, a pastor after God's heart, is the greatest treasure which the good Lord can grant to a parish, and one of the most precious gifts of divine mercy."[328]

A Recurring and Painful Scourge

It is a commonly known fact that no human can please all the people all the time. Invariably, there will be individuals who differ and sometimes sharply. A priest is but human. All he can do is to act in the light of his actual perceptions and, with due advice, in the best interests of his parishioners—a decision that can be progressively refined with newer insights and changing pastoral exigencies.

---

[326] John 18:38, 19:1-2
[327] Address to the bishops of the United States in Washington DC (April 16, 2008).
[328] St John Vianney. Quoted in "Letter of His Holiness Pope Benedict XVI Proclaiming a Year for Priests". www.vatican.va

Regrettably, those who differ often work insidiously to a priest's personal detriment by framing slanderous allegations and writing highly critical letters to the local bishop. Some even resort to what is as blatantly cowardly as it is morally depraved and irreparably ruinous—an anonymous letter.[329]

So many innocent priests have been the target of such a despicable act of cowardice and treachery. For instance, one bishop received an anonymous letter about a priest who was a religious and was serving in a diocese in the United States. The bishop sent for the priest and, without giving him a chance to explain or defend himself, ordered him to return to the Philippines. The priest asked to see the letter for himself; the bishop flatly refused.

In another instance, a bishop would write letters to himself about some priests in his diocese. Thereafter, he would call them and reprimand them. Reportedly, the dishonest and devious bishop got careless and started signing the anonymous letters!

A biographer tells us that the saintly Cure d'Ars was once grievously harmed by the calumnious rumours irresponsibly spread by a local gossip monger. One day, the guilty perpetrator was so gripped by remorse that she turned up at the presbytery and humbly begged Fr. John Vianney for his forgiveness. The magnanimous pastor graciously and willingly granted it. But the repentant visitor insisted on a penance. So, the report continues, she was instructed to take a bag of feathers and release them

---

[329] *Calumny* is defined by the *American Heritage Dictionary* (1992) as a "false statement maliciously made to injure another's reputation." The *Catechism of the Catholic Church* (1994) places calumny as a serious sin under the Eighth Commandment, "Thou shall not bear false witness against your neighbour." The Catechism states, "He becomes guilty of calumny who, by remarks contrary to the truth, harms the reputation of others and gives occasion for false judgements concerning them" (2447). The Catechism notes that calumny offends "against the virtues of justice and charity" (2479). Calumny and its close relative detraction (derogatory comments that reveal the hidden faults or sins of another without reason) have been part of life since the dawn of time. But opportunities for breaking the Eighth Commandment have proliferated with the advent of the Internet, especially since the rise of the phenomenon known as "blogging."

from the top of the bell tower. "That is very easy, Father. Please give me something more difficult."

"Very well," said the wise priest, "once you release the feathers from the top of the bell tower, I want you to go around and collect them all."

"But that is impossible, Father," interjected the woman. "The wind will have carried them far and wide."

"You are absolutely right, madame! It is equally impossible to recover one's reputation after it is has been destroyed by idle and malicious gossip."

Anonymous letters should never be entertained or retained on record, principally because they are unsigned and, therefore, unreliable. In the words of a Latin text *"spurgendum est*," they must be destroyed with contempt!

Anonymous Letters

The Holy See has always taught that anonymous letters are to be disregarded and ignored, mainly because they do not have any probative value.

On May 7, 1923, the Sacred Congregation for the Sacraments issued the decree, *Doctrina Catholica*. Its rule 77, #1 states, "No document is entitled to credit unless it is proved to be authentic and genuine."[330]

The Sacred Congregation for the Sacraments, August 15, 1936, promulgated the decree, *Provida Mater*. Article 165 states, "Anonymous letters and other anonymous documents of any kind usually cannot be considered as an indication, unless, and to the extent that, they report facts which can be proved from other sources."[331]

The jurisprudence of the Roman Rota is fully concordant with these statements.[332]

---

[330] Cf. *Acta Apostolicae Sedis*, Vol. 15, 389, ff.

[331] Cf. *AAS*, Vol. 28, 313, ff.

[332] Cf. Sacra Romana Rota: Decisiones 22, n. 9, 373; Vol. XXV, decision 35, n. 12, 303.

The Supreme Tribunal of the Apostolic Signatura has the same philosophy of jurisprudence with regard to documentation.[333]

Many commentators express the same opinion. Wanenmacher writes, "As long as the authorship of the document has not been duly established, there is no legal proof forthcoming." Anonymous letters cannot be brought as evidence in a trial.[334]

The same opinion is also articulated by Felix Cappello, SJ,[335] and Conte A. Coronata.[336]

"A bishop should always welcome priests with a special love since they assume in part the bishop's duties and cares and carry the weight of them day by day so zealously. He should regard his priests as sons and friends."[337] (Decree on Bishops, Vatican II, #16c).

The Eighth Commandment and Canon Law

"You will not bear false witness against your neighbour." [338] This is the precise injunction of the Eighth Commandment, issued by none other than our Creator God, the Supreme Lawgiver. In other words, every human being has a God-given right to a good reputation. And this is how canon law frames it: "No one may unlawfully harm the good reputation which a person enjoys, or violate the right of every person to protect his or her privacy" (Canon 220).

Two rights are recognised and protected here: the right to one's good name or reputation and the right to privacy—this latter having been inserted only after the final draft was submitted to the Sovereign Pontiff. So no one may "unlawfully" infringe either right. The right to one's good reputation is manifestly based on the natural law and is rooted in the

---

[333] Cf. Private Reply, Apostolic Signatura (November 24, 1973); reported in *Communicationes pro Religiosis*, Vol. 56 (1975) 373-383; and *Periodica*, Vol. 64 (1975) 296-303.

[334] Cf. Francis Wanenmacher, Canonical Evidence in Marriage Cases (Philadelphia: Dolphin Press, 1935), 236.

[335] Cf. *Summa Iuris Canonici*, Vol. III., Edition 4, n. 280.

[336] Cf. *Institutiones Iuris Canonici*, Vol. III, Edition 5, n. 1330.

[337] Decree on Bishops, Vatican II, #16c.

[338] Exod 20:16

dignity of the human person. The book of Genesis makes this point clearly and emphatically: "So God created humankind in his image, in the image of God he created them; male and female he created them."[339] So a person's dignity as a human being and his/her rights as a man or a woman come from none other than the Supreme Lawgiver. Consequently, to unlawfully harm the good reputation a person enjoys, priests included, is to break this sacred and inviolable bond and, therefore, to commit a grave sin.

In the Pastoral Constitution of the Church in the Modern World (*Gaudium et Spes*), the fathers of the Second Vatican Council decreed: "(Today) there is a growing awareness of the exalted dignity proper to the human person, since he stands above all things, and his rights and duties are universal and inviolable" (#26-27).

Canon 221 §1 states: "Christ's faithful may lawfully vindicate and defend the rights they enjoy in the Church before the competent ecclesiastical forum in accordance with the law." Stated differently, it is a formal statement that all may lawfully vindicate and defend the rights they enjoy in the Church—and precisely before the competent ecclesiastical forum (i.e. the appropriate tribunal). So everyone in the Church has the right to which this canon refers. Tribunals in the Church have hitherto—for the most part—been concerned with cases of alleged nullity of marriage. This canon clearly signals the need for a wider vision of judicial or quasi-judicial service to all the people of God—priests included! Consequently, when a bishop fails to afford these protections to his people, especially priests, he is violating justice. Even more, his may be a serious and sinful cooperation in evil.

The Fathers of the Second Vatican Council have been forthright in their condemnation of injustice and their promotion of justice. This is what they said to those involved in civic and political affairs: "Prudently and honourably let them fight against injustice and oppression, the arbitrary rule of one man or one party, and a lack of tolerance. Let them devote themselves to the welfare of all sincerely and fairly, indeed with charity and political courage" (*Gaudium et Spes* #75).

If this is the expectation of civic and political leaders, even more is it the bounden duty of bishops, as shepherds and leaders, to safeguard the rights of their own priests. One prominent canonist in the United

---

[339] Genesis 1:27

States has spoken of the glaring failure of bishops in this regard: "The current climate regarding abuse of a minor has caused many bishops to place diocesan public relations and finances paramount to the reputation and rights of the priest when such accusations are levelled."[340]

In other words, usually after an accusation has been made, a priest is swiftly removed from his parish residence and, in some cases, with little or no opportunity to get legal or canonical advice. Fr. Cecil is a striking example of such a hapless priest. Few bishops, like those of Fr. Abe and Fr. Bede, will contact the priest indicating that there is an allegation and then invite him to come in for a discussion after he has obtained canonical and/or civil counsel.

The following words of the illustrious prelate and eminent theologian, the late Avery Cardinal Dulles, are particularly pertinent:

> At the time when accusations are made, it is often impossible to judge their truth, and this impossibility may persist indefinitely if the accusations are denied and probative evidence is lacking. When dioceses routinely announce that accused priests have been "removed from public ministry because of a credible accusation of sexual abuse to a minor," such priests are, in effect, branded as guilty. An accusation is deemed credible unless it is manifestly groundless. When priests are treated as guilty, they suffer the loss of their good name and as a consequence find it difficult in the future to function effectively in their God-given vocation, assuming that they are restored to ministry.[341]

So a bishop must, at all costs, uphold the rights of his priests. Should he fail, either intentionally or unintentionally, then he is to be considered negligent in his duties, since he is the chief magistrate and shepherd of his diocese. Rev. Michael Orsi, EdD, Ave Maria School of Law, Naples, Florida, has this thought-provoking and salutary reminder for every bishop:

---

[340] Michael Orsi. "Abusive Bishops & the Destruction of Priests' Reputations" in Opus Bono Sacerdotti. Opusbono.org.
[341] *America* (June 21, 2004).

Some American bishops have made a travesty of Canon Law and have sacrificed their priests' reputations to quell a crisis basically of their own making. In doing so, they jeopardise the souls entrusted to their care as well as their own. If they are so willing to sacrifice their own brother priests and deacons, how can anyone take them seriously when they call for justice in society and preach the dignity of persons as a basic moral principle?[342]

---

[342] Michael Orsi, "Justice for Priests and Deacons" in Due Process. Law & Love. Vol.2, January 2010. justiceforpriests.org.

13

Ensuring a Level Playing Field

Thus says the Lord of hosts:
"Render true judgements, show kindness
And mercy to one another;
. . . do not devise evil in your hearts."
—Zechariah 7:9-10

How can one perceive of justice
without the right to defence?
—Pope John Paul II

At the very outset, it is important to state clearly and emphatically that this study should not be construed as a biased defence of beleaguered priests and deacons or as a prejudiced attack on bishops. While most priests are not aware of their own rights under canon law, bishops are not sufficiently cognizant of their bounden duty—both by natural and canon law—of exercising "a special concern for priests, to whom they are to listen as their helpers and counsellors. They are to defend their rights and ensure that they fulfil the obligations proper to the state" (Canon §384). In a word, it is vitally important that bishops and priests work together to ensure a level playing field at all times and in all circumstances. In the words of the late Pope John Paul II: "How can one perceive of justice without the right to defence?"[343]

---

[343]   Pope John Paul II. Op.Cit.

The following plaintive complaint was submitted by a priest in New Jersey to David Rice:

> I wanted out of a system where there is no term of office, no control, no appeal. And where everything is cloaked under silence. And that's how it is: Bishops are in for life; if they're unjust, there's nowhere to appeal, no higher court, no due process. And half the human race is excluded from all power—I mean the women. It's against the UN Declaration of Human Rights. I believe in the Church, but these are human abuses. It's just ecclesiastical city hall, and I couldn't just fight it.[344]

Guilty until Proven Innocent

In a very interesting article entitled "Guilty until Proven Innocent," Fr. Austen Ivereigh, MA, DPhil, of Heythorpe College, Oxford, informs us of the Cumberlege Commission review of the Church's child-protection policy. And this is his initial observation: "While treatment of the abused has improved, disturbing evidence has emerged that priests who have been accused and not charged are left in limbo, suspicion still hanging over them."[345]

Ever since a dithering Caiaphas succumbed to public pressure and maintained that the destruction of an innocent man was justified to save a nation, the law of Christian countries has consistently upheld the presumption of innocence and the need for definite and incontrovertible evidence before an accused can be convicted. In the Church's legal tradition, this is known as *favor rei—the accused enjoys the benefit of the law and is deemed innocent until he is proved guilty.* Said Pope John Paul II in 1979: "Due process and individual rights should never be sacrificed for the sake of the social order."

---

[344] David Rice, *Shattered Vows: Priests Who Leave* (William Morrow & Co. Inc., 1990), 29.

[345] Austin Ivereigh, *Justice for Priests and Deacons*, Vol.1, no. 1 (September 2007): 10.

In the wake of the explosive revelations of the sexual abuse of minors by members of the clergy in 2002, the bishops of the world reacted with drastic measures to repair the scandal and restore justice through penal sanctions. Quasi-judicial bodies were established and duly authorised to implement their policies. In the United Kingdom, for instance, there was COPCA (the Catholic Office for the Protection of Children and Vulnerable Adults), the child-protection agency of the Catholic Bishops' Conference of England and Wales, set up at Lord Nolan's report on abuse in 2001.

Fr. Austen Ivereigh frankly confesses that Nolan was well aware of the possibility of false or malicious allegations and the haunting danger of reputations being irreparably destroyed. Yet, continues Fr. Ivereigh, "COPCA's policies have ridden roughshod over these qualms. 'Nolan would be turning in his grave,' more than one canonist has told me." So there is a pressing need for a level playing field.[346]

Archbishop Vincent Nichols of Birmingham, the bishop in charge of COPCA, candidly acknowledged last year that an accused priest is unlikely ever to be reinstated. Of the 40 clergy in England and Wales who had been accused by 2005, only two had been restored to ministry; four were dismissed. Of the 41 reports made in 2006, 24 resulted in no further action by the police, while 14 are still being investigated. Ivereigh adds, "And what is the fate of those whose cases have been dropped by the police? Many of them live in limbo, their reputations and vocations cast to the wolves. All too often, they leave the priesthood."[347] *So a priest is guilty until proven innocent—and this is the deplorable stance of the very ones who brazenly preach about justice in season and out of season!*

Fr. Paul Bruxby, the Brentwood canonist who defends accused priests, informs us that most of the 20 priests he is defending have been assessed as "low risk"; yet, five or six years later, they are unable to return to their parishes. "They feel shunned by their bishops and describe themselves as lepers. They feel hopeless, and sometimes imagine committing suicide."[348]

---

[346] Austin Ivereigh, ibid.

[347] Ibid.

[348] Paul Bruxby, *Justice for Priests and Deacons*, Vol. 1, no. 1 (September 2007), 10.

"Woman, where are your accusers? Has no one condemned you?"

She said, "No one, sir!"

And Jesus said, "Neither do I condemn you. Go your way, and from now on do not sin again." [349](John 8:10-11)

These surely must have been encouraging words uttered by those messengers of God's unconditional love and unfathomable mercy. And yet when they would have hoped to be the beneficiaries of both compassion and benevolence themselves, by some curious quirk of circumstances, they would be deemed guilty until proven innocent.

Very rightly, Fr. Bruxby believes, in line with canon law, there should be moral certainty about an accusation—not least because some accusers are mentally disturbed.[350] A priest who owned a rental apartment let it out to a female occupant. When the individual failed to pay her rent, she was granted an extension. Eventually, the recalcitrant tenant had to be evicted. She vengefully retaliated by accusing the priest of sexual misdemeanours. He was stood down from the ministry while the allegation was investigated. Surprisingly, the tenant issued a signed declaration that the allegation had been fabricated. The priest was exonerated and duly reinstated. By canon law bishops are obliged to investigate the truth of a claim before removing a priest from the active ministry—a process known as a "preliminary investigation."

Regrettably, this is not being done: "Priests are removed, irrespective of the strength of the allegation," so said Fr. Brendan Killeen, a Northampton, U.K., canonist.[351]

Fr. Ivereigh relates the story of Fr. Dominic McKenna, a 56-year-old parish priest of Our Lady of Hal in Camden Town, London. In January, 2005, he was astounded beyond belief at hearing of an allegation of sexual abuse levelled against him by a man. Reportedly, it had occurred in Ireland some 30 years ago!

---

[349] John 8:10-11

[350] Ibid.

[351] Brendan Killeen, *Justice for Priests and Deacons*, Vol. 1, no. 1 (September 2007), 10.

COPCA took the allegation seriously, and Fr. McKenna was banished to a Hertfordshire safe house for two years. Westminster's bishops were supportive and his fellow clergy kept him going with regular phone calls. Sadly, his identity as a priest had been shattered, and he felt utterly disheartened. The Crown Prosecution Service eventually dropped the charge, and the judge pronounced a "not guilty" verdict.

Regrettably, COPCA insisted on a risk assessment. On the basis that such an enforced risk assessment could be self-incriminating and injurious to the priest's reputation, Fr. McKenna was advised by a canon lawyer to represent his objection before the Congregation for Clergy in Rome. Surprisingly, the response was expected to take anything from three to four years. As a lesser evil, the compliant priest submitted to a series of four-hour assessment interviews at the Birmingham Cathedral and was made to fill in questionnaires asking explicit questions about his fantasies—a blatant invasion of his privacy. He still shudders when he recalls that harrowing experience.[352]

Fr. Ivereigh adds:

Back in Westminster, mounting indignation on Fr. McKenna's behalf was indicative that six years on from the British clerical sex-abuse crisis, public opinion was changing. Protests meant that once the assessment was over he was allowed to return last Christmas to his overjoyed parish. He has told his story to the Cumberlege Commission, set up to review the way the Church complied with the Nolan Report, and he outlined the concerns he shares with canonists. A priest, he believes, should not be asked to leave his parish until charges are brought; and he should only be risk-assessed if there is reasonable certainty that he poses a risk, or a guilty verdict has been served.[353]

---

[352] Ibid.

[353] Ibid.

Fr. Paul Bruxby comments:

The assessments are not independent; they are ordered by the bishops and, because they almost never clear a priest, are self-incriminating. Nor do they necessarily spot abusers—as the case of William Hofton, a Westminster priest who was declared low risk but who in 2004 was subsequently convicted for serious abuse, painfully illustrated.[354]

"What are they assessing?" queries Fr. Dominic McKenna. "Are you assessing me on something I've never done? Or assessing me on whether I might repeat in the future what I've never done in the past?"[355]

"The implementation of child-protection norms," says Fr. Ladislas Orsy, SJ, an American canonist, "has caused a very deep resentment within the clergy—an emotional break between the bishops and their priests."[356]

The scales of justice certainly need to be righted. It is now time, canonists agree, to send Caiaphas packing. Defending the basic rights of priests who, like any and every human being, are rightly entitled to justice, is as important as creating a safe environment for minors. And, like every other human being, a priest too must be presumed innocent until proven guilty. This is a sacrosanct and inviolable right.

---

[354] Ibid.

[355] Dominic McKenna, *Justice for Priests and Deacons*, Vol. 1, no. 1 (September 2007), 11.

[356] Ladislas Orsy, *Justice for Priests and Deacons*, Vol. 1, no. 1 (September 2007), 11.

14

Discretion Is the Better Part of Valour

Thus says the Lord of hosts: "Render true judgements,
show kindness and mercy to one another."
(Zechariah 7:9)

How can you perceive of justice without the right to defence?
—John Paul II

On April 16, 2007, Pope Benedict XVI addressed the bishops of the United States of America. In the course of that address, this is what he said:

> Priests, too, need your guidance and closeness during this difficult time. They have experienced shame over what has occurred, and there are those who feel they have lost some of the trust and esteem they once enjoyed. Not a few are experiencing a closeness to Christ Jesus in his Passion as they struggle to come to terms with the consequences of the crisis.

With genuine and heartfelt concern, the Sovereign Pontiff wisely added: "At this stage a vital part of your task is to strengthen relationships with your clergy, especially those cases where tension has arisen between priests and their bishops in the wake of the crisis. It is important that you continue to show them your concern, to support them, and to lead by example."

165

Priests—Not Servants, but Sons and Friends

These words of solicitous concern and paternal wisdom are based on the theology of the Episcopal office in regard to a bishop's relationship with his priests. Canon 192 deals with the removal from an ecclesiastical office. As is commonly known, removal is a very grave matter. It is primarily disciplinary in character; exceptionally, it may take the form of a penalty. As such, removal takes place either by a decree of the competent authority or automatically by virtue of the law (Cf. Canon 194). As a precautionary measure, the competent authority is directed to the stipulations of Canons 193 and 195, with the added insistence that they be observed carefully, lest the rights of the one removed be harmed unjustly.

Canon 193 deals with three situations in which removal from office may be decreed by the competent authority. A parish priest, for instance, may be removed from office only for *grave reasons*, such as mental or physical illness or irreformable incompetence, despite strenuous efforts by the appropriate authority to remedy the situation. In weighing up the gravity of the causes, the competent authority must take full account of the circumstances involved, the effect on the officeholder and, above all, the effect on the common good and the salvation of souls. And like administrative acts concerning the external forum, notification of removal must be written.

Canon 384 explicitly enjoins that a bishop is to have special concern for his priests, to whom he is to listen as his helpers and counsellors. He is to defend their rights and ensure that they fill the obligations proper to their state. In other words, since the cooperation of the *presbyterium* is essential to the pastoral care of the faithful in a particular diocese, the law obliges the diocesan bishop to demonstrate special care and attention towards his priests. He is required to seek their advice *informally* as "sons and friends" and *formally* through structures such as the Council of Priests and the College of Consultors.

In particular, the bishop takes on certain obligations towards his priests. First, he must defend all their rights, those accruing both from natural justice and from the law of the Church. Second, he must make sure they have what they need to carry out their obligations. Third, he must provide whatever is necessary for their ongoing spiritual and intellectual formation and in whatever way this can be done in the local circumstances. And fourth, he must ensure that priests enjoy a remuneration that befits their condition and due provision is made by way of social welfare, for infirmity, sickness, and old age (Canon 281 §2).

This was expressly reiterated by the Fathers of the Second Vatican Council: "On account of this sharing in his priesthood and mission let priests sincerely look upon the bishop as their father and reverently obey him. And let the bishop regard his priests, who are his co-workers, as sons and friends, just as Christ called his disciples no longer servants but friends."[357]

These sentiments are emphatically repeated in the Decree on Bishops' Pastoral Office in the Church:

> A bishop should always welcome priests with a special love . . . He should regard his priests as sons and friends . . . He should be concerned about the spiritual, intellectual and material condition of his priests, so that they can live holy and pious lives and fulfil their ministry faithfully and fruitfully . . . With active mercy a bishop should attend upon priests who are in any sort of danger or who have failed in some respect.[358]

A Widening and Worrying Chasm

Very regrettably, the *de facto* situation between many bishops and their priests is very far from the *de iure*. There certainly is a widening and worrying chasm. For one thing, priests are finding it extremely difficult to regard their bishops as a father and friend. One priest, who is so typical of countless others, meets with his bishop only when he is to be transferred. As a matter of fact, it is rather distressing to have priests refer to diocesan appointments as "the chess game" in which they are no more than pawns that can be shifted at the whims of the bishop and often with the connivance of scheming and influential individuals—clerical and lay.

Some bishops are no better than corporate managers relating to their priests as employees, who can be hired and fired as and when they

---

[357] LG #28.
[358] CD #16.

deem fit.[359] One priest has never had a single application for a desired position entertained. On one occasion, he actually gave his application to the bishop and was given the assurance that it would be discussed at the next meeting of the diocesan consultors. That was never done—as one consultor unwittingly acknowledged later. Positions were filled even before they were formally announced. Some grapevines do divulge secrets!

Equally sad is the fact that priests are unable to regard their bishops as spiritual fathers, who have an active concern for their well-being.[360] One priest painstakingly prepared his report prior to a pastoral visitation by his bishop with the hope that he would receive the required support. It was yet another exercise in futility. Ironically, the priest had been appointed to the position principally because no one else was interested or willing to comply. Both justice and charity postulate that a promise of respect and obedience, trustfully made on the day of ordination to the ordaining prelate, does not render a priest a tool of convenience, to be used when required, and discarded when not.

In the light of his personal experiences, one priest reports of the situation in many dioceses: when a priest is placed on administrative leave and prohibited from acting or presenting himself as a priest, he is essentially cut off from all diocesan communications. His whereabouts are a secret closely guarded by the chancery, so that even his personal friends or brother priests are unable to be in touch or render whatever moral, financial, emotional or spiritual support that may be necessary.[361]

To add insult to injury, the bishop distances himself from the priest, rarely contacting him, and often only doing so through a chancery official. Some bishops have intentionally failed to provide the means of a decent livelihood to which the priest has a canonical right. In some instances, the priest concerned has referred the matter to the Holy See. In one such case, the bishop deliberately failed to respond, for as long as four years.

---

[359] Rev. Nicholas R. A. Rachford, JCL, a priest of the Byzantine Catholic Eparchy of Parma, Ohio, *Due Process, Law and Love*, Vol. 2, no. 1 (Jan. 2010), 10-11.

[360] Ibid., 10.

[361] Ibid., 10.

Even when the Holy See upheld the priest's recourse, the bishop failed to comply with the given directive.[362]

On one occasion, a priest was accused of sexual impropriety with an 18-year-old young lady. The bishop placed the priest on administrative leave and refused to give him any assignment, even though no canonical trial had taken place and, consequently, there was no proven guilt. When the priest took recourse to the Congregation for the Clergy, he was acquitted of any wrong-doing. The bishop was formally informed that he had acted illegally and that the priest should be reinstated. But he refused to comply.[363]

In response to the reports of child abuse and the concerted determination to eradicate it once and for all, every diocese has formulated and issued a Charter for the Protection of Children and Young People and the Essential Norms for Diocesan/Eparchial Policies Dealing with Allegations of Sexual Abuse of Minors by Priests or Deacons. These are laudable initiatives that are to be sedulously promoted with both justice and charity. Unfortunately, they have often led to the abuse of power by bishops in relation to their priests.

As can be expected, such abuses of power further widen the chasm between bishops and priests. Even more, this estrangement makes it difficult for priests to trust their bishops, or even to confide in them. The ramifications, as one can imagine, are far-reaching—from the loss of morale in the *presbyterium*, to dissensions and divisions in the diocese, to the loss of potential vocations to the priesthood or religious life, to disintegrating parish communities, and to the eventual loss of the Christian faith.

Natural Law Is Divine Law

The Church teaches that the right to due process is a fundamental human right of natural law. And natural law is divine law. So the presumption in all cases must be *innocent until proven guilty*. How, then, can any priest be convicted and penalised when he has never enjoyed the opportunity to defend himself against an allegation, which could be

---

[362] Ibid., 10.
[363] Ibid., 10.

baseless and calumnious? Once again, natural law is divine law. So how can anyone justifiably and morally take away a divine right?

The Code of Canon Law sets out people's rights within the Church and provides a legal structure for vindicating these rights. Indeed, since Vatican I, the official Church has frequently stressed its commitment to human rights, and has even included a kind of "Bill of Rights" in the 1983 Code. As a matter of fact, human rights experts speak of "equality of arms" to indicate that the prosecution and the accused should have equal assistance from the law in their contest. To use a more colloquial expression: there should be a level playing field for both sides. What assurance, then, does a priest enjoy of a level playing field in relation to his bishop?

Rev. Maurice Dooley, DD, JCL, a priest of the Archdiocese of Cashel and Emly, Ireland, is very frank and forthright when he says:

> There are certain fundamental human rights known even to those unskilled in law. These include the presumption of innocence until proven guilty, the right to defend oneself, the right to avail of expert legal advice, the right of the accused to know all the allegations invoked against him, the right that judges be unprejudiced and base their decisions solely on legally acceptable evidence, and so on. These and other basic principles are, however, safeguarded by precise legal norms in the Code of Canon Law. *These laws are not optional: whether he likes them or not, a bishop is bound by them, and rights given in the law must be respected.*[364] (emphasis mine).

1. Canon 221 §3 clearly states that no penalties can be inflicted except in accordance with the law, and only for actions which are specified as crimes in the law. With this, the protection of rights of the faithful is extended into the domain of penal law.

---

[364] Maurice Dooley, DD, JCL, is a priest of the Archdiocese of Cashel and Emly, Ireland; *Due Process, Law and Love*, Vol. 2, no. 1, (Jan. 2010): 11-13. (*my emphasis*).

The current code, unlike the one of 1917, is more restricted in this sphere: if no penalty is stated in the law, then one cannot be imposed—except as permitted by the limited provisions of Canon 1399.

2. When a bishop imposes penalties directly (administratively), he is governed generally by the same laws as when penalties are imposed by a court in a trial (judicially) (Canon 728 §1).

3. No penalties can be imposed unless the crime is canonically proven to have occurred and to be gravely imputable (Canon 1321 §1). By contrast with the 1917 code, the present code establishes a very important principle that, ordinarily, only those violations of a law or a precept which arise out of *malice* are to be punished. Thus, if it is proved that someone violated a law or precept *deliberately* (i.e. with malice), then that person is subject to whatever penalty is prescribed in the law or precept. On the other hand, if it is proved that the violation was not deliberate but, rather, the consequence of culpable ignorance or negligence, then the person does not incur a penalty.

4. Censures, including any kind of suspension, cannot be imposed without a prior warning to the offender to cease being contumacious (Canon 1347 §1) and must be remitted once contumacy has ceased (Canon 1358 §1). Since the purpose of medicinal penalties is the reform of the offender, the law requires that every effort be made to attain this end before the imposition of penalties. Thus, the validity of a censure is made contingent upon the issuing of a warning to the offender by the appropriate ecclesiastical authority. The law requires that at least one warning be given, urging the offender to amend.

5. A bishop has no power to dispense himself or anyone else from procedural or penal laws (Canon 87 §1).

6. An accused person is never bound to admit the offence with which he is charged (Canon 1728 §2); it is up to the prosecution to prove its case (Canon 1526 §1).

7. Decisions must be made on the basis of moral certitude, derived solely from what is proven in a proper Church investigation (Canon 1608).

8. It is absolutely forbidden to use information given to the decision-maker that is not in the dossier of the case and available

to the accused (Canon 1604 §1). The accused must be given access to all the evidence assembled in the case (Canon 1598). If the right of defence is denied, the decision made is immediately invalid (Canon 1620 §7). The right of defence is understood to be required by the very nature of the process. Therefore, if any of these elements is denied to any party to the controversy, then the judgement will be irremediably invalid.

Most regrettably, bishops feel free, it would seem, to act as if these laws did not exist, or that in the present crisis, that they do not apply to them. So they simply ignore the law, invent concepts, such as "administrative leave," unknown to the law, pay no heed to the complaints of the penalised priest, and effectively act as judge, jury, and executioner.

Priests Are Citizens of the State and Therefore are Entitled to Justice

The Sixth Amendment to the Constitution of the United States of America directs: "The accused shall be informed of the nature of the cause of the accusation; to be confronted with the witnesses against him, to have compulsory process for obtaining witnesses in his favour, and to have the assistance of the counsel for his defence." This principle of law is also denied to Catholic priests. Many are told only that an allegation of sexual misconduct has been made against them. They are not allowed to confront their accusers; they often face officials of both church and state by themselves; they are not provided with the opportunity for self-defence; and they are forced to live **as though they were** sexual deviants, even though no proof has been offered. The allegation alone is enough to destroy a priest, so much so that, even if found not guilty, his life as both a priest and a man is negatively impacted in society. Little to nothing is ever done to correct that injustice.

Bill Donohue, the president of the Catholic League, said while being interviewed in 2005 on *Today*, "There is no segment of the American population with less civil-liberties protection than the average American Catholic priest."[365]

Avery Cardinal Dulles, when he wrote for the Jesuit magazine *America* in 2004, observed, "The Church must protect the community from harm, but it must also protect the human rights of each individual who may face an accusation. The supposed good of the totality must not override the rights of individual persons."[366]

The Constitution of the United States was written to protect the rights of all Americans, no matter what the crime or alleged offence, and no one should be denied the protection, especially priests of the Roman Catholic Church.[367]

---

[365] Gary Watson, JD, El Paso, Texas; *Due Process, Law and Love,* Vol. 2, no. 1 (Jan. 2010): 14.

[366] Ibid., 14.

[367] Ibid., 14.

15

A Well-Formed Conscience—God's Herald and Messenger

Conscience is like God's herald and messenger;
it does not command things on its own authority,
but commands them as coming from God's authority,
like a herald when he proclaims the edict of the king.
This is why conscience has binding force.
—St Bonaventure

A story is indeed the shortest distance between reality and truth. Several years ago, a preacher from out of state accepted a call to a church in Houston, Texas. Shortly after his arrival, he had an occasion to ride the bus from his home to the downtown area.

When he sat down, he discovered that the driver had mistakenly given him a quarter too much change. As he considered what to do, he thought to himself, *You'd better give the quarter back. It would be wrong to keep it.* Then he thought, *Oh, forget it, it's only a quarter. Who would worry about this little amount? Anyway, the bus company gets too much fare; they will never miss it. Just accept it as a "gift from God" and keep quiet.*

When his stop came, he paused momentarily at the door, and then he handed the quarter to the driver and said, "Here, you gave me too much change."

The driver, with a smile, replied, "Aren't you the new preacher in town?"

"Yes," he replied. "Well, I have been thinking a lot lately about going somewhere to worship. I just wanted to see what you would do if I gave you too much change. I'll see you at church on Sunday."

When the preacher stepped off the bus, he literally grabbed the nearest light pole, held on, and said, "Oh God, I almost sold your Son for a quarter." Indeed, our lives are the only Bible some people will ever read.

> Watch your thoughts; they become words.
> Watch your words; they become actions.
> Watch your actions; they become habits.
> Watch your habits; they become character.
> Watch your character; it becomes your destiny.
> —Anonymous

What Is Conscience?

The Catechism of the Catholic Church gives us a succinct and classical definition: "Conscience is a judgement of reason whereby the human person recognises the moral quality of a concrete act that he/she is going to perform, is in the process of performing, or has already completed" (CCC #1778).

Turning to the story, the preacher did the right thing—as a commuter on a public bus, he paid his fare correctly and honestly. That was the right decision. However, he later realised that he had mistakenly been given a quarter more in change. And for a moment, he felt himself torn by an inner conflict. Should he do the right thing and return it to the bus driver? Or should he retain it and for two seemingly good reasons: first, the amount was miniscule; and second, the bus company was making hundreds of thousands of dollars every day? Surely a missing quarter would not make a substantial or even noticeable difference. As a conscientious and well-informed person, however, the preacher realised that he could either choose to do the right thing and return the extra money or retain it dishonestly. The former would be unquestionably right, the latter undeniably wrong. And so, very wisely and courageously, he opted for the former with the most remarkable result. Actions indeed speak louder than words and people are more influenced by what they see than by what they hear.

So conscience is like a voice within us that mysteriously tells us what to do or avoid doing. In other words, it is a judgement of reason, a judgement of the intellect or mind: *"Do that because it is right; don't do that because it is wrong."* Even young children know what is right and should be done and what is not right and should be avoided. Of course, that mysterious inner voice needs to be progressively and systematically refined so that it can unfailingly point us in the right direction, by consistently making the right choice. In a word, *there is an imperative need for one and all, regardless of age, to have a well-formed conscience.*

Follow Your Well-Formed Conscience

In order for conscience to make correct judgements, it must first learn the objective truth that God teaches through his Church on moral issues, so that it can then apply this teaching to the case at hand. In this sense, conscience is like a sextant, which a sailor uses to determine his position by focussing it on the stars. Without the stars, the sextant is of no use. Similarly, without the light of God's law, as taught by the Church, conscience has nothing by which to guide it. It is blind.

For example, every licensed driver is bound to obey traffic regulations, especially with regard to speed limits. In general, motorists can drive at the normal speed of 60 kilometres per hour. However, in a metropolitan area, where there are crowds of people milling about at any time of the day, the speed limit is reduced to 50 kilometres per hour; and in residential areas, for the sake of further safety to one and all, especially children, the speed limit is further reduced to 40 kilometres per hour. The all-important purpose of this law is to ensure the safety of one and all—drivers, pedestrians, and residents. And this stems from the moral law, which declares that human life is sacred and must, therefore, be respected. *Thou shall not kill!* And so, deliberately and recklessly flouting speed limits poses an imminent threat to both people and the driver, thereby endangering innocent lives and so violating God's sacred law.

And so, conscience is not a law unto itself; it is not autonomous. Indeed, the Catechism mentions "assertion of a mistaken notion of autonomy of conscience" as one of the factors that "can be at the source of errors of judgement in moral conduct."[368] Returning to the story at the start of this chapter, should commuters defraud a travel company of the due income, the collective amount could be exceedingly high and the consequences serious to the organisation as a whole and to the employees

---

[368] CCC. Part 3. Section 1. Ch.1. Article 6.

and commuters in particular. As is well known, shoplifters cause colossal losses to the organisation, which, in turn, is compelled to raise the prices of commodities, to recover their lost income and thereby make them more expensive to the honest and conscientious patrons. Consequently, it is erroneous to follow one's conscience if it leads one to violate the natural, civil and moral law. In a word, while a wrongly formed conscience is the voice of whim, pride and convenience, a rightly formed conscience puts us in touch with God with nothing short of the most desirable results—inner peace and lasting happiness.

This is the principal reason why our late Holy Father, Pope John Paul II, in his memorable encyclical *Veritatis Splendor*, quotes St. Bonaventure on the binding force of conscience: "Conscience is like God's herald and messenger—it does not command things on its own authority, but commands them as coming from God's authority, like a herald when he proclaims the edict of the king. This is why conscience has binding force."[369]

There Is No Religion Higher than Truth

The newspapers once reported the baffling and pathetic fraud of an attractive, competent, efficient and trustworthy accountant. Secretly, she had been syphoning funds from the organisation into her personal account. From a few covert transactions, the aberration became almost obsessive-compulsive.

One day, she bought herself a brand-new car. Her husband was surprised, but delighted, to hear that she had won a lottery. A week later, he walked into the garage to find yet another new car. As he entered the house in shocked disbelief, she teasingly dangled a pair of car keys and said, "Surprise! Surprise! That's my gift to you, darling!" His joy truly knew no bounds. Shortly thereafter, the couple undertook substantial renovations to the house, both within and without, and to the tune of a quarter of a million dollars. Of course, the icing on the cake was the purchase of a luxury yacht for the extravagant price of $80,000. As the saying goes, "When it rains, it pours."

---

[369] In II *Librum Sent.*, dist. 39, a. 1, q. 3; in *Veritatis Splendor*, 58.

Such a range of astounding developments almost overnight roused the curiosity and the envy of both friends and neighbours. Someone obviously blew the whistle, and an investigation was conducted. The lady's dishonesty was detected, and she was arrested and charged. Later, a magistrate sentenced her to three years' imprisonment with a non-parole period of eighteen months.

On emerging from the court, the lady was asked by one of the journalists: "Why did you, a supposedly trustworthy employee, do something so brazenly dishonest?"

Her response was brief and candid: "I did it to impress my friends."

"Indeed, money is a good servant, but a bad master."

"There is enough in the world for everyone's need, but not enough for everyone's greed."[370] The lady was truly contrite, and resolved to make due restitution in the near future. There is no religion higher than truth.

Living in the Truth

The Eighth Commandment plainly and unequivocally states: "You shall not bear false witness against your neighbour,"[371] Stated simply, each and every one of us is morally bound to be truthful, in both word and deed, especially in interpersonal relations. And this moral prescription flows from the fact that we have been fashioned unto the image and likeness of God, who neither deceives nor can be deceived, for God is Truth. This is why Christ Jesus did not hesitate to categorically and boldly proclaim: "I am the Way, the Truth and the Life . . . I have come as light into the world, so that everyone who believes in me should not remain in darkness."[372]

It is indeed a fact of experience that in every human being, there is an innate and irrepressible desire for the truth. In the precise words of the Fathers of the Second Vatican Council:

> It is in accordance with their dignity as persons—that is, beings endowed with reason and free will and therefore

---

[370] Frank Buchanan (1878-1961), *Remaking the World* (1947).
[371] Exodus 20:16; Deuteronomy 5:20.
[372] John 14:6; John 12:46

privileged to bear personal responsibility—that all men should be at once impelled by nature and also bound by a moral obligation to seek the truth, especially religious truth. They are also bound to adhere to the truth, once it is known, and to order their whole lives in accord with the demands of truth.[373]

In a word, each and every human being is morally bound to seek, treasure, and transmit the truth at all times, thereby ensuring trust and harmony in interpersonal relations. Said St. Thomas Aquinas with unambiguous candour, "Men could not live with one another if there were no mutual confidence that they were being truthful to one another."[374]

Offences against Truth

1. **False Witness and Perjury**—A person is guilty of false witness when, in a court of law, he or she intentionally and maliciously accuses another of something that was neither said, nor intended, nor actually done. And when this is stated under oath, it is perjury. As is patently clear, such rash allegations can do irreparable harm to an innocent individual leading to the exoneration of the guilty, the condemnation of the innocent, and the imposition of a punishment that is as undeserved as it is unjustifiable. History is replete with instances of persons falsely accused in a court of law and unjustly punished only to be vindicated later. "A false witness will not go unpunished, and the liar will perish" (Proverbs 19:9). "The Lord hates cheating and delights in honesty" (Proverbs 11:1).[375]

2. **Rash Judgement**—A person is guilty of rash judgement when he or she wrongly assumes that another is guilty without first ascertaining the actual facts of the situation. For instance, a local gossip-monger once informed her circle of friends that one of the local men was having an affair with a single woman. When asked to corroborate her report, the woman said that she had seen his

---

[373] The Decree on Religious Freedom *(Dignitatem Humanae)*, #2.2.

[374] St. Thomas Aquinas, STh II-II, 109, 3 ad 1.

[375] These proverbs underscore the importance of being honest.

utility van parked outside her home "all through the night," when in reality, it was only there for a hurried errand. This baseless and scurrilous rumour reached the man concerned. So the very next night, he decided to give the mischief-maker a taste of her own medicine: he deliberately parked his utility van right outside the gossip-monger's house all through the night, and for a week! The shoe was very much on the other foot. "Don't gossip. Don't falsely accuse your neighbour of some crime, for I am Jehovah."[376]

3. **Detraction**—A person is guilty of detraction when, without an objectively valid reason, he or she discloses another's faults and failings to those who did not know them. For instance, an employee could have quit a previous job for a host of personal reasons, one of which could be a personality clash with either the employer or a colleague. Knowing this and with no justifiable reason, another individual could intentionally use this information to mar the applicant's prospects of securing another job. Interpersonal differences at a workplace are definitely no reflection on the merit of a duly qualified and diligent applicant. "O Lord, I prayed, be kind and heal me, for I have confessed my sins. But my enemies say, 'May he soon die and be forgotten!'"[377]

4. **Calumny**—A person is guilty of calumny when he or she deliberately and maliciously distorts the truth in order to harm the reputation of another, and so poisons the minds of his or her listeners. For example, the gossip-monger in the instance above

---

[376] Leviticus 19:16. God's program for successful living demands honesty in both word and deed. Dishonesty and misrepresentation lead to suspicion, mistrust, and hatred, ultimately destroying our relationships. Human relationships can only grow and thrive if we are willing to tell the truth, the only real basis for trust between people. When there is honesty in our relationships, we can confidently look to others in times of need.

[377] (Psalm 41:5) Many people wish us well as we seek to recover. Others, however, seem to gloat over us, continually trying to predict our next failure. We will feel pressure from such people during times our relationship with God is weak. At such vulnerable moments, our enemies are hard at work trying to ruin our lives through lies, deception, and words of discouragement.

was guilty of calumny, because she was intentionally fabricating a lie in order to defame an innocent man, who was honestly doing his allotted work. "Do not pass along untrue reports. Do not co-operate with an evil man by affirming on the witness stand something you know is false."[378]

A Villainous Plot—a Ghastly Tragedy

Along with *Hamlet, King Lear,* and *Macbeth, Othello* is one of Shakespeare's most notable tragedies, and thus a pillar of what most critics consider the apex of his dramatic art and phenomenal ingenuity.

Iago is a soldier under the command of Othello, a Moorish general, who is passionately in love with a beautiful young lady, Desdemona. Unfortunately, the Moor fails to realise that he has a fierce and resolute competitor in a wealthy Venetian, Roderigo, who is hell bent on winning his prospective bride. And so, the scheming Roderigo shrewdly pays Iago a considerable sum of money to spy on the unsuspecting Othello.

Iago dislikes Othello, and his hatred is further fuelled by the general's choice of Cassio as his officer or lieutenant—a prestigious position that the ambitious soldier had ardently coveted. "Men should be either treated generously or destroyed, because they take revenge for slight injuries—for heavy ones they cannot."[379]

Well aware of Cassio's high regard for Desdemona, the crafty Iago manipulated him into consuming alcohol excessively so that he would do something that he would later regret. With Cassio out of the way, Iago turned to Montano and informed him that Cassio had a serious drinking problem. This was done with the deliberate intent of maligning Cassio in the eyes of Montano and so ruining his prospects for the future. Even more, Iago urged Roderigo to attack the drunken Cassio. In the ensuing scuffle, Cassio wounds Roderigo and then Montano, who tried to break

---

[378]   (Exodus 23.1) "You must not lie" (Exodus 20:16). This prohibits false testimony. The truth eventually comes out (see 1 Timothy 5:24-25), so honesty is not only the right policy, but also the smart one. Even if someone seems to be getting away with lies for a time, that person must still answer to God. In the end, he will be held accountable.

[379]   Niccolo Machiavelli (1469-1527), *The Prince* (written 1513), ch. 3.

up the fight. On hearing of Cassio's misdemeanour, Othello had him demoted from his prestigious position as lieutenant. "Revenge is a kind of wild justice."[380]

The plot now thickens. With vengeful malice, Iago and Roderigo informed Brabantio, the father of Desdemona, of her relationship with Othello, the Moor. This enraged the father, who promptly despatched a band to apprehend Othello for what he regarded as an abuse of his cherished daughter.

Secretly, the conniving Iago cautioned Othello about the contemplated arrest by Brabantio's men. Further, he deceitfully poisoned the mind of the Moor by insisting that it was Roderigo, and not himself, who had instigated Brabantio's actions against him. Othello is not fazed and is fully assured that his well-founded reputation would stand him in good stead. Not much later, he and Desdemona were married.

Brabantio was livid with rage, and rashly accused Othello of resorting to magic in order to win his daughter. He would have liked to wreak vengeance, but for the fact that Othello was called away to discuss a crisis in Cypress. Seizing the opportunity to strike while the iron was hot, the spiteful Brabantio complained to the duke and his senators that Othello had bewitched his innocent daughter, Desdemona, and even had intimate relations with her.

Both Desdemona and Othello were summoned by the duke for a personal investigation. They were honest and forthright in professing their mutual love, and rejected any suspicion of either coercion or trickery. The duke was convinced, and urged Brabantio to accept the marriage graciously rather than reluctantly. By way of a compromise, he ordered Othello to Cypress, in order to fight the Turks, and entrusted Desdemona to the care of Iago and his wife, Emilia, with the specific instruction to have her rejoin Othello later.

Roderigo was both disappointed and pained that he would be unable to win the bride of his dreams. This he conveyed to Iago, who cunningly decided to exploit the situation to his financial gain by suggesting that soon Othello would tire of Desdemona.

So Iago had a double-edged axe to grind: his loathing of Othello and his detestation of Cassio, who had been chosen to fill the position of lieutenant that he had ardently coveted. And, being a wily opportunist, he

---

[380] Francis Bacon. Essays. 1625. "Of Revenge".

also resolved to further exploit the wealthy Venetian, Roderigo. And so, he hit upon a vicious plan; he informed Othello that Cassio, his seemingly trustworthy lieutenant, was indulging in an adulterous relationship with his beloved but unfaithful wife, Desdemona.

This so infuriated Othello that, in a rage of unbridled jealousy, he used a pillow to smother his beloved wife, in spite of her repeated and earnest claims of total innocence and a haunting premonition that she was in for a violent and tragic end. Even in her final moments, the loyal and magnanimous wife would not hold her murderous husband responsible. "Murder's out of tune. And sweet revenge grows harsh."[381]

Even Emilia, the wife of Iago, was fully convinced that some very evil person had maliciously and irreversibly poisoned the mind of Othello against his innocent wife, Desdemona. Little did she suspect that that very evil person was none other than her own husband, Iago.

Earlier, the unscrupulous Iago had been personally retaining the gifts that the besotted Roderigo had intended for Desdemona, but had entrusted to him as a bearer. Fearing that he would be found out, Iago urged Roderigo to eliminate Cassio, and did actually cooperate in wounding him. "Revenge is a kind of wild justice."

Eventually, when Othello realised that he had been systematically and deviously duped and malevolently driven to an unpardonable crime, he killed himself with a concealed weapon and let his crumbling body fall on that of the beloved but deceased Desdemona. "For the wages of sin is death . . ."[382]

The Morality of Falsehood

The disciples of Christ Jesus have to "put on the new man, created after the likeness of God in true righteousness and holiness."[383] And this is to be achieved by "putting away falsehood . . . all malice and all guile and insincerity and envy and all slander."[384]

---

[381] William Shakespeare, *Othello*, act 5, scene 2, line 113.
[382] Romans 6:23
[383] Ephesians 4:24. Peter 2:1
[384] Ephesians 4:24; 1 Peter 2:1

1. Detraction and Calumny

As is patently clear, detraction and calumny destroy the reputation and honour of another person, to both of which every human being has a God-given right. This is why the term *character assassination* has been rightly coined. A person who knowingly and maliciously indulges in either detraction or calumny is guilty of taking away, without any justification, something as sacrosanct as another's life. In other words, it is tantamount to the heinous crime and grievous sin of murder—once destroyed, it is virtually impossible to recover. So detraction and calumny offend against the virtues of both justice and charity.

Well aware of the grievous consequences of both detraction and calumny, St. James has this very apt and thought-provoking admonition:

> For all of us make many mistakes. Anyone who makes no mistakes in speaking is perfect, able to keep the whole body in check with a bridle. If we put bits into the mouths of horses to make them obey us, we guide their whole bodies. Or look at ships: though they are so large that it takes strong winds to drive them, yet they are guided by a very small rudder wherever the will of the pilot directs. So also the tongue is a small member, yet it boasts of great exploits. How great a forest is set ablaze by a small fire! And the tongue is a fire." [385]

And then, as a further precautionary measure, St. James wisely adds: "Those conflicts and disputes among you, where do they come from? Do they not come from your cravings that are at war within you? You want something and do not have it; so you commit murder [character assassination]. And you covet something and cannot obtain it; so you engage in disputes and conflicts."[386]

St. Paul is bluntly honest with the members of a much-fractured community:

---

[385] James 3:2-6
[386] James 4:1-3

For you were called to freedom, brothers and sisters; only do not use your freedom as an opportunity for self-indulgence, but through love become slaves to one another. For the whole law is summed up in a single commandment, "You shall love your neighbour as yourself. If, however, you bite and devour one another, take care that you are not consumed by one another."[387]

Well aware of Cassio's high regard for Desdemona, the crafty Iago manipulated him into consuming alcohol excessively so that he would do something that he would later regret. With Cassio out of the way, Iago turned to Montano and informed him that Cassio had a serious drinking problem. This was done with the deliberate intent of maligning Cassio in the eyes of Montano and so ruining his prospects for the future. Even more, Iago urged Roderigo to attack the drunken Cassio. "Revenge is a kind of wild justice."

2. Flattery and Adulation

Equally reprehensible and deplorable are flattery, adulation or complaisance, which encourage and confirm another in malicious acts and perverse conduct. This is what the Psalmist candidly laments: "Help, O Lord, for there is no longer anyone who is godly; the faithful have disappeared from humankind. They utter lies to each other; with flattering lips and a double heart they speak."[388] And the author of the book of Proverbs wisely counsels: "A lying tongue hates its victims, and a flattering mouth works ruin."[389] Adlai Stevenson humorously adds: "I suppose flattery hurts no one, that is, if he doesn't inhale."[390]

Ingratiation is a deliberate effort made by a person so as to gain favour with another, often through flattery. Many an unsuspecting and naive individual has fallen an innocent and hapless victim to the wiles of a crafty

[387] Galatians 5:13-15
[388] Psalm 12.2
[389] Proverbs 26:28
[390] Adlai Stevenson (1900-1965), Television Broadcast, March 30, 1952.

and deceptive schemer, who cunningly exploited the other in and through the masterful use of flattery.

Even Queen Victoria, it is reported, was susceptible to flattery. Benjamin Disraeli confessed that he put it on thick in dealing with the queen. To use his precise words, he "spread it on thick with a trowel." But Disraeli was one of the most polished, astute and adroit men who ever ruled the far-flung British Empire. He was a genius in his line. What would work for him, however, would not necessarily work for us. For, in the long run, flattery will do more harm than good, for it is counterfeit, and, like counterfeit money, it will eventually get the user in trouble.

Of course, flattery seldom works with discerning people. It is shallow, selfish and insincere. The difference between genuine appreciation and blatant flattery is simple. One is sincere; the other is insincere. One comes from the heart, the other from the teeth. One is unselfish, the other selfish. One is universally admired; the other is universally condemned.

For instance, below a bust of General Obregon in the Chapultepec Palace in Mexico City have been inscribed the following wise words from the general's very own philosophy: "Don't be afraid of enemies who attack you. Be afraid of the friends who flatter you." And King George V had a set of six maxims displayed on the walls of his study at Buckingham Palace. One of these maxims said, "Teach me neither to proffer nor receive cheap praise."[391]

That is exactly what flattery is—cheap praise; it is telling the other person precisely what he/she thinks about himself/herself. In a word, flattery is suspect. Not only does it make one wary, but it also induces in the recipient an immediate dislike for the flatterer.

3. Lies

A lie consists in speaking a falsehood with the intention of deceiving another.[392] Without mincing his words, Christ Jesus denounced lying as the work of the devil: "You are of your father the devil . . . there is no truth

---

[391] Anonymous
[392] St. Augustine, *De Mendacio*, 4, 5; PL 40,491.

in him. When he lies, he speaks according to his own nature, for he is a liar and the father of lies."[393]

Lying is the most direct offence against the truth. To lie is to speak or act against the truth, in order to lead someone into error. By disrupting a person's relation to truth and to another, a lie offends against the fundamental relation of man and of his word to the Lord. Clamouring for the blood of Jesus, the frenzied rabble lied: "We found this man perverting our nation, forbidding us to pay taxes to the emperor, and saying that he himself is the Messiah, a king."[394] As a matter of fact, this is what Christ Jesus did earlier say: "'Show me the coin used for the tax. Whose head is this, and whose title?' They answered, 'The emperor's.' Then he said to them, 'Give therefore to the emperor the things that are the emperor's, and to God the things that are God's.'"[395]

The gravity of a lie is measured against the nature of the truth it deforms, the circumstances, the intentions of the one who lies, and the harm suffered by its victims. "'What accusation do you bring against this man [Christ Jesus]?' asked Pilate. They answered, 'If this man were not a criminal, we would not have handed him over to you.' Pilate said to them, 'Take him yourselves and judge him according to your law.'"[396] Later, a wavering Pilate acknowledged, "'Look, I am bringing him out to you to let you know that I find no case against him.' The bloodthirsty mob shouted, 'Crucify him! Crucify him!'"[397] So to lie is to speak or act against the truth, in order to lead someone into error. By injuring a person's relation to truth and to another, a lie offends against the fundamental relation of man, and of his word to the Lord.

By its very nature, lying is to be condemned. It is a profanation of speech, whereas the purpose of speech is to communicate known truth to others and so facilitate stable and trustworthy interpersonal relations. The intention of deliberately leading another into error, by saying things contrary to the truth, constitutes a failure in both justice and charity. The culpability is greater when the intention of deceiving entails the risk of

---

[393] John 8:44
[394] Luke 23:2
[395] Matthew 22:19-21
[396] John 18:29-31
[397] John 19:4-6

grave consequence for those who are led astray. "From then on Pilate tried to release him [Christ Jesus], but the Jews cried out, 'If you release this man, you are no friend of the emperor. Everyone who claims to be a king sets himself against the emperor.'"[398]

Since a lie violates the virtue of truthfulness, it does real violence to another. It affects his ability to know, which is a condition for every judgement and decision. It contains the seed of discord and all consequent evils. Lying is destructive of society; it undermines trust among humans and tears apart the fabric of social relationships. "There is no worse lie than a truth misunderstood by those who hear it."[399]

4. Reparation and Restitution

Every offence committed against justice and truth entails the obligation to both reparation and restitution, even if a person is contrite and has been forgiven in and through the Sacrament of Reconciliation. The ideal restitution is a frank and sincere apology to the person offended. For instance, a priest, who had been wrongly accused, was required to step down from his position as a parish priest while the necessary inquiry was conducted. When his innocence had been established, the bishop celebrated a Mass in the parish with the priest serving as a concelebrant. This effectively helped to restore the priest's good reputation with the parishioners, and to facilitate the continuation of his pastoral ministry. So every offence against justice and truth entails the obligation to both reparation and restitution.

If an individual is unable to do so personally and directly, he/she may resort to an alternative secretly and indirectly, through the financial support of a charitable cause or a deserving person. In other words, if someone who has suffered harm cannot be directly compensated, he/she must be given moral satisfaction in the name of charity. This duty of reparation and restitution also concerns offences against another's loss of reputation. The moral obligation and material restitution must be evaluated in terms of the extent of the damage inflicted. *And it obliges in conscience.*

---

[398] John 19:12
[399] William James (1842-1910), *The Varieties of Religious Experience* (1902).

16

Persistence Pays

Listen to what the unjust judge says.
And will not God grant justice to his chosen ones
who cry to him day and night?
I tell you, he will quickly grant justice to them.
—Luke 18:1-8

In the gospel according to the evangelist Luke, Christ Jesus, the masterful teacher, relates a poignant parable that proves strikingly and conclusively the efficacy of persistence. There once was a power-intoxicated and arrogant judge who neither feared God nor respected people. Swollen with his own importance, he was truly a law unto himself. Repeatedly, he had been approached by a desperately helpless widow seeking redress against an obnoxious and oppressive adversary. Callously and unscrupulously, the conceited judge ignored her. But the tenacious widow did not cease pestering him for justice.

One day, the stern and inflexible judge felt a surprising change of heart. "Even though I do not fear God or respect man, this importunate widow is bothering me. Lest she wear me out with her persistence, I had better grant her what she so insistently desires." So her persistence did eventually pay. Seizing the opportunity to teach us a salutary lesson, Christ Jesus makes an apt comment: "Listen to what the unjust judge says. And will not God grant justice to his chosen ones who cry to him day and night? I tell you, he will quickly grant justice to them."[400]

Under Jewish law, if a matter was brought forward for arbitration, one man could not constitute a court. There was need for three judges—one chosen by the plaintiff, one by the defendant, and one independently appointed. So one thing is patently clear: the judge in the story was not a Jewish judge.

He clearly was one of the paid magistrates appointed either by Herod or by the Romans. And such judges were notoriously apathetic and rapaciously dishonest. Unless a plaintiff had influence and money to bribe his way to a verdict, he had no hope of ever getting a case settled fairly and equitably. As a matter of fact, these judges were reported to pervert justice for a dish of meat. In a word, money did speak and most eloquently.

By contrast, the desperate widow was both penniless and defenceless. And so, there wasn't the remotest possibility of her securing justice at his hands. But she had one weapon and the only one that she could relentlessly wield—her dogged persistence. One commentator even says that the arrogant judge relented for fear of a physical assault and a possible black eye. And, against all odds, her persistence did win the day.

Fr. Edgardo Abano

On April 19, 2008, Maria Maria posted an item entitled "Justice Delayed to Fil-Am Priest."[401] It concerns the pastor of the Parish of St. Frances Cabrini, Piscataway, New Jersey, which has its own website: SaveOurPastor.org. The pastor, Fr. Edgardo Abano, is a Filipino American and a priest of the Diocese of Metuchen. He has served as pastor of St. Frances Cabrini Parish (church and school) since 1992. He was ordained in the United States on May 18, 1985, and served in four parishes before being assigned to Piscataway.

> September 25, 2007, Glenn Obrero, 25, a seminarian at the
> Immaculate Conception Seminary at Seton Hall University

---

[400] Luke 18:1-8

[401] http//www.pinoywired.com, ww.zoominfo.com, Profiles. Rev.Edgardo.D. Abano, or saveourpastor.org.

in New Jersey, filed a complaint of sexual contact against Fr. Abano, 51, pastor of St. Francis Cabrini Church and School and the Diocese of Metuchen. Obrero alleged Fr. Abano touched him on the chest and buttocks for three years. The bishop's office instantly referred the matter to the Police Department of Piscataway. Thereafter, there was an investigation with the Middlesex County Prosecutor's Office in New Jersey.

On October 19, 2007, the investigators taped a phone conversation in Tagalog they set up with Glenn Obrero at the police station, where he called Fr. Abano, a day after the priest's birthday.

On October 23, 2007, a Mr. Bong Nepomuceno, court translator, submitted his transcript of the taped phone conversation to the investigators.

On October 23, 2007, the Piscataway police arrested Fr. Abano at the rectory, charging him with sexual contact. He was denied his request to change his clothes and was brought to the police station for booking in his undershirt, shorts and slippers. That very night, he was released on $1,500 bail.

On October 23, 2007, the arrest of Fr. Abano was carried by local and international news and media services, including the Filipino Channel, ABS-CBN, which reported this around the world.

On October 24, 2007, Fr. Abano was asked by the diocese to sign a paper stating that he was voluntarily asking to be relieved of his responsibilities as pastor of St. Frances Cabrini, so as to concentrate on his case. Much against his will, he resigned from all positions in the diocese.

Fr. Abano hired a well-known criminal defence lawyer, Joseph Benedict, to represent him. Parishioners, friends and the Filipino Diocesan Community set up a legal defence fund and a round-the-clock prayer wheel, as well as a Web site—http://SaveOurPastor.org/, among other things, to show their whole-hearted support and belief in Fr. Abano's unquestionable integrity and indisputable innocence.

Benedict was curious to know how the adduced charge could be based on a translated taped conversation, when Fr. Abano strenuously and consistently avowed his innocence of the alleged crime. An expert was commissioned to listen to the tape and translate it from Tagalog to English for a second opinion.

The new translation submitted to Benedict clearly showed that the transcript submitted by Nepomuceno to the police and the Middlesex County Prosecutor's Office was incomplete and inaccurate. This, in effect, skewed the earlier transcript to show admittance of guilt by Fr. Abano.

Benedict stated, "The denials were there [in the new transcript], the complaints were there." He added, "I'm not sure that Fr. Abano would have been charged in the first place if they had an accurate transcript." He filed for trial by grand jury based on the new translation, which contradicted the key piece of evidence the prosecutor's office had on the alleged crime.

It was an unusual and risky move, but Benedict was convinced that this method would prevent a long trial, so that Fr. Abano could be reinstated and continue his ministries. There were court postponements along the way, but Benedict was determined to clear the innocent priest's name.

On February 2, 2008, Frank Cicerale, on behalf of all parishioners of St. Frances Cabrini, and supporters and friends of Fr. Abano, sent a letter to the local Ordinary, Bishop Paul Gregory Bootkoski, seeking information about the drastic actions against their pastor and the consequent repercussions on the parishioners. The bishop responded promptly that he found "no reason to meet", because he could not discuss the case while it was still ongoing.

On February 13, 2008, Frank Cicerale responded to the bishop's e-mail, that there was still a need for guidance and answers on future actions by the bishop's office, regarding the parish. Bishop Bootkoski did not respond to this e-mail.

On February 22, 2008, Fr. Abano and Glenn Obrero testified separately before a grand jury in New Brunswick, New Jersey. After only 45 minutes of grand jury deliberation, Middlesex Assistant Prosecutor Christie Bevacqua went to the conference room where Benedict and Fr. Abano were waiting to tell them that the jury issued a "no bill" finding, which meant that the prosecution had no case.

Fr. Abano was thankful for the decision, and wrote a message to his friends and supporters about the felicitous outcome entitled: "Case Dismissed! Praise the Lord!" In his message, Fr. Abano related that, during the deliberation by the grand jury, he was praying ceaselessly to Our Lady of Guadalupe and the Divine Mercy to uphold his innocence of such a calumnious charge. His prayers were answered.

On February 26, 2008, after the diocese was informed of the grand jury's decision, the office of Bishop Bootkoski released a statement saying that "he (the Bishop) would review the grand jury's findings and meet with Fr. Abano before making a decision about the priest's future." To that date, Bishop Bootkoski had not met with Fr. Abano, nor had he spoken to him directly.

On March 13, 2008, 21 days after the acquittal, Frank Cicerale sent a new letter via e-mail to Bishop Bootkoski, celebrating the "vindication of Fr. Abano by the courts." As such, he foresaw no further barrier to meeting with the local Ordinary in connection with the pastoral care of St. Frances

Cabrini parishioners. Bishop Bootkoski did not respond to the e-mail.

By April 17, 2008, 26 days after the acquittal, Fr. Abano had not heard from the bishop or his office about a meeting to discuss his future, including the resumption of his faculties and his priestly ministry. And so, he wrote to the bishop informing him of his decision to return to the Philippines to make a retreat.

Upon his return to New Jersey, Fr. Abano did touch base with the office of Bishop Bootkoski, but failed to receive any word on when he would be able to meet with the local Ordinary.

What has been hindering the evasive bishop? Note #7 of the Essential Norms for Diocesan-Eparchial Policies Dealing with Allegations of Sexual Abuse of Minors by Priests or Deacons by the United States Conference of Catholic Bishops (USCCB) stipulates that "the necessary observance of the canonical norms internal to the Church is not intended in any way to hinder the course of any civil action that may be operative."

Note #6 of Essential Norms directs: "When an allegation of sexual abuse of a minor by a priest or deacon is received, a preliminary investigation in accordance with canon law will be initiated, and conducted promptly and objectively."[402] During this investigation, the accused enjoys the presumption of innocence, and all appropriate steps shall be taken to protect his reputation. The accused will be encouraged to retain the assistance of civil and canonical counsel, and will be promptly notified of the results of the investigation (USSCB).

Even more, while the bishop must be compassionate and caring for the alleged victim, so too must he be compassionate and caring for the alleged abuser. Bishop Bootkoski had both the opportunity and the duty to confer with Fr. Abano about the veracity of the allegations, but he deliberately chose not to; nor would he relent thereafter. Members of the USCCB are quite explicit and forthright: "While we are very strong

---

[402] CICm c.1717; CCEO, c. 1468.

advocates against abuse, there must be better policies in the dioceses to protect the priests from 'fictitious claims.' The recent national sex abuse scandal of the Catholic Church in the USA has opened innocent church workers to fictitious sex abuse claims."

In spite of the fact that the grand jury did issue a "no bill" against the innocent Fr. Abano, Bishop Bootkoski made no attempt to meet with the acquitted priest or to have him canonically reinstated. This is a deliberate violation of Essential Norms #13, which very clearly states that "when an accusation has been shown to be unfounded, every step possible will be taken to restore the good name of the person falsely accused."

This is an obligation that binds the incumbent in both justice and charity. Bishop Bootkoski was swift and impulsive in referring the case to the police, without first consulting Fr. Abano about the veracity of the claim. Why, then, has he been so blatantly negligent and culpably irresponsible in rectifying the grave injustice suffered by the innocent priest?

"But if you had known what this means, 'I desire mercy and not sacrifice, you would not have condemned the guiltless.'"[403] (Matthew 12:7-8). Could there be anything more important than restoring the impeccable reputation of a priest in good standing for 25 years, both with his diocese in New Jersey and the universal Catholic Church?

"But if you had known what this means, 'I desire mercy and not sacrifice, you would not have condemned the guiltless.'"[404] The supposed shepherd and leader of the diocesan family, like the ruthless judge of the parable, made no attempt to heal the humiliation and suffering patiently endured by the mother of Fr. Abano, his sisters, their families and other relatives, since his unlawful arrest on October 23, 2007, by the Middlesex County Prosecutor's Office and the Piscataway Police. Said the magnanimous sister of Fr. Abano, "Right now, the focus of Fr. Abano is to clear his good name and the good name of his family. He wants to get back his faculties to practise his priestly ministry. This test of faith has only strengthened his resolve and conviction that he will continue his vocation as a priest, to serve God and his people."

---

[403] Matthew 12:7-8
[404] Ibid.

"But if you had known what this means, 'I desire mercy and not sacrifice, you would not have condemned the guiltless.'"[405] Said Lord Acton (1834-1902): "Power tends to corrupt and absolute power corrupts absolutely." In spite of the legitimate and earnest appeals from the loyal parishioners of St. Frances Cabrini, Bishop Bootkoski made no attempt to meet them, or even to send a representative to comfort them and to reassure them that they were working in the best interests of both the beleaguered pastor of 15 years and his devoted people. Only a couple of months later, at National Stadium, in Washington DC, on April 17, 2008, Pope Benedict XVI would say to the American people: "I ask you to love your priests, and to affirm them in the excellent work that they do."

Monsignor Charles Kavanagh

On August 4, 2004, Ray O'Hanlon posted a similarly heart-rending story on BishopAccountability.org entitled "Delayed Justice Angers NY Archdiocese Priests."[406]

> Monsignor Charles Kavanagh has been a leading cleric in the Archdiocese of New York. However, he is now a hapless man standing under the long shadow of a serious accusation.
>
> Since May of 2002, Msgr. Kavanagh has been on administrative leave from his position in the archdiocese, where for years he served as vicar of development, a job that is primarily focussed on raising funds and organizing major events. As a matter of fact, it was Msgr. Kavanagh who led the organization of the funeral of the late Cardinal John O'Connor in 2000. But his work came to a sudden halt two years later when an accusation was made by a former seminarian that Kavanagh had engaged in an inappropriate relationship with him twenty years earlier. Since the accusation surfaced, Kavanagh has continued to work in community-based projects, most especially in the Bronx

---

[405] Ibid.

[406] See also, irishecho.com/?p=58534

where he was pastor at St. Raymond's prior to being put on leave. But he has not been active in the workings of the archdiocese.

Several months ago, O'Hanlon informs us, 75 priests wrote a letter to Cardinal Edward Egan expressing frustration over delays in generally dealing with cases where priests are accused of inappropriate behaviour. But it is the delay in deciding the merits or otherwise of the case against Msgr. Kavanagh that has caused particular angst. That delay is rooted in new policies adopted by the Catholic Church in response to the recent spate of child abuse scandals.

Reportedly, the Kavanagh case file has been sent to the Vatican where it rests in the hands of the Congregation for the Doctrine of the Faith. Kavanagh has submitted statements to the congregation in his own defence and travelled to Rome earlier this year to speak for himself. But no word has been heard since from the Vatican. "Charlie is on administrative leave. If he had been suspended, that would have resulted in immediate action, but instead he is in a kind of limbo," said Fr. Edward Byrne, a classmate of Kavanagh from their seminary days forty years ago and one of the leading supporters among the archdiocese's priests.

"Principally, the frustration being felt is over the secrecy that surrounds the whole process. The accused person never seems to know what is going on," Byrne, who is pastor of St. Ann's Church in the Westchester County village of Ossining, said.

Byrne said that Kavanagh had thousands of supporters in the archdiocese backing his claim of innocence. Kavanagh's accuser, Daniel Donoghue, has charged that Kavanagh had what the *Journal News* in Westchester reported as "an intense, six year relationship with him and with romantic and sexual overtones."

The alleged relationship took place when Donahue, now 40 and living on the West Coast, was a freshman at Cathedral Preparatory School in Manhattan, a high school where young men considering the priesthood are educated. Serious though the charge is, however, it is the lack of some form of public due process that is stirring passion and argument among priests and laity in the archdiocese. "There has been no compassion or understanding for someone whose whole life is the ministry," says Fr. Byrne. "There is silence as opposed to dialogue. We're trying to find a way to engage in dialogue," he said.

At the time of this report, adds O'Hanlon, Kavanagh was not available for an interview. Reportedly, a year earlier, he was told that an archdiocesan board made up of laypeople had determined that he was guilty of the charge of having an inappropriate relationship and that he had been asked to resign by Cardinal Edward Egan. Kavanagh reportedly refused, and the matter was subsequently sent to the Vatican. Joe Zwilling, a spokesman for the archdiocese, said that the general issue of how accusations against priests in the archdiocese would be handled, (it had been earlier signed and submitted in a letter by 75 priests) had been discussed in meetings between priests and Cardinal Egan.

The Kavanagh case, he indicated, was being dealt with under a new procedure brought in by the church following the recent abuse scandals. "This is a new procedure, something we have not dealt with before so there is no precedent to go by," Zwilling said. "The Holy See wants to first make sure that the proper procedure is followed so that everyone's rights are respected."

Nobody wanted to see action in the matter that was taken in haste or inappropriate. "The archdiocese and Cardinal Egan are anxious that this case is resolved. Monsignor Kavanagh has the advice of his canonical advisers every step of the way, but we don't control the process," Zwilling said.

Fr. Ed Byrne, however, believes that procedure and process are delaying a determination that his old friend is innocent. "Charlie's case has been out there for two years, but the district attorney offices in the Bronx and Manhattan have not seen fit to bring charges. He has passed two polygraph tests and other students [from Cathedral Prep.] have written a letter on his behalf," said Byrne. "Justice delayed is justice denied. They taught us that at the seminary," added Byrne.

Where Is Justice for Falsely Accused Priests?

One of the least covered aspects of the clergy sex abuse crisis concerns priests falsely accused. It is hard to put into words what it is for a man who has dedicated himself to the love of God and others, who has sought not only to preach but to put into practice the Gospel, and who has tried to be a model of Christian conduct for his parishioners all of a sudden to be accused not only of being a hypocrite against his priestly promises but of being guilty of having committed some of the most despicable actions anyone could imagine.

In a penetrating study of this knotty problem, John Landry writes:

> Priests—except, obviously, those who have been falsely accused—can take some solace in the fact that mendacious incriminations are relatively rare. According to the 2004 study by the John Jay College of Criminal Justice, only 1.5 per cent of all sex abuse allegations against Catholic priests in the United States between 1950-2002 were determined to be false after investigation. Experts say, however, that the percentage of false accusations has increased somewhat since then as large monetary awards given in mediated settlements have enticed some dishonest claimants to come forward.
>
> A report prepared for the U.S. bishops earlier this year documented that in 2009, there were 21 allegations of the sexual abuse of minors against Catholic priests in America: eight of these were acknowledged as truthful by the offending clergy, four were determined to be without foundation, one accusation was recanted, and eight are still under investigation. Right now, according to the organisation Justice for Priests and Deacons, there are 300 American priests insisting on their innocence in cases before the Vatican.

"In the realm of clergy abuse, a priest or religious falsely accused of molestation is essentially ruined for life. Hence, we need to support not only the survivors of clergy abuse, but also those priests and religious who are innocent of the crimes of which they are accused. Yes, the percentage of false accusations is relatively small, but still . . . even one false accusation is one too many."[407]

Joe Maher, president of *Opus Bono Sacerdotii* (Work for the Good of the Priesthood), received the following e-mail from a priest with the fictitious name of Fr. John. It has been slightly edited.

Dear Mr. Maher,

I don't know where to begin. Those five words in the subject of this e-mail were some of the most difficult I ever had to write. A priest and friend gave me a flyer from Opus Bono two weeks ago and after I read of your ministry, I felt I was given a direction or a glimpse of hope that someone might understand. And so, with all humility I extend my arm and hand to you.

Until a priest has to personally experience the pain and degradation of being removed from priestly service, there is no one who can possibly "understand." This year, I will observe (I cannot say celebrate) my 40th anniversary of ordination as a Roman Catholic priest. This past June, I had a surprise visit to my parish office by two officials from the chancery, the vicar for priests and a canon lawyer (who happens to be a classmate of mine). They asked to see me privately and I was extremely nervous because of their attitude and demeanour. When the three of us were alone, they proceeded to tell me that a "credible allegation of sexual abuse" was made against me and that I had an hour to pack a bag and to come with them. Few details were given to me when I asked.

---

[407] John Landry, "False Accusations". 9 July, 2010. www.catholicity.com

They mentioned a name which I never had heard of before and that this "victim" was deceased. His widow and attorney came to the diocese to bring this supposed abuse to their attention. This was to have occurred some thirty years ago. I have served in my parish as pastor for almost 20 years without the slightest hint of an impropriety.

As I left them in utter disbelief, shame and humiliation, I discovered that the diocese had already sent out a "Fax Blast" concerning my removal. After the press and media extensively exposed my "credible allegation of sexual abuse" for two days, I found myself living in a hellish nightmare. After some two or three weeks later, the same two officials called me to another meeting and informed me that another "victim" came forth after the public disclosure to make a second allegation against me. (And I had thought that life could not have possibly gotten any worse.)

As God is my witness, I swear as I swore on a Bible before the diocesan officials, these allegations are totally and completely untrue. My mind and my soul are bruised, beaten and trampled down. My parishioners are most supportive, but I am not permitted to visit them and I cannot afford to call them by telephone. My health is not good and I had avoided many appointments with my doctors. This past Christmas Eve and Christmas Day were the worst emotionally devastating events I have had to endure. I was close to suicide. I suffer panic attacks, acute anxiety and severe depression. Worst of all, there is nobody that can really understand or share this onerous burden that I bear.

I am in financial ruin "to put the icing on the cake." I have exhausted my life savings trying to pay monthly expenses for car lease payments, auto insurance, telephone, and many credit card companies to mention a few.

Even when the day for my exoneration and restoration does come, I have already seen the future—there is none! Two weeks ago, a fellow priest of our diocese who was accused of sexual misconduct which allegedly occurred forty years prior was exonerated and was officially assigned to serve "in restricted ministry" at a convent motherhouse. When the media got hold of his new assignment, there was a public outcry that a "priest, accused of credible sexual abuse" would be assigned to an area which had schools and day-care centres nearby, and our bishop, bowing to "public pressure and shepherdly concern" reversed and revoked his official assignment the very next day; not even twenty-fours had elapsed.

Now I have abandoned all hope. I do not know where to turn for help, for someone who understands. I am ashamed. I am alone. I reach out for your hand.

Fr. John

This case is one of literally thousands of similar cases that this organisation has dealt with over the past eight years. Many of these men are scared for their safety and for their livelihood. For instance, a 75-year-old priest refuses to answer his telephone and keeps his shades drawn because he was falsely accused and is now scared to death that someone will turn up in order to cart him away. His family is all but gone, and he had nowhere else to turn after the state police showed up on his doorstep the day before. As is well known, it is common practice that once a priest is removed, he is cut off from all means of support: salary, insurance, and even a place to live. The most heart-rending plea invariably is: "I don't want to lose my priesthood! I just want to be able to offer the Eucharist and administer the Sacraments."

These Stone Walls

Stung by claims of cover-up when abuse was alleged in the past, Church leaders and some treatment professionals are now seriously focusing on the rights of accused priests. A letter published in an issue of *Our Sunday Visitor* (August 29, 2010) points out that "the Church is not just an easy target for the slurs of Jay Leno and the *New York Times*.

It's also an easy target for lawyers and false claimants looking to score a windfall." The writer certainly had in mind the heartbreaking story of Fr. Gordon MacRae, who was incarcerated for offences he strenuously maintains he did not commit. Yet there was no one to champion his cause. "To paraphrase the Gospel parable, this priest was beaten by robbers and left on the side of the road in our Church. A growing number of Catholics have become unwilling to pass him by, no matter how sick we are of the sex abuse story."

Equally supportive of Fr. MacRae is Ryan MacDonald, who courageously voiced his personal feelings in no uncertain terms:

> Many of the faithful are scandalized yet again when beloved priests disappear in the night, presumed by their shepherds to be guilty of crimes claimed to have occurred two, three, or four decades earlier. Many accused priests have been simply abandoned by their bishops and fellow clergy. Church laws governing their support and defence have been routinely set aside and many have languished under dark clouds of accusation for years. Some, far too many, have been summarily dismissed from the priesthood at the behest of their bishops without due process or adequate civil or canonical defence. The Puritan founds of New England would approve of the purging of the priesthood that is now underway, for it is far more Calvinist than Catholic.

Lest this seem too fictitious or harsh, Fr. MacRae relates the story of "The Exile of Father Dominic Menna." Fr. Dom is an 81-year-old Boston priest, who was removed from ministry and forced to move from his home a few months ago while the diocese "investigated" a claim of sexual abuse alleged to have occurred in 1959 when Father Menna was 29 years old. That's the problem with a "zero tolerance" policy. As the media-fuelled lynch mob settles down and people begin to think for themselves again, zero tolerance seems a lot more like zero common sense. The Archdiocese of Boston was "ground zero" of the Church's sex abuse scandal in 2002, but now many in Boston question whether they are ready to accept the character assassination of good priests like Father Menna just because someone sees a chance for a financial windfall.

With due justification, Fr. MacRae maintains that the *Boston Globe's* Spotlight Team may have won a Pulitzer for its 2002 archaeological expedition into ancient claims against priests, but its target wasn't sexual abuse. "I can prove that, and already have. A problem with sensational media 'spotlight' reports is that they focus an intense beam in one place while leaving the rest of the story in darkness."

Moved by this courageous communication from within prison, a priest from Florida wrote to Fr. Gordon MacRae. He frankly explained that he would never have considered writing to him until he, too, was falsely accused. His letter was very candid. He wrote of his presumption of guilt given the glare of publicity to which others had been similarly exposed. He presumed this, he wrote, until two men he never even heard of filed demands for compensation claiming abuse at his hands two decades earlier. Now he's living in his sister's guestroom, without income and barred from ministry pending an "investigation" that he fears will be little more than a settlement negotiation with him as an unrepresented pawn. The lawyers for his diocese are meeting with the lawyers for the claimants, but the accused priest cannot afford a lawyer. Like many priests so accused, he is entirely excluded from the closed-door settlement discussions. "I have heard time and again that laity want the Church and falsely accused priests to fight the allegations instead of settling them."

Fr. MacRae adds that the priest from Florida wrote to him because his bishop and diocese are demanding that he submit to a psychological assessment at a treatment centre for accused priests and he doesn't know what to do. It's an all-too-familiar story. This priest knew that when Fr. MacRae was falsely accused, he was working in ministry at one such facility as its director of admissions. With fraternal solicitude, Fr. MacRae urged that priest to be extremely cautious because he was in grave peril. And he said so from bitter personal experience. To quote his precise words: "At present, however, the Church leadership in the U.S., at least, exhibits another kind of zero tolerance. It's a zero tolerance of innocence. Accused priests who maintain their innocence, and insist on standing by the truth, are in for a rocky road . . . The time in which most priests can feel immune from all this is long past."

Finally, Fr. MacRae refers to the *Wall Street Journal* of September 27, which published an article entitled "Influential Pastor Pledges to fight Sexual Allegations." It's a story about a Baptist pastor accused by four young men. Among the *Journal's* vast online readership, his announcement

204

that he is fighting the claims was the fifth most viewed article of that day. Very discreetly, Fr. MacRae makes no comment on his guilt or innocence. But he reiterates his candid observation: "I have heard time and again that laity want the Church and falsely accused priests to fight the allegations instead of settling them."[408]

Incredibly True

"Say something nice about somebody and nobody will listen. Make it mean, malicious, scandalous and the whole town will help you spread the word," so said Harold Robbins in *Never Leave Me* (1953).

In 1754, a young woman, named Neria Caggiano, accused St. Gerard, a 28-year-old Redemptorist Brother of lecherous conduct. She had been dismissed from a convent and was seeking revenge on the one who had recommended her there. St. Alphonsus Ligouri, the founder of the Redemptorists, called Br. Gerard in to answer the accusation. Rather than defending himself, Br. Gerard remained silent. Very nobly and magnanimously, he did not want to damage his accuser's reputation. The superior thought he had no choice but to discipline Br. Gerard severely. And so, he forbade him from all contact and pastoral work with outsiders and even denied him the privilege of receiving Holy Communion.

These were extremely severe and harsh penalties. But Br. Gerard, true to the injunction of his Lord and Master, offered it up for the conversion and salvation of his accuser. Very simply, he said, "There is a God in heaven. He will provide."

Several months later, Neria became dangerously ill. Realising that she was at death's door and would soon have to face her Creator and Judge, she feared for her eternal salvation and resolved to repent by recanting her calumny. So she wrote a letter to St. Alphonsus frankly confessing that she had invented the charges. The founder, overjoyed at the innocence of his spiritual son, Br. Gerard, fully restored him. His exemplary trust in God even in the midst of such a gruelling ordeal quickly made him a model not only for the members of his religious family, but also for the universal Church. He is today the patron saint of those who are falsely accused.

---

[408]   Gordon MacRae. Op.Cit.

The story of St. Vincent de Paul is equally inspiring and powerful. As a young priest in Paris, the judge, at whose house he was boarding, found that a large sum of money was missing and rashly accused Vincent of having stolen it. Very calmly, Vincent insisted that he hadn't taken the money, but he was unable to prove his innocence any more than the judge could prove his guilt. Nevertheless, most people—including those who had been his friends—thought that Vincent was guilty. Repeatedly, Vincent would say, "God knows the truth." Six years later, the actual thief was arrested in connection with another burglary. Eager to ease his guilty conscience, the thief admitted stealing the money from the judge's home and strenuously maintained Vincent's innocence. Fr. Vincent was promptly exonerated to the great edification of all in Paris.

It is reported that the saintly Padre Pio, the renowned and revered stigmatist, was told by a cynical Church official that his "wounds" were psychologically induced. "Go to the fields," wrote Padre Pio in response, "and get close as possible to a bull. Concentrate on him with all your might. Do this, and see if you grow horns on your head!"

"Love is strong as death; jealousy is cruel as the grave." (Song of Solomon Ch.8. Vs 6)

> "O! Beware, my lord, of jealousy; it is the green-eyed monster which doth mock the meat it feeds on." (William Shakespeare, *Othello*, act3, sc.3,11.)

Again, it is reported that Padre Pio was rashly and calumniously accused of molesting women in the confessional. Never was such a report made; nor have any been corroborated. We now know that these claims were baseless, even though some in the media even today continue to maliciously exploit them. Regrettably few, if any, are aware of the extent to which Padre Pio suffered at the hands of his fellow priests and the Church leaders. The sole and vicious objective was to discredit the saintly priest who was so uniquely blessed.

Says Fr. Gordon MacRae, the one-time director of admissions for the Servants of the Paraclete—a treatment centre for priests accused of sexual offences:

> The irony is that if the claims against Padre Pio were brought today in America, he would be packed off to that very

'treatment' centre for an evaluation . . . He would be seen from day one as a 'priest offender,' and his denials would be interpreted as evidence of guilt.

Adds Fr. MacRae:

Justice has turned on its head when men who stand to gain hundreds of thousands of dollars for making a false claim are automatically called 'victims' by Church leaders now, while priests accused without evidence from decades ago are just as quickly called 'priest-offenders' and 'slayers of souls'.

Finally, Fr. MacRae poses this disturbing observation and question:

It horrifies me to realize that the dominant centre for accused priests in the U.S. operates with a stated bias that denies priests one of the foundational civil rights of American citizens: a presumption of innocence when accused. How does someone win when denial of the crime is used as evidence against the innocent, and often, the ONLY evidence?[409]

Even More Incredibly True

On March 18, 2010, Matt C. Abbott published an article "Priests Are Falsely Accused Regularly." He received many responses, one of which is being reproduced verbatim. It is written by "Father J," a priest of the Archdiocese of Boston.[410]

In response to your recent article: Priests are falsely accused regularly. There is no effort to protect priests from false accusations, simply because the interests of the bishops seem to be to protect themselves, the diocesan officials, and the

---

[409] Gordon MacRae. Op.Cit.

[410] www.renewamerica.com/columns/abbott/100323

207

property of the diocese. Canon Law is not followed; this is basically ecclesiastical lawlessness.

I know of a priest falsely accused, a holy priest, who has been ruined. The Archdiocese of Boston never investigated the case and some of the principal witnesses have died. The people who determine whether an accusation is "credible" are not the brightest bulbs on the tree and their main concerns are the interests of the archbishop.

I know of another priest who was accused and he raised money and got a lawyer and was cleared, but he was emotionally ruined. By the way, the diocese does not give financial help to priests in order to get lawyers. Most priests don't have significant financial resources. The dioceses also do nothing to restore the reputations of priests. The accusation is always on the front page and the clearing (if mentioned at all) is tucked in along with the legal notices.

I know of another priest who was accused, got his own lawyer with a small loan from the Archdiocese of Boston, and was cleared. The priest had been told by one archdiocesan official not to worry about the loan, but now the chancellor, who is paid $250,000 a year, sent a letter to the priest suggesting that an archdiocesan mortgage be put on his house. This is how priests are treated.

We priests have two targets on our bodies. The one on our front sides is aimed at by the representatives of the culture of death, and the one on our back sides is aimed at by the chancery. The fraternal link between bishops and their priests in many dioceses has been destroyed. Dirty little secret arrangements have been made with state and federal officials, so that the bishops won't be prosecuted, even though they and their staffs are the guilty ones who knew the priests who were abusing minors. These arguments make the bishop, who is supposed to be the spiritual father of the priest, into the prime enforcer of the civil law. These bishops and their staffs live in fear of prosecution, so they err on the side of harshness. Any accusation is thus credible. We are supposed to announce the Gospel with courage, but we are all alone. Any priest can be destroyed at any time.

We are supposed to be able to depend on our bishops and we cannot. The people of the parishes are supportive, but we can be cut off from them and have our faculties withdrawn at the drop of a hat. It seems as though bishops and their staff have no fear of God and do not think that they will be judged for destroying the reputation and ministry of a priest.

There is also the fact that dioceses have become businesses run by highly paid laymen. For them it is a 9 to 5 job. They have no sympathy for the life of a priest, it seems to me. And when they find a better gif, they will jump ship.

If the Catholic people want priests in the future, they had better seek justice for priests. A priest who abuses the young can hurt thousands of people, and a priest who is falsely accused is destroyed and thousands of people are hurt—their faith being shaken.[411]

A certain Lorraine Keess did send in this response:

I have read with great heartache your article "Was Your Priest Falsely Accused?" I will pray for the priest who wrote that gut-wrenching account of his accusation and any others that may be suffering the same persecution.

Through all the turmoil of the reality of real predators offending under the guise of priestly ministry comes the sinister reality of false accusations. Personally, I believe that there is an epidemic of false accusations and the subject has

---

[411] Ibid.

not been sufficiently explored. We fear that by exploring the issue of false accusations, this would make us look like deniers that any real offences have occurred, right? Also, in all likelihood we would be accused of adding to the pain of the victims of real abuse by addressing the subject of false allegations.

Catholics are between a rock and a hard place and I believe this to be the cunning strategy of the forces of evil. We must not be afraid to address the issue of false allegations in the midst of true abuse crimes that are coming to light in these trying times. The victims of false allegations need to be profiled and defended, too.

I am aware that both the Canadian and American Psychiatric Associations have made clear the ambiguity of memory, warning about those therapeutic techniques that supposedly uncover "repressed memories." This is important to know, especially in regard to allegations that go back so many years and suddenly come to the forefront.

Motivations for false allegations vary from outright lies that stem from malice or a desire to grab a windfall of money to a sincere belief that one has been violated after going through therapeutic techniques that conjure up a lost memory. Thanks for the article. I pray every day that the Lord will expose truth where it needs to be exposed.[412]

And this is what a certain Terry Carroll very candidly and courageously adds:

There's no question that the scandal of abuse is a dark time for our Church. I'm not sure, however, that the fallout from the scandal isn't worse than the offences themselves. This fallout doesn't just affect priests who are subject to the

---

[412] Ibid.

presumption of guilt by virtue of their collar. The need to protect ourselves has become a cancer throughout the faith community. How can we call it progress when we can't even allow communion to be brought to the sick and shut-ins without chaperoned ministers who have passed all manner of criminal background checks? How can it be progress when everyone must be assumed to be potentially harmful to us? Are we really safer, or do we just need to appear that way? In the desire to make sure everyone is safe, have we not sacrificed something more?

I have been accused of latent Donatism in my criticisms of faithless and disobedient clergy. Have we not spread this attitude to all the faithful? Is everyone now to be presumed unworthy of ministry unless first proven beyond reproach? Is no one worthy to pastor or minister unless first beatified?

As you know, my talents are not available in any setting where I must first prove, not that I am talented, but worthy of trust. I don't know how today's priests live from day to day without Xanax. I understand the courage it takes to wear a collar in public. It shouldn't be that way. Yes, there are truly unworthy priests who must be removed from ministry. There are truly unworthy laity who must be confronted and separated from the faith community as well. But this can't be the presumed norm. We are becoming what we always used to laugh about when we thought of Soviet society. No one can trust anyone else.

The former pastor in Wichita Falls could probably write a letter similar to the one below, and he was the victim of a pre-emptive not a reactive strike (no one ever said that he did anything, only that he might). And while we're rounding up the usual suspects, we let even worse deformations of the faithful from the pulpit and liturgy go unaddressed. I really don't know which is worse: priests who might sin and even do sin, or priests who have lost their faith and inflict their personal darkness on far more victims than abusers do.[413]

And, finally, this is what a certain Mike Malone boldly and rightly asserts:

> This is crazy and disgraceful! Where else can someone be accused, tried and convicted before a hearing or any kind of defence? I have often wondered just how many lawyers and their clients have been enriched by phoney allegations. Remember the famous quote laid out by Labour Secretary, Raymond Donovan, in 1987 after being cleared of fraud charges? He said: "Which office do I go to in order to get my reputation back?" . . . When is the Church going to defend priests and get evidence that is beyond a reasonable doubt?" [414]

---

[413]   Ibid.

[414]   Ibid.

17

A Formidable but Inescapable Challenge

Be merciful, just as your heavenly Father is merciful.
—Luke 6:36

Blessed are the merciful, for they will receive mercy.
—Matthew 5:7

So speak and so act as those who are to be judged by the law of liberty.
For judgement will be without mercy to anyone who has shown no mercy;
mercy triumphs over judgement.
—James 2:12-13

In a penetrating and thought-provoking article, Sr. Camille D'Arienzo, RSM, relates the following story: [415]

The well-known poetess, Maya Angelou, was raped when she was just seven years old. So brutal was the violation that she was hospitalized. From her bed of pain and shame, she revealed the rapist's name. He was arrested and released for lack of conclusive evidence. The very next day, his battered and lifeless body was discovered beside a road; he had been savagely kicked to death.

---

[415] Camille D'Arienzo, "Mercy toward Our Fathers: Difficult as It May Be, Forgiving Priests Guilty of Abuse Could Be the Key of Healing," *America* (August 18, 2008).

When the tragedy was reported to the little child, she confessed later that she felt personally responsible for the abuser's death. After all, she had divulged his identity. Like others before and after her, Maya felt culpable, if not for the rape but for its tragic consequences. As a result, she refused to speak for five years. In her self-imposed solitude, Maya became a voracious reader, avidly assimilating the wisdom of the ages from William Shakespeare to Langston Hughes.

As a regular churchgoer, Maya would listen attentively to the preacher and the varied inflections of his voice as he shared God's Word. Moved by the grace of God, Maya summoned the courage to break her silence, and she did so most eloquently, fully equipped with her exceptional knowledge even at that early age. Since then, she has systematically and progressively embraced the formula for self-healing: "One who has suffered a great evil must name it, learn from it, forgive it and move forward with courage and focus on the future. Forgiveness has no power to change the past, but it certainly has enormous power to mould the future."

This very same advice was reiterated many years later during a television show on evil by Bill Moyers: "Victims of evil must cope with the ugly graffiti that is scribbled on the walls of their psyche. Can they forgive the evildoers? Should they? An answer can be found in the wisdom of the Quakers, who remind us that 'forgiveness is a gift we give ourselves.'" [416] This is indeed a formidable but inescapable challenge.

A Formidable Challenge

Jesus said, "But to you who are listening I say: Love your enemies, do good to those who hate you, bless those who curse you, pray for those who ill-treat you. To him who strikes you on one cheek offer the other cheek also."[417] As is well known, there is no commandment of Jesus that has caused so much discussion and debate as the commandment to love our enemies. However, it is important that we examine it more closely in order to comprehend its precise meaning and the consequent obligation to conform.

---

[416] Ibid.
[417] Luke 6:29

Unlike English, Greek has three distinct words for "love." First, there is *eran*, which describes the passionate love of a young man for the girl of his dreams; hence the word *erotic*. Second, there is *philein*, which describes our love for our nearest and dearest. Such, for instance, is the affection that we feel for the members of our immediate family. It is patently clear that Jesus is referring to neither one of these here. It is both unnatural and impossible to feel either *eran* or *philein* towards one's enemies—persons who either harbour nothing short of the meanest dispositions towards us or have directly or indirectly harmed us.

The specific word used here is *agapan*, which describes an unconquerable benevolence and invincible good will towards another person, regardless of the ill will of the other. In other words, *agapan* is a matter of the *will* and not of the *heart*. It means that no matter what another does to us, we will never allow ourselves to retaliate with the same coin but nobly desire the highest good. Even more, we will make every endeavour, difficult though it may be, to reach the other and when the occasion presents itself, to be as gracious and kind as we can. In a word, regardless of what the other thinks, feels, or plans towards us, we will still persist in seeking nothing short of his/her highest good. And this is *agapan*—the trait that makes us like God, our Father in heaven, who makes his sun to shine on the good and the bad and his rain to fall on the virtuous and the not so virtuous.

This precisely is what Maya Angelou meant when she said: "One who has suffered a great evil must name it, learn from it, forgive it and move forward with courage and focus on the future. Forgiveness has no power to change the past, but it certainly has enormous power to mould the future."[418]

And this is exactly what Bill Moyers meant when he said: "Victims of evil must cope with the ugly graffiti that is scribbled on the walls of their psyche. Can they forgive the evildoers? Should they? An answer can be found in the wisdom of the Quakers, who remind us that 'forgiveness is a gift we give ourselves.'" This, once again, is a formidable but inescapable challenge.[419]

The Christian ethic quite patently is *positive*. That is to say, it does not consist in *not doing* but in *actively doing something for the good of others,*

---

[418] Ibid.

[419] Ibid.

even those who hurt or harm us. This is why it is rightly termed the Golden Rule: "Treat others as you would have them treat you. Do unto others what you would have them do to you."

Hillel, one of the great Jewish Rabbis, was once asked by a man to teach him the whole law while he stood on one leg. And this was the prompt and succinct answer: "What is hateful to thee, do not to another. That is the whole law and all else is explanation."[420]

Philo, the great Jew of Alexandria, said, "What you hate to suffer, do not do to anyone else."[421]

And Isocrates, the Greek orator, said, "What things make you angry when you suffer them at the hands of others, do not you do to other people." [422]

And when Confucius was asked, "Is there one word which may serve as a rule of practice for all of one's life?" he answered, "Is not Reciprocity such a word? What you do not want done to yourself, do not do to others."[423]

A Woeful Miscarriage of Justice

Msgr. Harry J. Byrne, JCD, recounts the instance of an innocent priest who was hastily and rashly removed from the pastoral ministry on the basis of what can best be described as "vengeful and emotional blackmail." [424]

As a canonist, Msgr. Byrne was requested to represent the case of Father X, who had been removed from ministry by the bishop of Metuchen, Paul Bootkoski. Reportedly, the bishop had received a communication from the chancery of the Archdiocese of San Francisco seeking the whereabouts of Father X. The letter went on to explain that a Ms. Z

---

[420] jewishencylopedia.com/articles
[421] Quoted by William Barclay in "The End of the World's Values", Idolphin. org
[422] Ibid.
[423] think.exist.com
[424] Monsignor Harry J. Byrne JCD, "Bishop as Cop, DA, Judge, and Appellant Bench!" *Justice for Priests and Deacons* (May 5, 2010). Or larryjbyrneblogspot.com, 5 May, 2010.

was seeking retribution from him for an alleged affair some twenty years ago. Her charges, adds Msgr. Byrne, were not canonically credible. Ms. Z was referred to a chancery social worker, who thereafter wrote to the Metuchen diocese, where Father X worked in the Parish of St. ABC. The social worker's letter stated that Ms. Z was seeking funds for counselling and support from Father X. And this was in compensation for the alleged affair between Father X and Ms. Z.

Focussing on the allegation of an affair, Bishop Bootkoski removed Father X from ministry. To add insult to injury, the bishop did not first inform Father X of the reported allegation, nor did he give the priest a chance to defend himself on the basis of the fundamental principle "*innocent until proven guilty.*" Further, the bishop made no effort to investigate the complaint objectively and fairly. "In so doing, Bishop Bootkoski has failed to comply with all the stipulations of Canon Law," maintains Msgr. Byrne.

Father X was told to vacate the rectory. The pastor of St. ABC agreed to pay Father X on a *per diem* basis for the days that he had worked prior to his abrupt and unfair removal. Even more, the pastor debarred the evicted priest from working with children. In other words, the reputation and ministry of the defenceless and helpless priest were irretrievably destroyed. In one fell blow, the hapless Father X had slumped from a respected and much-loved priest to a spurned social outcast!

Apart from being a grievous sin, this drastic action is a blatant violation of Canon 220, which very clearly and unambiguously states: "No one may unlawfully harm the good reputation which a person enjoys, or violate the right of every person to protect his or her privacy." Stated differently, two rights are recognised and protected here: the right to one's good name or reputation and the right to one's privacy.[425] *No one may "unlawfully" infringe either right.* The right to one's good reputation is manifestly based on the natural law, rooted in the dignity of the human person and acknowledged as such by Vatican II.[426] Of course, a person may by his or her conduct

---

[425] "The right to one's privacy" was inserted only after the final draft was submitted to the pope (John Paul II). For the history of the drafting of this canon cf. RCom SPD 30 at Cann. 32, 33; Sch 1982 36 at Can. 220.

[426] Cf. GS 26-27.

obviously forfeit this right as in the case of individuals who have been indicted for a serious public offence. In a word, Ms. Z's allegations as to the nature of their affair twenty years ago had no canonical significance.

Msgr. Byrne made several informal attempts, either by e-mail or phone, to discuss the crucial matter with the vicar general of the Metuchen diocese. The latter was initially sympathetic but regretted his inability to clear the name of Father X. Undeterred Msgr. Byrne requested a personal meeting with Bishop Bootkoski and Father X. This was rejected by the former.

So Msgr. Byrne decided to examine the matter himself. He found that Ms. Z had been stalking Father X for many years. As a matter of fact, "she had been punishing miscreants for reasons too lengthy to be presented," said Msgr. Byrne. This was relayed to Bishop Bootkoski. Further, Msgr. Byrne pointed out that the eviction of Father X from his residence and his final limited pay cheque would not be acceptable in ordinary business practice. No Christian employer would treat a dishwasher in such an unethical and unchristian manner! It might even have been in violation of New Jersey labour laws.

Reportedly, Bishop Bootkoski explained that the dismissal of Father X was based on a communication signed by an official of the San Francisco archdiocese. This, avers Msgr. Byrne, is simply not true! "I have the letter! It was signed by the social worker. Archbishop George Niederauer of San Francisco did participate in this case. I have his letter stating that only the social worker was involved; that she and she alone signed the letter; and that her sole interest was to help Ms. Z towards counselling and financial help. Niederauer wrote that his office, through the social worker's letter, did not say and had no intentions of saying anything about X's fitness or lack thereof for ministry."[427]

Msgr. Byrne persisted in reaching overseas to the Philippines, from where Father X hailed, and to Bishop Camilo D. Gregorio of the Prelature of Batanes. "Gregorio sent a letter glowingly endorsing Father X as 'very well loved and respected by both the clergy and the faithful he has worked with in all these past twenty-six years . . . and has been subjected

---

[427]   Ibid.

to a very painful experience through . . . a misapplication of the Dallas Charter."[428]

Further, Gregorio knew Ms. Z and provided a candid report of her mentality and her deliberate stalking of Father X. He discounted the alleged affair of twenty years ago as long absolved and repented for and not a reason to dismiss the priest from the ministry. The noble and compassionate bishop concluded with this plea to Bootkoski and other bishops: "Father X has been a victim of canonical injustice here. As bishops, we need to view such situations with humility, justice and charity, for we have an obligation to do what serves the best interests of one and all." "Be merciful, just as your heavenly Father is merciful" (Luke 6:36).

This is how Msgr. Byrne concludes this woeful miscarriage of justice:

> Bootkoski is a bishop! He is in charge. Many roles, however, conflicting! He was Father X's arresting officer, prosecutor, judge, and appellant bench—an absurdity in any jurisprudential sense! But he dealt with Father X in each role. There was no appeal! There is no appeal! The bishop has spoken! Father X's life has been disrupted personally, spiritually, economically, and in his priestly ministry for a year and a half. 'I, the bishop, have spoken!' And Bishop Bootkoski had completely misunderstood the letter from Archbishop Niederauer's Chancery and misunderstood who signed and sent it![429]

Blessed Are the Merciful!

In his famous Sermon on the Mount, Christ Jesus made it explicitly clear that to be forgiven we must be forgiving. St. James pulls no punches in asserting: "For judgement is without mercy to one who has shown no mercy."[430] Earlier, Christ Jesus did emphasise the very same truth when concluding the thought-provoking and challenging parable of the unforgiving debtor: "So also my heavenly Father will do to every one of

---

[428] Ibid.

[429] Ibid.

[430] James 2:13.

you, if you do not forgive your brother from your heart."[431] Consistent with this recurring theme, Christ Jesus included two verses in the Lord's Prayer that make it patently clear we must first forgive if we are to enjoy forgiveness: "Forgive us our debts as we also have forgiven our debtors." So forgiveness is a *sine qua non* in the Christian ethic. "For if you forgive men their trespasses, your heavenly Father also will forgive you. But if you do not forgive men their trespasses, neither will your Father forgive your trespasses."[432] In a word, it is the consistent and incontestable teaching of Christ Jesus that indeed only the merciful shall receive mercy.

However, there is even more to this beatitude. The Greek word for merciful is *eleemon*. But, as is often the case, the Greek of the New Testament as we possess it goes back to an original Hebrew and Aramaic. The Hebrew word for mercy is *chesedh*, and it an untranslatable word. It means far more than just sympathy. To sympathise with another person in the popular sense of the term is to feel sorry for someone in distress or grief. *Chesedh,* however, means something deeper and more demanding. It means the ability to get right inside the other person's skin until we can see things with his eyes, think things with his mind, and feel things with his feelings. The closest English equivalent is *empathy*.

So very clearly, *chesedh* is much more than an emotional wave of pity. It actually demands a deliberate effort of the mind and of the will. It denotes a sympathy which is not given, as it were, from outside, but which comes from a deliberate identification with the other person, until we see things as he sees them, feel things as he feels them, and think things with his mind as the magnanimous and fatherly Bishop Gregorio did towards the harried Father X. This is empathy at its noblest and purest—experiencing things together with the other person, literally going through what he is going through and so feeling not only for but with the person. And this is what Jesus is strongly advocating to us: "Be merciful, just as your heavenly Father is merciful" (Luke 6:36).

On one occasion, St. Luke tells us Christ Jesus visited his good friends Martha and Mary at Bethany.[433] This was invariably his practice when his journey took him to that part of the woods. With customary good will

---

[431] Matthew 18:35.
[432] Matthew 6:12, 14, 15.
[433] Luke 10:38-42.

and generosity, Martha set about feverishly preparing her special visitor a sumptuous meal that he would relish. That was her way of demonstrating her genuine respect, esteem, and affection for her honoured guest.

By contrast, her sister, Mary, sat beside Jesus literally gracing him with her reassuring presence and undivided attention. And she did so for a very special reason. With typical feminine intuition, the perceptive Mary realised that Jesus was deeply distressed; that a heavy load did weigh on his anxious mind; that his eyes, the windows of his soul, did manifest a hidden but painful trepidation. And she was right. Jesus was on his way to Jerusalem, where he knew full well that he was destined to be treacherously betrayed, to suffer grievously, and to be mercilessly tortured and brutally crucified.

So on that occasion and at that precise moment, food and drink were certainly not uppermost in Christ Jesus's hierarchy of needs. Consequently, Mary wisely chose the better part—the comfort of her presence, the support of her attention, and the reassurance of her affection. Hers was *chesedh* at its purest, noblest, and best. As we know, *chesedh* means something deeper and more demanding. It means the ability to get right inside the other person's skin until we can see things with his eyes, think things with his mind, and feel things with his feelings. This is "the better part" that Mary did wisely and rightly chose and for which Christ Jesus did warmly and gratefully commend her.

An Inescapable Challenge

On a cold night in January 2008, Joseph R. Maher, a successful businessman and president of *Opus Bono Sacerdotii*, addressed a group in Long Island, New York. *Opus Bono Sacerdotii* is an organisation that endeavours to provide help for priests who have been accused of the sexual abuse of minors and so expelled from the priestly ministry. In the audience were priests, victims of abuse, and members of *Voice of the Faithful*. Although the opening prayer called for healing and reconciliation, the tension in the room militated against both.[434]

In his talk, reports Sr. D'Arienzo, Joseph Maher humbly and honestly acknowledged with unfeigned humility and deep regret the mind-boggling

---

[434] Camille D'Arienzo, *America* (August 18, 2008).

plague of sexual abuse of minors by members of the clergy. He frankly admitted that, as a consequence, countless individuals had been wounded, reputations of the alleged perpetrators had been irreparably impaired, and trust in both clergy and the hierarchy had been irretrievably eroded. In response, the American bishops (USCCB) gathered in Dallas, Texas, in June 2002 and devised a charter of policies and programmes that have since proved effective in protecting young people. However, Mr. Maher continues, while the bishops at Dallas listened to other bishops, psychologists, criminal lawyers, law enforcement experts, and members of the faithful, one group was visibly absent—not one priest was invited to participate! Even more, the charter made no provision whatsoever for priests who would be falsely accused and wrongly condemned.

Springing to their defence, Cardinal Avery Dulles[435] sharply criticized the charter on this count and called for its revision. Even the National Review Board (NRB), a select group of prominent Catholic men and women appointed by the bishops to oversee the implementation of the charter, called for a periodic review of it.[436] Very justifiably, the board asserted that, had the bishops enforced canon law against the alleged abusers, the mind-boggling crisis would never have happened. This inexcusable negligence, the failure to protect priests against the scourge of false allegations, and other glaring flaws, led the NRB to declare without hesitation, "The Charter was the bishops' attempt to deflect criticism from themselves onto individual priests." Other harsh criticisms of the bishops by the NRB resulted in hostility with some members of the American hierarchy. Four bishops even tried unsuccessfully to block the USCCB from funding the mandated audits of dioceses.[437]

In his talk, Joseph Maher argued that a large number of accused priests are innocent and that, abandoned by their bishops and members of the laity, they are denied the resources to defend themselves and to clear their names. They were guilty until proven innocent! And then, Mr. Maher courageously spoke of the pressing need to give culpable priests the opportunity to reform and to return to the active ministry.

---

[435] Cardinal Avery Dulles, *America* (June 14, 2004).

[436] February 2004.

[437] Ibid.

Further, Mr. Maher said that many victims, who claimed abuse, were actually seeking financial gain. As can be expected, there were vehement protests from the floor, with members denouncing Mr. Maher for his assumed insensitivity. What had begun as a genuine attempt at healing the breach and commencing the slow path to healing eventually resulted in "the still open wound on the soul of the church" opined one attendee. The acrimonious conflict reached its nadir when one woman openly declared, "For such men no healing is possible."

How, then, are the reassuring words of Christ Jesus to be interpreted: "Just so, I tell you, there will be more joy in heaven over one sinner who repents than over ninety-nine righteous persons who need no repentance" (Luke 15:7)?

The Parable of the Unforgiving Servant

When Peter, the spokesman of the apostles, inquired: "Lord, if another member of the church sins against me, how often should I forgive? As many as seven times? Jesus candidly responded, 'Not seven times, but, I tell you, seven times seventy."[438] To substantiate his point and in no uncertain terms, Christ Jesus related the parable of the unforgiving servant. Unable to meet an overwhelming debt, he pleaded for clemency until such time he acquired the amount due. The concession was readily given by the large-hearted creditor. As he left with that onerous responsibility lifted off his shoulders, the servant met a fellow servant, who owed him a pittance. He demanded it, and when the fellow servant pleaded for clemency and the time to acquire the money due, the unforgiving servant literally throttled him and threatened to have him imprisoned until that petty amount was repaid in full.

William Barclay rightly maintains that Peter had good reason to pose such a curious question. It was rabbinic teaching that a man must forgive his brother three times. Rabbi Jose ben Hanina said, "He who begs forgiveness from his neighbour must not do so more than three times."

Rabbi Jose ben Jehuda was even more explicit, "If a man commits an offence once, they forgive him; if he commits an offence a second time,

---

[438] Matthew 18:21-22

they forgive him; if he commits an offence a third time, they forgive him; the fourth time they do not forgive him."

The biblical proof that this was correct was taken from Amos. In the opening chapters of Amos, there is a series of condemnations on the various nations for three transgressions and for four.[439] From this, it was deduced that God's forgiveness extends to three offences and that he visits the sinner with punishment at the fourth. It was not to be thought that a man could be more gracious than God, whose forgiveness was limited to three times.

Peter thought that he was going very far, for he takes the rabbinic three times, multiplies it by two for good measure, adds one, and suggests, with eager self-satisfaction, that it will be enough if he forgives seven times. Peter expected to be warmly commended, but Jesus's answer was that the Christian must forgive seventy times seven. In a word, there is no reckonable limit to forgiveness. It is in the light of this astounding revelation that the parable of the unforgiving servant needs to be rightly interpreted.

These are the salient implications of this Christian challenge:

1. A person must forgive in order to be forgiven. Stated differently, he who will not forgive another cannot hope that God will forgive him. "Blessed are the merciful, for they shall obtain mercy."[440]
2. Forgiveness is a *sine qua non* for God's forgiveness. "For if you forgive men their trespasses, your heavenly Father also will forgive you; but if you do not forgive men their trespasses, neither will your Father forgive your trespasses.[441] "And this stark admonition was reiterated by the apostle James: "For judgement is without mercy to one who has shown no mercy."[442] *So divine and human forgiveness go hand in hand.*
3. And why is this so? Returning to the parable of the Unforgiving Servant, the first servant owed his creditor a fabulous sum of money—the equivalent of £2,400,000. By contrast, his fellow

---

[439] Amos 1:3, 6, 9, 11, 13; 2:1, 4, 6.
[440] Matthew 5:7
[441] Matthew 6:14-15
[442] James 2:13

servant owed him the paltry sum of £5—one five-hundredth-thousandth of his own debt.

4. The point of this glaring contrast is that nothing men can do to us can in any way compare with what we have done to God, and if God has forgiven us the debt we owe him, we must forgive our fellow men the debts they owe to us. Nothing that we have to forgive can even faintly or remotely compare with what we have been forgiven.

The apostle Peter has framed this astounding contrast most eloquently: "You know that you were ransomed from the futile ways inherited from your ancestors, not with perishable things like silver and gold, but with the precious blood of Christ, like that of a lamb without defect or blemish" (1 Peter 1:18). Could there be anything more heinous than the wilful, brutal, and ignominious murder of the innocent Son of God, who had come so that we may have life and in abundance. And even as he wasted away on the cross and his quivering life ebbed out of him, Christ Jesus turned to his heavenly Father and prayed: "Father, forgive them, for they do not know what they are doing" (Luke 23:34).

Forgiveness Means "Fore-giving"

The sexual abuse of any human being, but especially an innocent and defenceless minor, is a grievous crime that needs to be justly and effectively addressed. Of this, there is no doubt whatsoever. As a matter of fact, the Catholic Church has made a firm commitment to strive for seven things in particular: truth, humility, healing for the victims, assistance to other persons affected, an effective response to those who are accused, an effective response to those who are guilty of abuse, and prevention of abuse.

The late Cardinal Avery Dulles framed it most succinctly: "Since World War II, the Catholic Church has become a leading champion of the inviolable rights of individual human persons. Applying this principle, the bishops of the United States in November 2000 published *Responsibility and Rehabilitation*, a critique of the American criminal justice system, in which they upheld the dignity of the accused and rejected slogans such as 'three strikes and you're out.' Among other things, the bishops stated: 'One-size-fits-all solutions are often inadequate . . . We must renew our efforts to ensure that the punishment fits the crime. Therefore, we do not support mandatory sentencing that replaces judges' assessments with rigid formulations.'"[443]

Yet while these practices have widespread support, there is little talk of forgiveness of the abuser as part of the formula that contributes to healing. Reportedly therapists advise against broaching the topic of forgiveness for fear of aggravating the victim's ire and impeding recovery. Attorneys forbid contact with the victim for fear of risking a lawsuit. And church leaders cautiously avert any initiative that could trigger an explosive media blitz further undermining their effectiveness as witnesses of the Gospel.

For instance, an Adelaide (South Australia) man honestly confessed that he sexually exploited his daughter and grand-daughter because that was the way he was brought up.[444]

The man, who cannot be named, pleaded guilty in the Adelaide District Court on Thursday, November 17, 2010, to persistent sexual exploitation of a child and gross indecency.

Judge Peter Herriman heard that the man had sex with his daughter on numerous occasions between 1976 and 1983 beginning when she was just six years old.

He also committed acts of gross indecency against his grand-daughter in 2004.

Prosecution counsel Melissa Wilkinson told the court the accused had many opportunities to reflect on his offending "but he has of course offended again against his grand-daughter some 20 years later."

Defence lawyer Joseph Saunders told the court his client had expressed remorse for his crimes and sought religious counsel to express his guilt.

Mr. Saunders said his client had told a psychiatrist "it was how I was brought up" because he himself was sexually abused as a child.

The man was sentenced on December 7, 2010.

The fact of the matter is that forgiveness does not mean forgetting, nor does it rule out the punishment appropriate to the criminal behaviour. This is what Rev. Richard P. McBrien writes:

---

[443] Cardinal Avery Dulles, SJ, *Rights of Accused Priests: Toward a Revision of the Dallas Charter and the "Essential Norms* (June 21, 2004).

[444] 9 News (Thursday, November 18, 2010).

> To be forgiven from a sin does not carry with it pardon for a crime or a guaranteed return to one's former employment. A murderer, for instance, who repents and confesses may be restored to the state of grace, but not to freedom.

In a word, every murder case is judged in terms of the mitigating factors, and different sentences are imposed.

"One-size-fits-all solutions are often inadequate . . . We must renew our efforts to ensure that the punishment fits the crime. Therefore, we do not support mandatory sentencing that replaces judges' assessments with rigid formulations." Stated differently, it is but meet and proper to consider extenuating factors in cases of alleged sexual abuse. There is an enormous difference between an obsessive-compulsive predator and one who errs in a moment of human frailty and is genuinely contrite. While both deserve compassion, the former needs to be effectively rehabilitated and the latter needs both forgiveness and encouragement. "To err is human; to forgive divine." Consequently, it would be unfair and unjust to tar both with the same brush. While the former has no option but to comply with the dictates of the law as well as be encouraged to seek rehabilitation, the latter certainly does not deserve to be totally excluded from the priestly ministry. "Every saint has had a past; every sinner has a future."[445]

Truth Is Indeed Stranger than Fiction

Ryan Anthony MacDonald is an independent journalist writing in New York. He is a convert to Catholicism, and he writes religious and legal commentary and book reviews. His revelations in *Truth and Justice* literally defy comprehension. As is patently clear to one and all, throughout the last seven years, the media has ruthlessly capitalised on the sexual abuse crisis in the Catholic priesthood. However, adds MacDonald, scant attention has been paid to the probability of false claims levelled against innocent priests. As one nationally known legal scholar has pointed out, *when one understands the role of the contingency bar in mediated settlements, it becomes a virtual certainty that some priests have been falsely accused for money.*

---

[445] See "Rights of Accused Priests" in *Justice for Priests and Deacons*, 19 November, 2011. justiceforpriests.org.

One such case, states MacDonald, was profiled in a two-part series of articles by Dorothy Rabinowitz.[446] A member of the *Wall Street Journal* editorial board, Rabinowitz won a Pulitzer for her compelling disclosures about false witnesses and witch-hunt sexual abuse prosecutions in American courts of law. Her coverage of the travesty of justice by which Father Gordon MacRae was convicted and imprisoned in 1994 got the attention of numerous legal scholars and civil liberties experts.

Conspicuously, however, notes MacDonald, Catholic news services and publications have uniformly ignored this case, or worse, have pro-actively refused any reference to it. Some Catholic publications, such as *NCR*, were quick to report some of the vast propaganda that surrounded MacRae's life sentence in 1994—a sentence imposed after he declined three "plea deals" to serve only one year in prison. However, the overwhelming evidence of fraud that has emerged from the background of this case has been shunned by most Catholic commentators, adds MacDonald.

The National Centre for Reason and Justice sponsors a website.[447] It contains a comprehensive case history for which MacDonald and others conducted substantial research. For instance, the late Avery Cardinal Dulles wrote that "the MacRae case must come to light and will be instrumental in a reform." Again, the late Fr. Richard John Neuhaus wrote "the case of Father MacRae reflects a Church and a justice system that seem indifferent to justice."[448] Others, adds MacDonald, in the American Church and Catholic media have been silent. *And that silence is becoming a scandal of its own.*

The following report by Ryan Anthony MacDonald is being reproduced verbatim not only for its startling accuracy but for its disturbing veracity:[449]

A careful reading of the detailed Case History published at www.GordonMacRae.net reveals that the central accusers

---

[446] Dorothy Rabinowitz, "A Priest's Story," the *Wall Street Journal* (April 27/28, 2005).

[447] www.GordonMacRae.net

[448] Richard John Neuhaus, *First Things* (August/September 2008).

[449] Ryan Anthony MacDonald, *Truth and Justice*, reproduced with the permission of the author.

in MacRae's 1994 criminal case originally accused another priest, Fr. Stephen Scruton. As the claims evolved, it became clear that Scruton was a central figure in the case, but one whose presence could not reconcile with the accusers' time frame. He was simply not in the claimants' community until the youngest of them was 16.

Nevertheless, Stephen Scruton has never denied the claimed sexual involvement that MacRae's accusers originally attributed to Scruton. Before MacRae's 1994 trial, Scruton fled the state to avoid a subpoena from MacRae's lawyer. Scruton refused to respond to all inquiries from MacRae's defence.

Because he could not be located, the jury never heard his name or the fact that he was accused by the same people who accused MacRae. Evidence of a relationship between Scruton and MacRae's accusers has never been explained. This evidence includes a series of cheques to each accuser drawn from parish accounts and filled out and signed by Rev. Stephen Scruton.

In November of 2008, 14 years into Father MacRae's 67-year prison sentence, Stephen Scruton was located in Massachusetts by an investigator reviewing this case. Scruton was reached by telephone. He was highly agitated and nervous when the investigator identified his purpose for calling. A male voice could be heard in the background clearly saying, "Steve, if this is something that will help Gordon, I think you should do it."

Scruton reluctantly agreed to be interviewed and a date was set for two weeks later. On the day of the interview, Scruton refused to open his door saying only that he had consulted with unnamed persons and now declines to be interviewed.

A summary was then mailed to Scruton outlining his presence in this case, and asking him to reconsider his decision not to co-operate by telling the simple truth. Within days of his receipt of that summary, Stephen Scruton suffered a mysterious fall down the stairs of his Newburyport, MA, home, and died a month later at the end of January, 2009.

Father Scruton took the truth with him. He was buried in his priestly vestments though there was no obituary, no traditional notification from his Diocese (Manchester, NH), and no public notice of any kind. Most regrettably, Father Scruton's unexplained presence in the case against Father Gordon MacRae—along with a rather vast collection of other exculpatory information—has been hiding in plain sight for nearly 15 years.

The late Rabbi Abraham Heschel[450] said that while it is important to consider all sides of destructive and broken relationships, it is essential to include God's perspective as well. God's own relentless pursuit of each sinner and saint finds expression in the father of the prodigal son, or the lover in Francis Thompson's poem "The Hound of Heaven." God eagerly longs only for the sinner's repentance and homecoming.

---

[450]   Jordan Horn "Prophet Sharing: Discussing the Legacy of Rabbi Abraham Joshua Heschel". 30 May, 2008. www.online.wsj.com.

18

Money Is a Good Servant, but a Bad Master

Money makes the law and the law protects the money;
and lawyers protect the people with money.
—Mark Giminez

Fiduciary trust? Putting the clients' best interests before one's commissions.
—Mark Gimenez

In 2003, the Archdiocese of Boston paid the mind-boggling sum of $85 million in settling 541 civil cases alleging that priests had sexually abused children and other parishioners. In a comparable compensatory gesture, the Diocese of Springfield paid $7.5 million to settle 45 similar complaints, and the Diocese of Worcester, reportedly with more reluctance, settled a few claims as well. It is reported that the Boston archdiocese had been running a substantial deficit for years. So while most of the 2003 settlements have been or will be covered by insurance, the disastrous financial fallout from the scandal continues. Further, contributions from the disillusioned and disgusted people have plummeted and for three stated reasons: the conduct of the abusive priests; the failure of the hierarchy in disciplining the wayward priests; and the frequent transfer of the individuals concerned to other parishes, where they could continue to prey on vulnerable children.

As the tidal wave of child-sex-abuse claims keeps escalating, the embattled dioceses are resolved to fight the claims and will have two crucial advantages, one that is new and another that it chose not to exploit the first time around. To quote the precise words of Harvey A. Silverglate: "A financially crippled local Church is entering a new round of claims, much better able to defend itself, making another all-encompassing massive settlement less likely."[451]

The reasons, adds Silverglate, are as follows:

1. There is considerable doubt about the veracity of many of the new claims, quite a few of which were made *after it became apparent that the Church was willing to settle sex-abuse cases for big bucks.*
2. In Boston and Springfield, the Church signed blanket settlements, meaning that it conceded liability across the board without regard to whether a claim seemed genuine or questionable.
3. The cases were settled *en masse*, with each assigned a dollar figure based on the egregiousness of the misconduct alleged and the amount of harm demonstrated (or at least claimed) by each plaintiff-victim.
4. The cases in this new round are likely to receive more scrutiny.
5. Some knowledgeable observers and participants suspect that public outrage has settled down sufficiently to allow the Church to sift the meritorious cases from those that are either false or highly exaggerated.[452]

The caution and restraint stem from the reported rhetoric of some of the plaintiffs' lawyers. In September 2003, *Boston Globe* reporter, Kevin Cullen, quoted Carmen L. Durson, who represented a large number of plaintiffs in the 2002 mass settlements and who has since submitted new claims to the Church, explaining why another crop of plaintiffs has suddenly arisen. These are her precise words to Cullen: "They felt it was safe to come forward now that they'd be treated okay." Adds Silverglate: "One wonders whether 'okay treatment' refers to the perceived ease of wringing a settlement from a battered, publicity shy, and scandal-averse Church leadership."[453]

---

[451] Harvey A. Silverglate, "Fleecing the Shepherd," *Boston Phoenix*, news and features.

[452] Ibid.

[453] Ibid.

Another lawyer, Michael Garabedian, who was prominent in the first round of cases, told Cullen that he represents 41 new plaintiffs against the Church. His explanation for why his clients have come forward only in the wake of the 2002 settlements was that they had feared the "stigma" associated with claiming abuse and the "emotional strain" of seeking redress.[454]

Especially controversial are the claims based on the phenomenon of "recovered memory," in which repressed memories are "recovered" via hypnosis or other therapeutic techniques. Many experts regard this as a largely bogus and unscientific practice, in which false memories result from suggestion or even convenience.[455]

John J. Stobierski of Greenfield, an attorney for 45 plaintiffs, whose cases against the Diocese of Springfield were settled in the first round, told the Globe that "people were either fearful or too sceptical to proceed earlier. I think they needed to see the diocese was serious about settling before they would come forward."[456] In a word, the new claimants waited shrewdly until they saw the money flow to other plaintiffs.

On October 20, 2010, Fr. Gordon MacRae posted this striking item on his blog:

> How does a priest accused from ten, twenty, or thirty years ago defend himself or ever restore his good name when a diocese simply writes a cheque with no other evidence of guilt than the claim itself? And unlike the lawsuits filed by the accusers of Bishop Eddie Long, the lawyer was given a $5.2 million cheque by my diocese—the first of several rounds of mediated settlements with the same lawyer who proclaimed, "I've never seen anything like it! Didn't even file the claims in a court of law." He simply wrote a letter demanding settlement, and got it! Last month, the *Concord*

---

[454] Ibid.

[455] "How to marry a rich man? Lie—about your past, your future, your needs and wants and 'desires,' about who you really are so he'll marry you. Lie to get married and stay married. Don't tell the truth and risk having your existence taken from you" (Mark Giminez, Accused).

[456] Ibid.

233

Monitor reported on another case handled by that same lawyer with amazing results.[457]

Justice has certainly turned on its head when men who stand to gain hundreds of thousands of dollars for making a false claim are automatically called "victims" by Church leaders now, while, priests accused without evidence from decades ago are just as quickly called "priest-offenders" and "slayers of souls".

Adds Fr. Gordon MacRae:

I once scoffed at the notion that evil surrounds us, but I have seen it. I think every person falsely accused has seen it." Most regrettably, the exposure of the sex abuse scandal in the Catholic Church has become like an ATM for lawyers and litigants at the expense of basic civil liberties for the priests accused.[458]

David F. Pierre Jr. has written an explosive revelation of the *double standard* with regard to allegations of sexual abuse and the attack on the Catholic Church. His is a courageous and compelling account of how money, the media, and wilful malevolence have distorted and driven the scandal and singled out the Catholic Church as a scapegoat for rampant abuse in our culture. This is what he has to say about the disturbing manner in which claims against Catholic priests were settled in the New Hampshire diocese without any legitimate determination of credibility:

In 2002, a New Hampshire diocese faced accusations of abuse from 62 individuals. Rather than spending the time and resources looking into the merits of the cases, "Diocesan officials did not even ask for specifics such as the dates and specific allegations for the claims," New Hampshire's *Union*

---

[457]   Fr. Gordon MacRae, "When Priests Are Falsely Accused, Part 2: Why Accusers Should be Named" (October 20, 2010).

[458]   Harvey A. Silverglate, "Fleecing the Shepherd", Op.Cit.

Leader reported. Getting money from the diocese could not have been any easier for the complainants. It was almost as simple as a trip to an ATM. "I've never seen anything like it," a pleased and much richer plaintiff attorney admitted.[459]

It has been reliably demonstrated, states Harvey A. Silverglate, that those looking for a repeat of the 2003 settlements may be facing serious obstacles. In the first round of litigation, the Church momentarily raised but declined to press what legal observers have long considered its ace in the hole: the "charitable limitation on liability," a legal doctrine that could well protect the Church from having to pay more than $20,000 to any one of the plaintiffs. This is a potent defence that can be effectively invoked in any case claiming the Church acted negligently in failing to properly supervise and assign priests, which is precisely the major legal claim being made against the institutional church. After all, the Church did not commit the acts of abuse but instead failed in its duty to assign priests in a manner that would protect the vulnerable victims. Adds Silverglate: "The Church declined to pursue the defence earlier for fear of compounding the public-relations damage inflicted by revelations about paedophile priests and the Church officials, who failed to stop them. In the first round of cases, the Church ultimately settled on average for far more than $20,000 each."[460]

The charitable-limitation defence, which exists today in only eight other states, says Silverglate, is a long-standing legal doctrine in Massachusetts. In the 19th century, Bay State courts began granting fully charitable immunity to philanthropic non-profits, such as churches and public hospitals. This immunity protected them from court judgements arising out of claims that the organizations or their authorized agents acted negligently and thereby inflicted harm upon an individual claimant. The theory behind such immunity was that allowing unlimited money-damage claims for negligence against such organizations would severely impair, if not cripple, their ability to carry out their charitable missions. Further,

---

[459] David F. Pierre, Jr., *Double Standard: Abuse Scandals and the Attack on the Catholic Church*, 125.

[460] Ibid.

235

it recognized the donors' right to see their contributions go to fund the charitable enterprise, not damage claimants.[461]

It is a known though regrettable fact that, in polite society, sexual abuse is hastily buried. Families build systems to protect the abuser from guilt. And if an outsider was presented with a claim of abuse, that claim was callously dismissed with no resolution for the abused, except possibly more serious abuse. Even more, there have been instances where families of abuse turned against the one who would speak the truth of what was happening, thereby re-victimizing the victim of abuse. Undoubtedly, there are many men, and even women, languishing in prisons because of being successfully prosecuted for crimes of sexual and even physical abuse. But when someone claims that a priest has sexually abused a young person, no matter how long ago, there is an added incentive: the monetary factor.

Some Catholic dioceses, particularly in North America, probably because of their guilt and shame over hiding abuse for so many years, changed the whole field of abuse. The pendulum had swung to one extreme; the sensible reaction would be to have it return to the centre before readjusting the clock, but it was impulsively and rashly made to swing to the other extreme and stay right there. In other words, instead of resolving the crisis rationally, justly, and effectively, it was gravely compounded by acquiescing to the avaricious demands of unscrupulous claimants without making any reliable endeavour to ascertain the truth. *As a consequence, there is a newer scandal—the scandal of depriving priests of the right to confront their accusers and the fundamental and inalienable right to be presumed innocent until proven guilty.*

Most regrettably, this is the skewed outcome of the zero tolerance policy advocated by the USCCB, followed similarly in Canada, that accepts all claims as valid and all priests against whom a claim of abuse has been made as guilty first. "Money makes the law and the law protects the money; and lawyers protect the people with money."[462]

Many claims, it must be admitted, are valid, and they need to be justly and appropriately met. However, assuaging those claims with filthy lucre, as any right-thinking individual would agree, is fraught with opportunity for a blatant abuse of the principles of justice, as has been the case so often.

---

[461] Ibid.
[462] Mark Giminez, *Accused.* www.markgiminez.com

Priests have made a lifelong commitment to serve both God and his people. Theirs is a selfless commitment with no strings attached. All they receive is a monthly stipend or salary, which is fractional when compared with the monthly incomes of their secular counterparts. A lawyer, for instance, can be paid $750 per hour; even telephone calls to a client or on his/her behalf are charged on the basis of the time expended. By sharp contrast, a priest receives approximately $500 a month! One priest falsely accused and wrongly removed from the pastoral ministry by his bishop has had no alternative but to crave the compassion and security of his solicitous sister for both board and lodging. And this travesty has occurred in spite of the fact that the priest, as an American and according to the U.S. Constitution, is entitled to competent counsel. This is the bounden duty of the bishop of the diocese, because a priest does not have the financial means of championing his own cause.

In the words of one author:

> When a Catholic priest becomes a non-person, unable to afford to defend himself, the possibility for justice for him goes out the window. The rights of a priest to protection under the law are different than the objectives of our Catholic dioceses, which are attempting to minimize scandal. He must defend himself separately, but can ill afford it, based on the life of secular poverty that almost all priests live.[463]

So the love of money becomes the root of all evil, even in the Catholic Church, which plays along. The pendulum has certainly swung to the other extreme. Father Gordon MacRae, for instance, is a priest who has been falsely accused and has spent 16 years as a guest of the State of New Hampshire and for claims that have been made but not substantiated. In other words, *as a priest, he is guilty until proven innocent.* When that will be is anyone's guess. His heart-rending story can be accessed over the Internet on *These Stone Walls*—a three-part series that will tear at the heartstrings of any person with a well-formed conscience and a passion for

---

[463] Posted by M. Brandon with regard to the Catholic Church, Faith, Fr. Gordon MacRae, *op.cit.*

justice in truth. This, says Brandon, very rightly is *the scandal within the scandal.* "What is fiduciary trust?" asks Mark Gimenez. "Put the clients' best interests ahead of your commissions."[464]

Fr. Gordon MacRae—an Unimaginable Travesty of Justice

Among the innumerable sad consequences of the sex abuse crisis are the injustices visited on priests falsely accused. A particularly egregious case is that of Father Gordon MacRae of the Diocese of Manchester, New Hampshire. *He was sentenced to thirty-three years and has been imprisoned more than twelve years with no chance of parole because he insists that he is innocent.* Even lawyers, who have closely examined the case, believe that the unfortunate priest was railroaded. Writing in *First Things*, a journal of the Institute on Religion and Public Life, the late Fr. Richard John Neuhaus wrote an editorial on this heartbreaking story and entitled it "A Kafkaesque Tale." Friends of Fr. MacRae have created a website—www. GordonMacRae.net—it provides a comprehensive narrative of the case, along with pertinent documentation, in which key members of the hierarchy do not come off as friends of justice, or, for that matter, of elementary decency.

The *Wall Street Journal's* Pulitzer Prize-winning journalist Dorothy Rabinowitz published, on April 27 and 28, 2005, an account of the travesty of justice by which Fr. MacRae was convicted. I will endeavour to highlight the salient points on the basis of a feature article that Ms. Rabinowitz did publish in *Society* (September/October 2005). [465]

Nine years after he had been convicted and sent to prison on alleged charges of sexual assault against a teenaged boy, Fr. Gordon MacRae received a letter in July 2003, from Nixon Peabody LLP, a law firm, representing the Diocese of Manchester, New Hampshire. The letter stated: "an individual named Brett McKenzie has brought a claim against the Diocese of Manchester seeking a financial settlement as a result of alleged conduct by you." The letter went on to explain that neither Fr.

---

[464] Mark Giminez. Op.Cit.

[465] Dorothy Rabinowitz, "A Priest's Story," *Society* (September/October 2005).

MacRae nor the Diocese of Manchester would be liable if only he would not object to a settlement agreement.

Promptly, Fr. MacRae responded through his lawyer declaring he had no idea who Mr. McKenzie was, that he had never met him, and that he was confounded by the request that he assent to any such settlement payment. Neither he nor his lawyers ever received any response. Fr. MacRae has little doubt that the stranger did get his settlement. "Money makes the law and the law protects the money; and lawyers protect the people with money."[466]

Assigned to St. Bernard's Parish in New Hampshire, Fr. Gordon MacRae was entrusted with the ministry to troubled teenagers, invariably referred to drug addiction centres. Initially unaware, the young priest was soon to learn the hazards that such a pastoral outreach would entail.

In the spring of 1983, 14-year-old Lawrence Carnevale cried bitterly when he learnt that Fr. MacRae was to be transferred to another parish. Such was his supposed esteem and affection for the priest that he would call over the telephone at the new rectory. Within a few months, the youth told his psychotherapist that Fr. MacRae had kissed him. Not much later, Carnevale was expelled from his school for carrying a weapon.

Thereafter, he told his counsellor that the priest had fondled him and run his hands up his leg. At roughly the same time, Carnevale accused a male teacher of St. Thomas High School of making advances to him and then made the same allegations against his study hall teacher at Winnacunnet High School. The wily and mendacious lad had called wolf once too often. Even Police Detective Arthur Wardell, who investigated, concluded in his report that this was a young man who basked in the attention such charges brought him and that there was no basis for them.

A decade later, Lawrence Carnevale had more revelations of abuse. In 1993, he alleged that Fr. MacRae had held a gun on him and had forced him to masturbate while licking the barrel. Prosecutors and their experts ascribed these groundless but damaging allegations to the accuser's newfound courage! In spite of the fact that the allegations could not be substantiated, they did play a decisive role in bolstering a 1994 criminal case against the beleaguered priest. Even the presiding judge did cite "the

---

[466] Mark Gimenez. Op.Cit.

torment and lifelong pain that Lawrence Carnevale had suffered at the hands of Fr. MacRae."

"Money makes the law and the law protects the money; and lawyers protect the people with money."[467]

In 1988, 17-year-old Michael Rossi, a patient at the Spofford Chemical Dependency Hospital, asked to meet with Fr. MacRae. The stated intention was to discuss his addiction with the priest. However, the young man's real intentions were more sinister and malicious. In the course of the conversation that ensued, Rossi suddenly became agitated, exposed himself, and began telling the priest about his other sexual encounters at the hospital. Fr. MacRae instantly walked away fully aware of the pernicious backlash of the Carnevale accusations. Discretion is indeed the better part of valour. He had barely reached the door—a threat that chastened the patient enough to zip up—when Rossi said: "This was confession, right?"

Gordon MacRae lost no time in informing his superiors of the incident. Msgr. Frank Christian offered his reassurances. Nonetheless, the innocent priest was suspended pending an investigation. History does repeat itself—he was guilty until proven innocent, and in yet another violation of his constitutional right to competent counsel, he was offered none. Two months later, state police who conducted an investigation declared the case unfounded and closed it. Regrettably, that acquittal only fed the suspicions of Detective James McLaughlin, sex crimes investigator for the Keene police department, then just beginning what was to become a considerable career in his field, particularly for stings involving child molesters. "Fiduciary trust demands that the clients' best interests are placed ahead of one's commissions."[468]

The plot begins to thicken. McLaughlin received a letter from an investigator stating that he had authoritative information about Fr. MacRae's involvement in the murder and sex mutilation of a Florida boy. It was a while before word from Florida police, dismissing the story as a hoax, caught up with the social workers and police in Keene. This did not deter Detective McLaughlin from interrogating some 22 teenage boys whom Fr. MacRae knew or had counselled. Despite determined and

[467] Ibid.
[468] Ibid.

repeated questioning, he could find no one with any complaints about the priest.

One teenager, Jon Plankey, claimed that Fr. MacRae had attempted to solicit sex from him. Reportedly, the young man asked for a loan of $75, explaining that he was prepared to do anything for money. Fr. MacRae declined the request for a loan. Earlier Jon Plankey had made a molestation complaint against a Job Corps supervisor and would go on to accuse a church choir director. He also accused a man in Florida of attempted abuse. Money is indeed a good servant, but a very bad master.

At that time, the mother of Jon Plankey worked for the Keene police. As the saga involving her son evolved, Mrs. Plankey contacted Msgr. Frank Christian (now auxiliary bishop) over the telephone. She informed the cleric that she had learned of the investigation on solicitation involving Fr. MacRae and her son and that a settlement would be in order if the diocese was to avoid a lawsuit and lawyers. The Plankeys' claims were duly settled out of court (after added claims that the priest had taken pornographic pictures of Jon).

Detective McLaughlin summoned Fr. MacRae and informed him that there was much evidence against him, that the police had an affidavit for an arrest, and that it would be in everybody's best interests for him to clear everything up and sign a confession! At that time, in view of the string of baseless and defamatory allegations, Fr. MacRae was on leave of absence from his parish duties. So, he was literally at the end of his tether.

The police did not help the situation when they assured him that he could save all the bad publicity. "Our concern is, let's get it taken care of; let's not blow it out of proportion . . . You know what the media does," they warned. When the helpless priest asked for a lawyer, he was told that "that would only muddy the waters and further damage the church." A report thereafter stated: "Though no sexual acts were committed by MacRae, there are often varied levels of victimization." Officer McLaughlin was commended for his excellent work!

It is impossible to extricate a succulent bone from the powerful jaws of a terrier; he who foolishly tries does so at his own peril. Fr. MacRae subsequently took a job at a centre for priests in New Mexico. One day, out of the blue, he received a strange letter from a Jon Grover, in his mid-20s, a member of a family he had known back in Keene, New Hampshire. The letter referred to many sexual encounters in detail and observed that "the sex between us was very special to me." Fr. MacRae wrote back to say that such a claim could only come from an impostor, because the real Jon Grover would have known that no such thing had taken place.

This was the first of several sting attempts by Detective James McLaughlin, whose own reports testify that he wrote the letters himself. To add insult to injury, Jon's elder brother, Thomas, deep into plans for a civil and criminal case alleging that the priest had molested him a decade earlier, took a role in a different sting effort. This was a series of phone calls to the priest, which Detective McLaughlin was supposed to record.

The possibilities of a lawsuit caught the attention of an increasing number of Grovers! Twenty-seven-year-old David Grover, who had heard of the financial settlements in the notorious Father Porter case in Massachusetts, told police that he had to pull his car over and weep, because he had been suddenly overcome by his memories of his victimization by Fr. MacRae. "Say something nice about someone and nobody listens. Make it mean, malicious and scandalous and the whole town helps you spread the word," so said Harold Robbins[469] and with justifiable cause.

In early May 1993, while in New Mexico, Fr. MacRae was arrested on the basis of the indictment in New Hampshire. With a lawyer but minimal funds, Fr. MacRae prepared for the battle, though nothing could have prepared him for the press release issued by his diocese shortly before his trial. Carried all over New England, it declared, "The Church is a victim of the actions of Gordon MacRae just as these individuals . . ." The newspapers had shrewdly edited the words "alleged actions." So an innocent priest was declared guilty even before he could go to trial. In his summation at the trial to come, the chief prosecutor did not neglect to remind jurors of the statement by the priest's own diocese. Said Christ Jesus, "One's foes will be members of one's own household."[470]

Throughout his testimony, Thomas Grover repeatedly railed at the priest for forcing him to endure the torments of a trial. He would not have much to fear in the end; in these proceedings, the presiding judge, the Hon. Arthur D. Brennan, refused to allow into evidence Thomas Grover's long juvenile history of theft, assault, forgery, and drug offences. The judge also took it upon himself to instruct the jurors to "disregard inconsistencies in Mr. Grover's testimony," and said that they should not

---

[469] Harold Robbins, *Never Leave Me.*
[470] Matthew 10:36

think him dishonest because of his failure to answer questions. The jury had much to disregard.

Thomas Grover alleged that he had been repeatedly assaulted sexually by Fr. MacRae in the rectory office and another time elsewhere. When asked why he did return after the first supposedly terrifying attack, Mr. Grover explained that he had an "out-of-the-body experience." Also that he had blackouts that caused him to go to each new counselling session with no memory that he had been sodomized and otherwise assaulted the session before. Fr. MacRae notes these counselling sessions were never held.

Mr. Grover further alleged that the attacks were not the only traumas inflicted. The priest had also chased him with his car, and he had a gun and threatened to kill him should he tell anybody "He even chased me through the cemetery and tried to corner me." As a final salvo, Mr. Grover spoke of the priest's stash of child pornography, an ever more prominent theme in the prosecution. Even today, Detective McLaughlin says, "There was never any evidence of child pornography."

Halfway through the trial and the escalating suspicions of the veracity of the wildly imaginative allegations, the prosecutors offered Fr. MacRae still another plea deal—an extraordinarily lenient one to two years for an admission of guilt. His lawyers waited with bated breath for the answer, which did not surprise them. Without mincing his words, the beleaguered priest candidly and courageously replied: "I am not going to say that I am guilty of crimes I never committed, so that the Grovers and other extortionists can walk away with hundreds of dollars for their lies." Within 90 minutes, the jury returned with a verdict of "Guilty!" And only because the honest priest would not compromise for a negotiated lie.

Among the witnesses testifying at the sentencing hearing was Lawrence Carnevale. At least two church staff members recall that, back in the 1980s when all this was beginning, the youth told them that he had a hit list and that Fr. MacRae was at the very top—an announcement that came just after Fr. MacRae stopped accepting the young Carnevale's non-stop collect calls to his new parish.

Also testifying at the sentencing hearing was Mr. Carnevale's psychologist, Allen Stern, who opined that the chief cause of Mr. Carnevale's lifelong psychological problems were "the sexual events that took place with Fr. MacRae." Was his diagnosis post-traumatic stress syndrome? "Not quite," the psychologist explained. "It was post-traumatic stress disorder delay."

At the sentencing, Judge Brennan charged that the priest had groomed and exploited vulnerable boys. In assaulting Lawrence Carnevale, the judge continued, the guilty priest had destroyed his dream of becoming a priest! To Fr. David Diebold, the only priest to come forward in defence of Fr. MacRae, the judge had nothing but harsh words. Above all, he was incensed at the lack of remorse of Fr. MacRae and his "aggressive denials of wrong-doing."

"The evidence of your possession of child pornography is clear and convincing."

As mentioned, Detective McLaughlin still says, "There was never any evidence of child pornography." The die had been definitively and irreversibly cast.

Having given his reasons, the judge then sentenced Fr. MacRae, 42, to consecutive terms on the charges, a sentence of 33 ½ to 67 years. *Since no parole is given to offenders who do not confess, it would be in effect a life term.*

In the years since Fr. MacRae's conviction, nearly all accusers who had a decisive part—along with some who did not—received settlements. Jay, the second of the Grover sons, who repeatedly insisted that the priest had done nothing amiss, came forward with his claim for settlement in the late '90s. *Strike while the iron is hot!* And in 2004, the subject in the Spofford Hospital incident, Michael Rossi—*"This is confession, right?"*—also came forward with his claim. "There will be others," predicts the innocent but defenceless Fr. MacRae, who dreads the cruellest blow ever—expulsion from the sacred priesthood that he loves so dearly and to which he has been devotedly and unswervingly committed. Indeed, money is a good servant, but a bad master.

19

The Insidious and Treacherous Lure of Lucre

The Church must be a mirror of justice.
—Pope John Paul II

There is no segment of the American population
with less civil liberties protection than the average Catholic priest.
Remember that what will always be of service to the Church is the truth.
Pursue the whole truth, and you are pursuing what is best for the Church.
—Bill Donohue

The Catholic Church is the safest place for children,
but the most dangerous for priests.
—Bill Donohue

Wednesday, December 8, 2010

Three weeks ago, a news item on the Internet revealed the tragic murder of a young newlywed on her honeymoon in South Africa. The taxi in which she and her husband were being driven was ambushed by a group of armed men, who reportedly were deliberating the rape of the innocent woman before murdering her. A later report stated that in the heated argument that ensued, one man's gun went off accidentally and the bullet struck the terrified woman in the neck killing her instantaneously. On a closer probe, detectives began to suspect more than just an accidental homicide.

This is what media reports had to say:

> A British businessman plotted to have his Swedish bride murdered on their honeymoon in South Africa, a court has been told in a sensational twist to an apparent robbery and shooting.

> Anni Dewani, 28, was shot dead after the taxi in which she was travelling with her husband Shrien Dewani, was hijacked on the outskirts of Cape Town on November 13, just weeks after their marriage.

Her body was later found in the neighbourhood of an impoverished township.

> Dewani, who returned to Britain days after the incident in which he was unharmed, has denied any involvement.

> Three men were originally charged with the murder, but, as part of a plea bargain, the High Court in Cape Town heard one of the accused allege that the victim's husband had ordered the killing. Reportedly, the taxi driver ferrying the newlyweds had been paid $2,000 to arrange the ambush and murder.

> "The deceased was murdered at the instance of her husband," Western Cape director of public prosecutions Rodney de Kock told Judge President John Hlophe in court, the national news agency SAPA reported.

> A judicial spokesman refused to say if Dewani, who accompanied his wife's body back to Britain, would be charged.

> The claim that the husband plotted the murder was made by Zola Tongo, the driver of the taxi in which the couple had been travelling in Cape Town.

Tongo was sentenced to 18 years in jail on Tuesday after pleading guilty to murder and aggravated robbery.

National Prosecuting Authority spokesman Eric Ntabazalila told AFP that Tongo had given evidence that he was approached by the British businessman and promised $2074 "to remove someone from the scene."

Tongo, who gave evidence under a plea bargain deal with the state, then enlisted two accomplices to carry out the murder, according to Ntabazalila.

"That is part of a different investigation. I cannot comment on that, police would have to act on that," Ntabazalila said.

The two other men accused of Dewani's killing are due to face trial on February 25.

Prior to the killing, the honeymooners had dined in a seaside restaurant in a town outside Cape Town and were on their way back to the city when Anni Dewani allegedly asked to see township nightlife, reports said.

The murdered bride was also robbed of a Giorgio Armani wristwatch, a white gold and diamond bracelet and a Blackberry phone, the charge sheet stated.

National Prosecuting Authority spokesman Eric Ntabazalila told AFP that Tongo had given evidence that he was approached by the British businessman and promised A$2074 "to remove someone from the scene."[471]

---

[471] See reports in dailymail.co.uk, bbc.co.uk and mirror.uk dated 29 November, 2010.

God or Mammon?

Well aware of the pernicious influence of an obsessive avarice, Christ Jesus unambiguously and courageously declared: "No one can serve two masters; for a slave will either hate the one and love the other, or be devoted to the one and despise the other. You cannot serve God and wealth."[472] (Matthew 6:24).

In the ancient world, a slave, in the eyes of the law, was not a person but a tool of convenience that could be used when necessary and discarded when not. In other words, a slave had no rights whatsoever but was totally subject to the unscrupulous whims of his ruthless master, who could beat him, sell him, throw him out, and even kill him. In a word, a slave was no better than a living, helpless, and defenceless tool.

Second, in the ancient world, a slave literally had no time that he could claim as his own. He had to be at the beck and call of his master at any time of the day or the night, in much the same way that a tradesman would use his tools whenever the need arose. By contrast, a worker today is employed to do a specific job and for a definite period of time for all of which he is paid a just living wage. Thereafter, the worker is free to do as he pleases until he is next required to report for work. So his leisure time is his and can be profitably utilised in pursuing his chosen preferences. The slave, on the other hand, had literally no moment of time that belonged to him. Every moment belonged to his owner, and he was perpetually at his master's disposal.

When translated to our relationship with God, the committed Christian belongs solely and exclusively to God, our Creator and undisputed Master. In other words, the Christian has no time off from being a Christian; there is just no time when he can relax in his unswerving commitment to God. So being a Christian is a full-time job.

A loving, devoted, and industrious mother, for instance, spends every waking hour in the service of her immediate family—providing for their needs, comforting them when distressed, guiding them in times of doubt or perplexity, nursing them when they are sick, chiding them when they tend to do the wrong thing, assisting them in their academic work, and ensuring that they dutifully fulfil their obligations to God and to people.

---

[472] Matthew 6:24

Unlike a slave and in spite of this unswerving and intensive commitment, the mother still has the opportunity to pursue her preferences for rest, leisure, recreation, and personal development. This is how the dutiful and hardworking mother expresses her exclusive and unswerving commitment to God. And therein lies that noble mother's pathway to personal holiness. "Not everyone who says to me, 'Lord! Lord!' will enter the kingdom of heaven, but only the one who does the will of my Father in heaven.".[473]

This is how the Fathers of the Second Vatican Council framed it: "Married couples and Christian parents should follow their own proper path to holiness by faithful love, sustaining one another in grace throughout the entire length of their lives. They should imbue their offspring, lovingly welcomed from God, with Christian truths and evangelical virtues."[474]

Cut from the same cloth is the devoted and industrious priest, who spends every waking hour in the service of his parish family—providing for their spiritual needs through his sacramental ministry, comforting them when distressed, guiding them in times of doubt or perplexity, ministering to them when they are sick or bereaved, gently chiding them when they tend to do the wrong thing, assisting them in their progressive growth in the Christian faith, and ensuring that they dutifully fulfil their obligations to God and to people. Unlike a slave and in spite of this unswerving and intensive commitment, the priest still has the opportunity to pursue his preferences for rest, leisure, recreation, and personal development. This is how the dutiful and hardworking priest expresses his exclusive and unswerving commitment to God. And therein lies that noble priest's pathway to personal holiness. "Not everyone who says to me, 'Lord! Lord!' will enter the kingdom of heaven, but only the one who does the will of my Father in heaven" (Matthew 7:21).

This is how the Fathers of the Second Vatican Council aptly commended the conscientious and industrious priest: "In the first place, the shepherds of Christ's flock ought to carry out their ministry with holiness, eagerness, humility and courage, in imitation of the eternal High Priest, the Shepherd and Guardian of our souls. They will thereby make this ministry the principal means of their own sanctification."[475]

---

[473]   Matthew 7:21
[474]   The Dogmatic Constitution on the Church, #41.
[475]   The Dogmatic Constitution on the Church, #41.

Material possessions and financial income are necessary but only as a means to an end. The Christian who makes these an end in itself—the be-all and end-all of his life—now has a new master, Mammon. As such, he is a slave totally subject to the whims and the caprices of an unrelenting and implacable master. In a word, he is a living tool with no time to call his own and perpetually enmeshed in the insidious and treacherous lure of lucre. In the insightful words of Frank Buchanan (1878-1961), "There is enough in the world for everyone's need, but not enough for everyone's greed."[476]

Greed Is One of the Seven Deadly Sins.

Fr. Gordon MacRae is a Catholic priest, who has been wrongly accused and unjustly imprisoned for a phenomenal period of time only because he firmly and unequivocally insists on his innocence. "There is no segment of the American population with less civil liberties protection than the average American Catholic priest." [477] In 2002, as a dutiful priest, he wrote a private letter to his bishop, John McCormack, in which he stoutly maintained his innocence of the baseless claims for which he was imprisoned. These are his precise words:

> I was accused falsely, and in the context of being a Roman Catholic priest. If I was not a priest, I would not have been accused. To pretend that somehow the claims against me are not related to the context of my priesthood is false. This is something that most Church officials long recognised, but many have put aside the rights of priests in open disregard of Church law.[478]

Further, he wrote that he would withdraw his defence and remain silently in prison for the remainder of his life if the bishop deemed it good for the Church. The bishop candidly replied that he could not ask

---

[476] Frank Buchanan, *Remaking the World* (1947).
[477] Bill Donohue, in Gordon MacRae. Thesestonewalls/About. Op.Cit.
[478] Fr. Gordon MacRae, *"Are Civil Liberties for Priests Intact?"* (June 16, 2010).

Fr. Gordon to surrender his civil and canonical rights. Providentially, the Catholic League's Bill Donohue prevailed upon Fr. Gordon that staying the course of truth and justice would be not only in his own interest, but that of the Church as well. These are his precise words, "Remember that what will always be of service to the Church is the truth. Pursue the whole truth, and you are pursuing what is best for the Church."[479] Said Pope John Paul II: "The Church must be a mirror of justice."[480]

Gripped by the insidious and treacherous lure of lucre, the media has been fixated with "scalp hunting" even to the point of an obsession. For instance, an editorial in the *New York Times* wrongly and rashly opined, "The Catholic Church is working against the interests of child abuse victims in state legislatures around the country." Reportedly, the *Times* was referring to the fact that the Church in the United States opposes bills in several states that would extend civil statutes of limitations so that Catholic institutions, especially, can be sued long after current laws allowing such suits have expired.[481]

As is clearly evident, the passing of such bills would bankrupt diocese after diocese across the country because there would be no end to the unproven claims that would float to the surface demanding settlements. Adds Fr. Gordon MacRae, "the opposition of the U.S. Bishops to the promulgation of these proposed bills is a good sign that they have finally caught on to the relationship between accusations against priests and the enticement of guaranteed financial settlements." In a word, the very existence of the Catholic Church in the United States of America could be at stake.

Militating against the promulgation of any such bill, Fr. Gordon MacRae wrote:

> The prison system in which I have spent the last fourteen years houses nearly 3,000 prisoners. Estimates of those convicted of sexual offences range from 25 to 40 percent. This translates into a population of 1200 sex offenders in

---

[479] Bill Donohue, in a posting by Fr. Gordon MacRae (June 16, 2010).

[480] John Paul II. www.mariancatechist.com/burke

[481] New York Times. Editorial, "Justice for Child Abuse Victims". 15 May, 2010.

this one prison with thousands more in the state's parole system or otherwise monitored by the state as registered sex offenders. Three among these (6,000) convicted men are Catholic priests . . . The thousands of other men convicted of sexual abuse are accused parents, grandparents, step-parents, foster parents, uncles, teachers, ministers, scout leaders, and so on, and for them the typical time lapse between abuse and the victim reporting it was measured in weeks or months, not years, and certainly not decades.[482]

"There is no segment of the American population with less civil liberties protection than the average Catholic priest."[483]

The following startling revelations by Fr. Gordon MacRae, after sixteen years of being wrongly and unjustly incarcerated, will astound readers both lay and clerical:

1. Children are in far more danger in some of their homes and schools than they are, or ever have been, in any Catholic Church.
2. The vast majority of men in prison for molesting children are married men. This issue has nothing whatsoever to do with celibacy, in spite of dissidents' obsessive insistence on using it for their own agendas.
3. *Only Catholic priests, and no one else, face claims of sexual abuse that are decades old. This happens solely to Catholic priests, and it is because of the enticement of money.* Numerous other prisoners have served short sentences because of plea deals, but none have faced a charge that is decades old.
4. Even as the witch hunt unfolded, every prisoner was aware of a dozen cases of men who served their sentences for child sexual abuse, got out of prison, and then created new victims, in spite of

[482] Fr. Gordon MacRae, "Are Civil Liberties for Priests Intact?" (June 16, 2010).
[483] William Donohue. NBC "Today". 13 October, 2005. 4thepriests. wordpress.com. 2 January, 2011

supervision of the State either through parole or state-mandated sex offender registration.

5. The first action taken today when a priest is accused is to minimize his priesthood and separate him with as much distance as possible from the support of his diocese and the life of the Church.

6. This is what makes the possible outcome of forced laicization a cruel and deeply unjust conclusion. I was put in harm's way because I am a Catholic priest and because it is widely known that claims against priests, however ancient, are lucrative.

7. Even prison guards see this point. Prison guards are often accused of wrong-doing in the context of their work as prison guards. One asked me one day how the Church defended me. I told him that the Church did not defend me at all, that from the moment I was accused, I was suspended and entirely on my own for both finding and funding a defence. He was appalled and said that no sane person would ever work in a prison if that was what happened when guards were accused.

8. I was accused for only one reason: a long practical policy of quietly settling all claims against Catholic priests regardless of merit to keep publicity to a minimum. The lure of money, and corporate decisions to settle every claim, now drive the scandal. As Ryan MacDonald wrote in a recent issue of the *Catholic World Report*, "Greed ranks right up there with lust among the Seven Deadly Sins . . ." Priests have no understanding of how tenuous their own rights are when mine could be so easily trampled upon.[484]

As the International Year of the Priest (2009) draws to a close, the cruellest tyranny of all is best summed up in something Dorothy Rabinowitz wrote in *A Priest's Story*. It is that thing I fear the most, more than false witness itself, more than prison, more than the endless demonizing aimed in my direction. It is the end of priesthood itself, and the fact that it can be taken from me even as I lay here in prison

---

[484] Fr. Gordon MacRae. Op.Cit.

slowly dying, suffocating under the avalanche of agendas and rhetoric that mark the sex abuse crisis in the Church.[485]

Reportedly, Fr. Gordon MacRae was accused by two persons of having sexually abused them in early adolescence and during counselling sessions. By way of compensation, they were awarded $700,000. "An essay by Ryan MacDonald entitled 'Should the Case against Fr. Gordon MacRae be Reviewed?' contains a retraction from one of Fr. Gordon's accusers. The retraction is verbatim, and it is very chilling. This person claimed that he was offered a substantial amount of money to falsely accuse Fr. Gordon. He also wrote of the reputations of those who also accused him. It is just incredible that this went on for 16 years before being retracted. So there always is hope."[486]

To this, a certain Charlene posted this comment on Fr. MacRae's blog:

> Ah, Mary, it is highly unlikely that Fr. Gordon's accusers would have a change of heart. You see, if they ever confessed that they accused an innocent priest solely to gain $700,000, they would face charges of FRAUD, and it would be highly likely that they would go to prison. So, between the money and the threat of prison looming, chances are zero to none that they would ever confess to their crime. But they know and our Lord knows—he will be the final arbiter.[487]

Indeed, money is a good servant, but a bad master.

Finally, Fr. Gordon MacRae tells us of two inmates in prison who, knowing full well that he was a priest, approached him with a curious request. They wanted to know the name of a priest—any priest—who had served in the area where they were growing up as young adolescents. Their sole and malicious intent was to frame an allegation of sexual abuse and so make a claim of a handsome monetary compensation. As is patently clear,

---

[485]   BishopAccountability.org. See also, Dorothy Rabinowitz. Op.Cit.

[486]   Ryan MacDonald, *Should the Case against Fr. Gordon MacRae Be Reviewed?*

[487]   Fr. Gordon MacRae. Op.Cit.

their target was pointedly specific and their sinister plot unashamedly opportunistic. A prison guard was privy to this conversation and was stunned beyond belief at the brazen audacity of the two inmates and the perfidious malice of their malicious plan. Oddly, the alleged culprits sought a vulnerable person and no other because they knew for sure that the anticipated outcome was guaranteed. "I once scoffed at the notion that evil surrounds us, but I have seen it. I think every person falsely accused has seen it," so said Fr. Gordon MacRae.[488]

Ryan MacDonald continues:

> I am also aware that Fr. Gordon took and passed two polygraphs [lie detector tests] before his trial while his accusers, under the guidance of their contingency lawyers, refused to take polygraphs. There is a lot that is wrong with this case.[489]

Said Harvey A. Silverglate:

> There is considerable doubt about the veracity of the new claims, quite a few of which were made after it became apparent that the Church was willing to settle sex-abuse cases for big bucks. Indeed, in Boston and Springfield, the Church agreed to blanket settlements, meaning that it conceded liability across the board without regard to whether a claim seemed genuine or questionable. The cases were settled en masse, with each assigned a dollar figure based on the egregiousness of the misconduct alleged and the amount of harm demonstrable (or at least claimed) by each plaintiff-victim. But the cases in this new round are likely to receive more scrutiny. Indeed, some knowledgeable observers and participants suspect that public outrage has settled down sufficiently to allow the Church to sift the

---

[488]   Ibid.
[489]   Ryan MacDonald. Op.Cit.

meritorious cases from those that are likely false or highly exaggerated.[490]

An Egregious Double Standard

Fr. Gordon MacRae relates the heartbreaking story of Fr. Jim, who is 74 years old and has served in the priestly ministry for 50 years. In 1992, he was accused of an incident involving a 16-year-old girl that reportedly had occurred in 1972—twenty years earlier! Fr. Jim denied any wrong-doing, but admitted to a hug, in which he could have unintentionally touched her breast. For the rest, he was a priest of impeccable character and integrity.

And so, Fr. Jim's bishop convinced him—20 years later—that settling the claim for the demanded $40,000 was the easiest solution. The defenceless and helpless priest had no alternative but to comply. Of his own accord, he agreed to leave parish ministry and spend the next ten years serving as a chaplain in an urban hospital. The incident was forgotten until 2002.

The Dallas Charter resulted in Fr. Jim's name being released as a "credibly" accused sex offender. He was banished from any ministry and told to leave the premises of the rectory, where he stayed with other priests. Today, at the age of 74 and after 50 years of devoted and creditable service, Fr. Jim lives alone in an urban rented room. Last year, he was subjected to a canonical trial in the case for which "prescription"—the Church's statute of limitations—had expired decades ago.[491]

Well aware of the ruthless persecution to which his faithful followers would be unscrupulously subjected, Jesus said:

> I will send them prophets and apostles, some of whom they will kill and persecute, so that this generation may be charged with the blood of all the prophets shed since the foundation of the world, from the blood of Abel to the blood of Zechariah, who perished between the altar and

---

[490] Harvey A. Silverglate, "Fleecing the Shepherd: Will the Church Settle the Sexual-Abuse Cases This Time Around?"

[491] Fr. Gordon MacRae. Op.Cit.

the sanctuary. Yes, I tell you, it will be charged against this generation."[492]

Said Fr. Gordon MacRae in concluding this heartbreaking story:

> Justice requires that the bishops not argue the statute of limitations issue from two polar opposite positions according to how it suits their own interests. I am not saying this to be a dissident or to be seen in confrontation with the Church. I am saying this because I love the Church, and this double standard is destined to be the next wave of the scandal. As Archbishop Charles Chaput wisely wrote in *First Things* ("Suing the Church"—May 2006): "Statutes of limitations exist in legal systems to promote justice, not hinder it."[493]

And the Truth Shall Set You Free

Way back in the seventeenth century, Blaise Pascal said: "He that takes truth for his guide, and duty for his end, may safely trust to God's Providence to lead him aright." Indeed, it is only a wise man, and most often a holy man, who actually takes truth for his guide.

Fr. Mark Gruber is one such exceptional man. John the Baptist stood for the truth and against the established authority; he was shamelessly beheaded. Christ Jesus stood for the truth and against the established authority; he was brutally tortured and savagely crucified. Mahatma Gandhi stood for the truth and against an oppressive foreign regime; he was vengefully persecuted and violently murdered. Martin Luther King Jr. stood for the truth in championing the cause of a racially discriminated people; he was hounded, vilified, and assassinated. Fr. Mark Gruber stood up to an administration at St. Vincent College with which he respectfully disagreed. In other words, he had the courage of his convictions and boldly abided by them. This did not please the established authority, and his promising career was destroyed.

---

[492] Luke 11:49-51

[493] Fr. Gordon MacRae, "Are Civil Liberties for Priests Intact?" (June 16, 2010).

Undeterred, the brave priest filed a suit against his oppressors with the clear objective of protecting both his reputation and his sanity. However, when it became clear that his spirited defence could violate the sacrosanct and inviolable seal of confession, Fr. Mark Gruber rescinded his suit. An innocent penitent could be deposed in that vile charade. His opponents claimed a victory, as hollow as it was.

"Jerusalem, Jerusalem, the city that kills the prophets and stones those who are sent to it! How often have I desired to gather your children together as a hen gathers her brood under her wings, and you were not willing! See, your house is left to you, desolate."[494]

Said a staunch supporter of Fr. Mark Gruber:

Man's perfidy never ceases to amaze me, my own included. To think that lies are truth, and that God will somehow turn his back and pretend along with you that it is not really a lie defies all logic, but from personal experience, I can tell you that that did not stop me many times. So, Fr. Mark is caught up in the lies of others, the need to be right, and they are basking in the glory of being right today. However, that glow that they feel from the heat is not of the Sun/Son, but the fires of Hell being stoked for those who would defy God and harm one of His precious children, while hurting the faith of His other children in this perfidious display . . . If this were the end of this charade, it would be a time for mourning, but God is not done with this situation, and will use the redemptive suffering of Father Mark Gruber for His purpose, and His ends . . . Father Mark is very Christlike in his silence, and is a model for us all.[495]

"A faithful friend is a sturdy shelter; he who finds one finds a treasure."[496] (Sirach 6:14).

This ATM Couldn't and Didn't Spew Money

Thursday, December 23, 2010

---

[494] Matthew 23:37-38
[495] Freedom Through Truth, "Truth For His Guide".5 November 2010. Freethroughtruth.blogspot.com
[496] Sirach 6:14

Even as I conclude this particular chapter, the Internet carries the following intriguing report entitled: "Sacred Site Sex Charges Dismissed in Court."

A man allegedly told a Japanese woman she would die if she did not have sex with him on a sacred site, a Darwin court has been told.

A committal hearing at Darwin Magistrates Court heard the tourist accused the man of duping her into sex at Ubir Rock in Kakadu after telling her he could see her dying in hospital in three years' time if she did not have sex with him, the *NT News* reports.

However Magistrate Michael Carey dismissed four charges of sexual intercourse without consent against the man because the woman's evidence "did not hang together" and was contradictory in some places.

"There is no way [a jury] would convict on her evidence," Mr. Carey said.

The woman said she was raped by the man four times over two days at his Jabiru home in October 2009 after he had offered to fix the woman's flat tyre.

When she was interviewed by police, the woman—who spoke limited English—said she had "no option but to follow because I was scared."

"I was told I could no longer say no in this sacred place," she said.

"I was told if I reject I will die, someone did because of rejecting."

Mr. Carey said the woman did not indicate lack of consent to the sexual encounters.

"There is no way," said the presiding magistrate, "a jury would convict on her evidence."

Why, then, does a defenceless priest, falsely accused and wrongly imprisoned for 17 years, have to wait interminably for justice?

A Witch in Salem

Sadly priests have no alternative but to cope by themselves. Repeatedly, they are unfairly blamed for situations that are beyond their influence or control. Often, they are publicly ridiculed by the media, heedlessly patronised by their leaders, and callously dumped on by various groups with differing agendas and tacit or explicit dissensions, leaving them with no alternative but to comply only because they have no one to articulate a pertinent and competent response on their behalf.

This was forcibly brought home to Fr. Brendan Hoban, an Irish priest, recently when, in chatting with an eminent Dublin lawyer, he said: "Being a priest today in Ireland is like being a witch in Salem." And he certainly did not mean it flippantly. Comments Fr. Hoban: "As we know the infamous witch-trials in Salem are a vivid cautionary tale about the dangers of unfair and sometimes false accusations and lapses in due process."[497]

Reportedly, a certain Frances Babic addressed a letter to the editor lamenting the silence of Cleveland's priests in the face of church closings by the Catholic bishop of Cleveland, Richard Lennon. In his response, Fr. Donald Cozzens has this to say:

> We priests have remained silent because it is our way of life. We priests have remained silent as evicted parishioners of closed parishes coped with feelings of disorientation and spiritual abandonment while searching for new parish communities—and others decided not to search at all. We priests have remained silent about our own tattered morale and the widespread spirit of discouragement in the people of our diocese.[498]

Fr. Cozzens suspects that Frances Babic and other Catholics are thinking: *What have you priests got to lose? You have no family to support, no mortgage to pay off, no children to educate, and you enjoy unparalleled job security. Why then do you remain silent?*

"Here is why I think we priests remain silent," opines Fr. Cozzens. "From our seminary days, we have been educated and formed in a quasi-militaristic, quasi-feudal clerical society. On the day of our ordination, we promised obedience and respect to our bishop and to his successors. In such a closed world, it is as difficult for a priest to publicly question or criticize his bishop as it is for a junior military officer to

---

[497] Fr. Brendan Hoban, *The Inaugural Meeting of the Association of Catholic Priests,* Portaloise Parish Centre, September 15, 2010, published in *The Swag,* Vol.18, No.4 (Summer Edition) 8-10.

[498] Fr. Donald Cozzens, writer in residence at John Carroll University and author of *Sacred Silence: Denial and the Crisis in the Church* (Liturgical Press, 2002). Quoted in *The Swag,* Vol.18, No.4 (Summer Edition), 15.

publicly question or criticize his commanding officer. Public questioning or public criticism, regardless of its merits, is perceived by many priests and many Catholic laity as disloyalty. *And disloyalty is the capital sin of both the military and Catholic clergy.*"[499]

Moreover, Catholics look upon their bishop as the representative of Christ for their local church. For the faithful, and, in particular for priests, public questioning or criticism of their bishop is tantamount, in the eyes of some, to flagrant disrespect for both the office and the person of the bishop.[500]

The book of Ecclesiastes tells us that there is "a time to remain silent and a time to speak."[501] In times of crisis, mature believers need to ask what they can do to help their church regain its equilibrium and renew its spirit. *"This is especially true,"* adds Fr. Cozzens, *"of its leaders, its priests".*[502]

Said the theologian-turned-poet, Rev. Kilian McDonnell, very wisely and candidly:

"No grand betrayals—
we lacked the impudent will—
we died of small treasons."[503]

---

[499]   Ibid., 15.

[500]   Ibid., 15.

[501]   Ecclesiastes 3:7.

[502]   Ibid., 15.

[503]   Rev. Donald Cozzens. "Why Our Priests Remain Silent". www.cleveland. com/opinion, 15 October, 2010.

20

Zero Tolerance, Zero Sense

One of them, Nicodemus—the same man who had come to Jesus
earlier—said to them, "But surely our Law does not allow us to pass
judgement on anyone without first giving him a hearing
and discovering what he is doing?"
—John 7:50-53

The March 28, 2011, issue of *Time* carried a most interesting and thought-provoking contribution by the reputed journalist, Nancy Gibbs, strikingly entitled "Zero Tolerance, Zero Sense."[504] The subtitle succinctly encapsulated the gist: What's the lesson learned when rules don't allow for mistakes?

As is well known, rules are made and laws are framed with a view to ensuring justice for one and all. In other words, they must be justly and uniformly applied without making meat of one and flesh of another. This, regrettably, according to Ms Gibbs, is very far from the truth. "Two good kids, two broken rules. Two parables of justice, except one offers a bracing lesson in honour and the other just leaves you heartsick at the latest evidence that zero tolerance often makes zero sense."[505]

To substantiate her point, Ms Gibbs relates the story of Brandon Davies, a star Brigham Young University basketball player, whose team

---

[504] Nancy Gibbs, "Zero Tolerance, Zero Sense," *TIME* (March 28, 2011), 59.
[505] Ibid.

was heading towards its first Final Four ever. Unfortunately, it emerged that Brandon had violated the Mormon school's strict honour code with its injunction to "live a chaste and virtuous life"—he had apparently slept with his girlfriend. Normally, such an act would never create a stir or ruffle a feather on most campuses, where athletes' failing grades, drunken sprees, and loutish behaviour are ignored as long as the players perform successfully in boosting the university's image and prospects.

As a concession, Brandon could have been permitted to play while the honour-code office investigated the incident. Even his teammates were distraught at the prospect of missing him and magnanimously said that they bore him no malice and even considered him a brother. But the authorities were firm and inflexible on the principle of *zero tolerance*. Even the crowd roared in ovation when Davies returned to the arena not as a player but as a spectator nobly determined to cheer his team. Sadly, they lost by 18 points. This is how Los Angeles *Times* sportswriter Bill Plaschke commented: "BYU knows all this stuff, and it suspended the kid anyway; and if you don't believe in its code, you have to love its honour."[506]

By contrast, Ms Gibbs relates the story of Nick Stuban, a 15-year-old Boy Scout in Fairfax County, Virginia. He was a conscientious student, a gifted footballer, a dutiful Christian, and the only child of parents who had retired from the military. Sadly, Nick's mother suffered from Lou Gehrig's disease, as torturous an illness as one could ever watch consume a close and loved relative. With tender and loving care, the devoted adolescent would take care of her, suctioning her tracheal tube in the middle of the night when the alarm went off.

One day, Nick bought a single capsule of a synthetic compound that acts like marijuana but is not illegal. Someone reported it to the school officials. Like Brandon Davies, Nick Stuban frankly confessed and acknowledged that it was a dumb thing to do. But in November, a school review board suspended him; he was separated from the friends who supported him, from the team, the Scouts, and those in driver's ed. He pleaded in vain with officials to be allowed to return. Two months later, in January, a desperate Nick Stuban committed suicide.

Adds Ms Gibbs: "Thus Fairfax County has become the latest to reconsider whether the edicts born of fear and Columbine actually make any

---

[506] Ibid.

sense or keep anyone safe. The original rules against drugs and knives soon swelled, with schools that once called parents now calling the police."[507]

The following instances have been listed by Ms Gibbs:

- Middle-schoolers were being suspended for puddle stomping and Alka-Seltzer possession or referred to a drug-awareness program for accepting a breath mint.
- A six-year-old in Delaware was suspended and threatened with reform school for taking to school a camping item that served as a fork, spoon, and knife.
- A nine-year-old was questioned by police about a plan to launch a spitball with a rubber band; he had to undergo psychological counselling before he could go back to class.
- A twelve-year-old New York girl was led off in handcuffs for scribbling on her desk with an erasable marker.
- A high school sophomore was suspended for breaking the no-cell-phone rule when he took a call from his father . . . who was serving in Iraq.
- A Florida honour student faced felony charges when a dinner knife—not a steak knife or a butcher knife—was found on the floor of her car, which she had parked at school. Said the principal: "A weapon is a weapon is a weapon."

Indiscriminate and inconsistent "zero tolerance" does indeed make no sense. As is well known, an automobile is a lethal weapon, and every driver is a potential murderer. Riding in an elevator is seriously hazardous, and every trip is fraught with death-defying danger. Painful though it is, an injection from a medical practitioner is often the best antidote against disease or infection. Occasionally, however, it could have severe repercussions. This does not deter people from trustfully submitting to the treatment of a qualified, authentic, experienced, and judicious doctor of medicine.

This is why Ms. Gibbs very rightly and wisely maintains:

---

[507] Ibid.

Making distinctions is part of learning; and so is making mistakes. When authorities confuse intent and accident, when rules are seen as more sacred than sense, when a contrite first-time offender is treated no differently from a serial classroom menace, we teach children that authority is deaf and dumb, that there is no judgement in justice. It undermines respect for discipline at a stage when we want kids to internalize it.[508]

And she concludes with this poignant observation: "Sometimes justice is at its most merciful when it is blind."[509]

Zero Tolerance sans Common Sense

Fr. Praxides (Prax) had just celebrated his Sacerdotal Silver Jubilee. With his bishop's expressed permission and the official acceptance of another in a foreign country, he decided to spend a year in the service of a parish so as to glean some new pastoral experiences. Within the first few weeks, he endeared himself to one and all by his gentle, cheerful, and friendly pastoral outreach.

One evening, he decided to take a walk around the immediate neighbourhood. A lady recognised him as he was passing her house and invited him to come in. Fr. Prax did so willingly. The lady explained that she was a single parent and that all she had to live for was her only child—a little girl about six or seven in age.

On the pretext of preparing the priest a cup of coffee, the lady went into the kitchen while her little daughter sat and spoke to the priest. At one stage, the little child wanted to display some of her elementary artwork. The priest was impressed and warmly commended the little girl. As a gesture of his commendation, he put his arm around the child's shoulders with no malice whatsoever. At that very moment, the mother walked in and accused the priest of touching her little daughter "inappropriately."

Promptly, she informed the police, who lost no time in arresting the innocent priest *solely on the basis of the fabricated report and the non-negotiable*

---

[508] Ibid.

[509]   Ibid.

principle of zero tolerance. A handful of loyal and indignant parishioners were fully prepared to vouch for the integrity and innocence of the priest, but to no avail. Fr. Prax was accused, convicted, and condemned solely on the principles of zero tolerance, even though the allegation was as spurious as it was calumnious. The priest, solely by virtue of being a priest, was guilty until proven innocent.

The matter was quickly reported to the local bishop, who was very compassionate and supportive. After bailing out the priest, he personally had him live in the bishop's residence while the process was duly conducted as per the standard practice in such sensitive situations. As can be expected, the media was quick to capitalise on the titillating story, exposing the priest by name while shielding his accuser under the veil of anonymity. The case went to the local court, and the bishop did engage lawyers to plead the innocence of the priest.

In the meantime, the lady visited the parish priest and tried to cajole him into a dubious compromise. She said that she would drop the charges against Fr. Prax if she was given $30,000.00. She explained that, as a single parent, she was finding it extremely difficult to make ends meet and urgently needed the money. With that wily ruse, she literally fell on her own sword.

Not only did the parish priest refuse, but he reported the matter to the bishop, who, in turn, relayed it to the defending lawyers. The presiding judge, after due investigation, dismissed the case on the grounds of insufficient evidence and unconditionally acquitted the innocent priest. Regrettably, the harm done to his morale, reputation, and ministry was irreparable, so that the priest of his own accord opted to return to his diocese in order to resume his pastoral ministry.

This is a patent case of the glaring abuse to which an innocent priest is willy-nilly subject solely on the non-negotiable but gravely flawed principle of zero tolerance. The indiscriminate application, as is clearly evident in this most unfortunate case and numerous others, can lack both common sense and basic justice. Oddly, the truly guilty party went scot-free—that was her questionable prerogative once again on the principle of zero tolerance, which clearly amounted to zero common sense.

Let us for a moment consider a parallel case. With a view to reducing an alarming death toll, averting accidents, and ensuring the safety of one and all, the national law in Australia stipulates that the blood alcohol limit for drivers of a motor vehicle, motorcycle, or scooter on any public road should not exceed 0.05. It originally stood at 0.08, but that did not prove effective, and so it was unanimously revised and reduced. In a word, there is zero tolerance for any driver who irresponsibly and recklessly flouts this very stringent law.

Accordingly, the police have been authorised to conduct random breath tests (RBT) for both alcohol and drugs. However, even before an intoxicated driver is penalised, he/she is tested three times—first at the scene, then in an RBT bus that is equipped with more sophisticated equipment to detect excesses, and finally at the police station only to make assurance doubly sure both for the police and the driver. Once the offence is firmly established, the penalties imposed are, according to the stipulated directives, proportionate to the level of excess, which could vary from low to medium to high. So even with this very stringent law and the application of zero tolerance, there is room for both leniency and stringency—all intended to serve as an effective deterrent.

The Presumption of Innocence Is Fundamental and Inescapable

The apostle John tells us that on one occasion, the enemies of Jesus despatched officers with the authority to arrest him only because he appeared to be blazing a new trail that they personally found unsettling and threatening. To their stunned disbelief, the officers returned without Jesus only because they were so captivated by his wisdom and eloquence. To quote their own testimony: "Never has anyone spoken like this!"[510] In a word, to them, not only was Jesus a very honest and erudite person, but even listening to him was an unparalleled experience.

Having met Jesus on an earlier occasion, Nicodemus sounded a note of caution. Undoubtedly, it was a timid reaction, but nonetheless a sincere attempt to defend Jesus: "Our law does not judge people without first giving them a hearing to find out what they are doing, does it?"[511]

With this, Nicodemus was drawing the attention of the bystanders to the explicit teaching of the Law: "You shall not spread a false report. You shall not join hands with the wicked to act as a malicious witness. You

---

[510] John 7:46
[511] John 7:51

shall not follow a majority in wrong-doing; when you hear witness in a lawsuit, you shall not side with the majority so as to pervert justice; nor shall you be partial to the poor in a lawsuit."[512] It is, therefore, morally wrong to condemn a person without giving him/her a chance to defend himself/herself.

This very teaching is authoritatively repeated in the book of Deuteronomy: "I charged your judges at that time: 'give the members of your community a fair hearing, and judge rightly between one person and another, whether citizen or resident alien. You must not be partial in judging; hear out the small and the great alike; you shall not be intimidated by anyone, for the judgement is God's."[513] So every person, regardless of caste, creed, or community, is entitled to an impartial hearing and a just judgement, which, in the last analysis, is endorsed by God who can neither deceive nor be deceived.

Oddly, this was not the case with the unsuspecting and innocent Fr. Prax. The blow was far too traumatic, so that he, of his own accord, decided to return to his country, diocese, and ministry. Fortuitously, the compassionate and magnanimous bishop personally bore the expenses for Fr. Prax's travel. But the damage done had literally scarred the hapless priest ineffaceably. How very true is the poignant observation of Ms. Nancy Gibbs: "Sometimes justice is at its most merciful when it is blind."[514]

Zero Tolerance Obfuscates Truth and Justice

Kate (not her real name) is an 18-year-old Air Force cadet who voluntarily consented to having sex with an army cadet a little senior in age on March 29, 2011. Later, it was discovered that he was not a nice guy. Without her knowledge, her partner had tuned the camera of his computer onto the couple engaged in sexual intercourse and had it broadcast via Skype to half a dozen fellow cadets sitting in a room nearby. The pictures were snapped by one or more of the voyeurs and distributed around the Australian Defence Force Academy (ADFA).[515]

---

[512] Exodus 23:1-3.
[513] Deuteronomy 1:16-17.
[514] Nancy Gibbs. Op.Cit.
[515] *The Weekend Australian* (April 9-10, 2011), 1-2.

Defenceless and helpless, Kate rang and left a message at the Ten Network, as she knew no one in the media. Her sole purpose, she frankly explained, was to ensure that something similar would not happen to other naive women. She never asked for, nor has she been offered, money.

Kate was interviewed by the boss of ADFA, Commodore Bruce Kafer, who assured her that she had the support of the ADFA staff. In the very next breath, she was informed that she "needed to think about how [the media exposure] would affect the young men involved in the Skype incident." Allegedly, Kafer informed Kate that "his concern was not just for her welfare but for theirs as well."

Further, Commodore Kafer wanted Kate to address her division of cadets because "they'll be angry." Specifically, he said that it might help if "she apologised to her classmates for bringing the division into disrepute by going to the media." Constrained by circumstances, Kate did.

During her address, one cadet yelled out, "Name and shame the dirty slut." Other cadets took up the cry, yelling, "Do it!" The officer present cancelled Kate's planned address, fearing the worst from the volatile cadets.

Kate explained that as the officer enjoys a rank equivalent to a brigadier, she felt she had no choice but to comply. That did not stop colleagues, both male and female, and others from heaping abuse and sarcastic remarks even as she walked down the corridor. Her bedroom had to be changed, as it had been plastered with shaving foam, and she stopped eating in the mess because of the malicious gossip and nasty whispers. As can be expected, there has been universal revulsion at such a traitorous betrayal.

Sue McLean, a former police officer with decades of experience in investigating sex crimes, says the psychological effect on Kate would have been similar to a serious sexual assault. The Australian Federal Police investigating the matter are seriously examining if the Skyping without Kate's knowledge "negates her consent" and so amounts to "fraudulent misrepresentation," which, under law, can be treated as rape.

On November 27, 2000, 15-year-old Eleanore Tibble hanged herself after being told to resign or face discharge from the Tasmanian Air Training Corps following alleged fraternisation with 30-year-old senior instructor Leading Aircraftsman M. Harper. Her discharge was rescinded 15 days before her death, but the Air Force failed to inform her. A 2004

Human Rights and Equal Opportunity Commission Report found senior personnel had humiliated her instead of treating her as a victim.

In 2006, a legal battle that had gone almost to the High Court was resolved in an out-of-court settlement that Ms. Susan Campbell, the mother of the deceased, said had included changes to the handling of cadets, as well as an award in Eleanore's honour. Commenting on the traitorous betrayal of Kate, Ms. Campbell said:

> I had hoped the culture had changed. But this unfortunate girl has faced punitive action when it hasn't emerged that anything is happening to the perpetrators . . . They still haven't got it right. We are looking at someone who may be so traumatised by this ugly, horrible event that she finds herself unable to face the shame . . . Again, it's this male dominated culture that is putting the spotlight on a female.

And she knows what she is saying: "It took me six interminable years of toiling to get them to admit that their own investigation, which found them to be lacking, needed to be exposed . . . My heart goes out to that young lass—18 years of age, at the very beginning of her career—being crucified outside of due process. Here we are again."

The Unassailable Truth about Zero Tolerance

Marcus is a former cadet and now a very successful barrister.[516] Twenty-two years ago, he literally had the world at his feet as a very successful and promising student, a multi-talented sportsman, and a cadet under-officer in the school cadet unit.

Being very keenly interested in a military career and the army, he was most fortunate in being offered an Australian Defence Force scholarship to the recently opened Australian Defence Force Academy (ADFA). There, he was assured of the finest military training and a first-class university education before commencing a career as an army officer.

In January 1989, Marcus was duly sworn in as an officer cadet and flown to Canberra to commence officer training. Arriving at ADFA, he

---

[516] *The Weekend Australian* (April 9-10, 2011).

was allocated to a division and introduced to the Corps of Officer Cadets. He was only 17, unsuspecting and hopeful, when he had his innocence shattered at the hands of the Australian Defence Force.

He never imagined that the bullying and harassment would be so rampant in of all places the Defence Forces. "I know I am not alone and that there are hundreds of others who have lived through the same mistreatment and carry the same scars. They are a silent majority, and are a skeleton in the closet that the ADF does not acknowledge or talk about.

"After 20 years, I can now speak out and describe the physical, sexual and psychological abuse I was subjected to, and the inappropriate culture that existed, and still lingers in the ADF." Marcus candidly relates the horror of having a gang of people break into his room at night, hold him down, beat him, and anally rape him. The concomitant anger and the humiliation literally defy expression. "I had no alternative but to live with it."

After a short stay in hospital, Marcus was transferred to RMC Duntroon to finish his military training. It was made clear to him that if he complained, his career would be irreparably ruined. He would be stigmatised by the sexual nature of the assault because homophobia was the norm, and at that time, homosexuality was still illegal in the ADF. "Even though I was the victim, it seemed to be my fault. As a proud young male, this was difficult to cope with." Zero tolerance, zero sense.

Shortly after he was attacked, Marcus reports that the same gang attacked and gang-raped a female cadet in his division. No one was charged, and nothing was done about it. As a matter of fact, one of the perpetrators had the audacity to say openly that "she was a drunk slut; she had it coming." That person is now a senior officer in the ADF.

The root cause of the deteriorating problem according to Marcus was the fact that after 20 months of limited military training, the senior class was given hierarchical superiority over the first-year cadets. It was no surprise that this power was ultimately abused.

When reports of inappropriate conduct began to surface and could no longer be ignored, a review was commissioned into the widespread allegations of sexual harassment and bullying. Most reviews, adds Marcus pointedly, of this type are generally innocuous and purposefully do not make any findings. However, the Grey Review conducted a thorough investigation and found that bastardisation was rampant at ADFA, stating: "Unfortunately, some cadets at the defence academy are dishonest, emotionally stunted, insensitive bullies and cheats." Drastic changes were recommended. The supreme power of the senior cadet was removed, and male and female cadets were segregated. The day-to-day management and training of cadets was placed in the hands of trained officers.

When Marcus left the ADF and graduated from law school, he wrote to the defence minister and outlined what had happened to him. The ADF investigated his allegations and found there was "no record" of his allegations on his cadet file. When the Grey Review investigated Marcus's allegations and that of others, it found: "On occasions, Divisional Officers (DO) have not kept a record of a significant incident which affected a cadet. On other occasions, a record has been kept which does not accurately reflect the true nature of an incident, or alternatively, an accurate record has been kept but is not held on an official file. There is, therefore, no record of it on either the cadet's training file or an official academy file." (*The Australian*)

Unlike the half-hearted defence investigation, the Grey Review examined Marcus's medical records, which were held separately from ADFA files and which revealed hospitalisation as a result of injuries inflicted by other cadets. Says Marcus: "With the passage of time and the cynicism of the lawyer I have become, I am not surprised that no one at ADFA carefully wrote down the details of the attack on me by a gang of serial rapist senior cadets, most of whom would go on to be commissioned officers in the ADF."

As a successful barrister working in criminal law, Marcus regularly sees people incarcerated for the same crimes that were perpetrated against him at ADFA. However, the criminals in his case were never brought to trial, but were given instead commissions and careers in the ADF. Regrettably, no one took the time to say to anyone in the ADF that what happened at ADFA prior to 1998 was wrong. No one said to any of the graduates of ADFA: "What was done to you at ADFA was wrong, what you did to other cadets at ADFA was wrong."

In firing a final salvo, Marcus courageously and candidly says, "Every time an ADF harassment scandal erupts, the old wounds ache a bit. As a trained leader, I can see the root of the problem and some of the potential answers, but no one is listening."

Not an Isolated Instance of Blatant Injustice

The same is true of Fr. Gordon MacRae, who at 57 has been languishing in jail for the past 16 years for crimes that he did not commit but of which he was falsely accused and rashly declared "guilty until proven innocent" on the gravely flawed principle of *zero tolerance.*

On October 13, 2005, Bill Donahue, Catholic League president, appeared on NBC's *Today* show to contest a panel of contingency lawyers promoting lawsuits alleging sexual abuse by priests. In the heated debate, the lawyers and litigants tarred the Catholic Church and priests with the same brush as evil, perverse, and lecherous offenders. But Bill Donahue had the last word and literally floored his vehement opponents with one masterful stroke of genius: "There is no segment of the American population with less civil liberties protection than the average American Catholic priest."[517]

In 1994, Fr. Gordon MacRae was tried and pronounced guilty of crimes that a growing number of people believe never occurred at all. Ironically, he was offered a "plea deal." That is to say, if he confessed that he was guilty, then he could leave prison after one or two years instead of being incarcerated for 67! To admit guilt, when in reality, he is guiltless, would be self-incriminating, dishonest, and unethical, even if it could opportunistically redound to his early release. Conversely, protesting his innocence would *ipso facto* condemn him to 67 years in prison and for claims that have never been corroborated by substantial evidence and for fabricated crimes alleged to have occurred almost 30 years ago.

What caught Bill Donohue's attention was "A Priest's Story"[518]—a two-part series on the MacRae case by Dorothy Rabinowitz, a Pulitzer Prize-winning investigative journalist on the *Wall Street Journal* editorial board. At a time when many Catholics reeled over the scandal in the Catholic Church, Dorothy Rabinowitz took a hard look at the facts of the case of Fr. Gordon MacRae—facts that the rest of the news media had distorted or conveniently omitted. The result was a disturbing account of greed, false witnesses, and as the late Father Richard John Neuhaus

---

[517] Posted by Ryan A. McDonald on February 14, 2011 @ 12.00 a.m. in *Becoming Christlike,* featured on front page.

[518] Dorothy Rabinowitz, *The Wall Street Journal* (April 27/28, 2005).

described, "a Church and a justice system that seem indifferent to justice."[519]

Providentially, the *Wall Street Journal* series caught the attention of some civil liberties experts and lawyers, who have found the case most disturbing. Fortuitously, their investigation is nearing completion. The probe has revealed some shocking evidence of fraud and larceny—and Church officials all too eager to accommodate both—but no evidence whatsoever that the claims against this priest might be true. It is hoped that resources will be raised to bring a new appeal in the case of Fr. Gordon MacRae in the not-too-distant future.[520] Even so, Fr. MacRae's eye-catching, thought-provoking, and conscience-grabbing blog, *These Stone Walls*,[521] has been deemed by many to be the finest example of priestly witness amid the plethora of scandals that have rocked the Catholic Church in the course of the past decade.

In November 2005, the Catholic League journal, *Catalyst*, published the first of two major articles by Fr. Gordon MacRae about the scandal in the Catholic Church. "Sex Abuse and Signs of Fraud" was a well-researched account of how some have taken advantage of this phenomenal crisis to score windfall settlements based on fraudulent claims. The article made its way to the late Cardinal Avery Dulles, who promptly wrote to the imprisoned priest:

> Your article is an important one, and hopefully will be followed by many others. Unfortunate though your situation is, you are in a position to carry on an effective apostolate on behalf of unjustly accused priests. The time is bound to come when the tide will shift and even the bishops will be ready to hear the priests' side of the story. The change will come, but not before the public is prepared for it by articles

---

[519] Richard John Neuhaus, *First Things* (July 2009).

[520] Ryan A. MacDonald, Ibid.

[521] "While imparting a side of the abuse scandal that the major media refuses to provide, *These Stone Walls* is informative, thoughtful, and spiritually empowering ... One visit will make anyone reconsider all the one-sided hysteria we've heard in the media for the last two decades" (David F. Pierre Jr., Author of *Double Standards*).

such as yours. Your writing, which is clear, eloquent, and spiritually sound, will be a monument to your trials.[522]

That anticipated time is at hand, for the tide of competent personnel and enlightened opinions is fast turning. *These Stone Walls* and Fr. Gordon MacRae's unrelenting and courageous defence have been endorsed and sponsored by the National Centre for Reason and Justice (www.ncrj.org) a Boston-based organization whose board of lawyers, journalists, and wrongful conviction specialists examined and unanimously approved the case of Fr. Gordon MacRae for sponsorship. *These Stone Walls* has also been endorsed by numerous civil liberties and wrongful convictions organizations and websites.

There could not be a better and more persuasive conclusion than that of Fr. Gordon MacRae.[523] In responding to a priest who, like him, had been falsely accused and was, as a consequence, seething with anger and vindictiveness, this is how Fr. MacRae responded:

> It's ironic that this priest is often angry with me because he doesn't think I am angry enough. I assure you, he is wrong on that score. But being angry and feeling let down does not excuse me from doing the right thing. It does not excuse me from fidelity to the Gospel, fidelity to the Church, and fidelity to my own sense of right and wrong. At the end of the day, I am still wrongly imprisoned, but I have the freedom to choose the person I am going to be while wrongly imprisoned.[524]

---

[522] Cardinal Avery Dulles, posted by Ryan A. McDonald on February 14, 2011 @ 12.00 a.m. in *Becoming Christlike,* featured on front page.

[523] "No priest should be required to sacrifice his life to satisfy the demands of lawyers, insurance companies, and a rabid news media feeding on scandal. The case of Rev. Gordon MacRae opens a new chapter in the story of scandal in the Catholic Church."

[524] Fr. Gordon MacRae, posted by Ryan A. McDonald on February 14, 2011 @ 12.00 a.m. in *Becoming Christlike,* featured on front page.

One of them, Nicodemus—the same man who had come to Jesus earlier—said to them, "But surely our Law does not allow us to pass judgement on anyone without first giving him a hearing and discovering what he is doing?"[525] (John 7:50-53).

"Innocent until proven guilty" is indeed a fundamental and inalienable right of paramount importance even 2,000 years later.

---

[525] John 7:50-53

EPILOGUE

Saturday, July 9, 2011

Thousand Oaks, California

As I open the *Los Angeles Times*, my eyes fall on two pieces of topical information: first, the arrival at LAX of Britain's Duke and Duchess of Cambridge, Prince William and Princess Catherine; and second, the death notice of Betty Ford (93), wife of former president Gerald Ford, whose candour helped dispel taboos over cancer and substance abuse.

Skimming through the other pages of Section A, my attention is grabbed by two prominent features: first, a thought-provoking article by columnist Sandy Banks, entitled "Perception Gender Divide," and second, a stimulating article by Robert L. Shapiro (O.J. Simpson's defence attorney) entitled "In Casey Anthony's Case, the Law Worked."

The first focuses on the highly emotive, controversial, and polarizing case of Dominique Strauss-Kahn, the ex-IMF chief. The second closely examines the pertinent legal details of yet another highly emotive, controversial, and polarizing case, that of Casey Anthony, who was found not guilty of murdering her infant daughter, Caylee.

Returning to the first feature, Sandy Banks very frankly informs us of the widely differing comments that followed her earlier column on sexual assault allegations against a prominent French politician accused of attacking a hotel maid. On the one hand, most women she heard from were gratified by her willingness to believe the maid's account. On the other hand, admits Banks, "men by the dozens weren't buying that. For them, Dominique Strauss-Kahn is the victim here." While the women felt appeased, the men were enraged. To quote just one indignant male respondent: "Clearly you have to know and believe that men with power and money are targets for those who are without."

Moving onto the second, Robert L. Shapiro explains that the vehement protest to the acquittal of Casey Anthony "reveals how little many Americans know about the justice system." The Fifth Amendment guarantees that defendants can't face "double jeopardy," which means the government can't prosecute a person a second time for the same crime if the jury returns a verdict. Stated differently, only if the jury doesn't reach a decision can prosecutors elect to retry a case.

Shapiro explains: "First, prosecutors overcharged the case. Undoubtedly the mother (Casey) had failed to report her infant daughter (Caylee) missing for a month and lied when she did. The badly decomposed remains could not provide any clear evidence of the cause of death. Yet prosecutors chose to bring a charge of first-degree murder and ask for the death penalty." And why? They tried to gain a tactical advantage, and it backfired.

What the prosecutors failed to take into account was that in death penalty cases, jurors require a higher standard of proof. And this is but inevitable in view of the fact that such an extreme punishment is irrevocable. Adds Shapiro, "Our constitution-based criminal justice system places a high value on protecting the innocent. Among its central tenets is the idea that it is better to let a guilty person go free than to convict someone without evidence beyond a reasonable doubt."

Why, then, were the public so outraged with the eventual acquittal? Part of the blame must fall on the media. Says Shapiro, "This case got a lot of armchair quarter-backing from self-appointed experts, many of whom have never tried a murder case. Even more, by offering punditry rather than serious analysis and reporting, the media turned the trial into entertainment."

In the last analysis, concludes Shapiro, "Casey Anthony was not found innocent; she was simply not found guilty of murder because the prosecution did not prove each and every element of the charges they brought against her beyond a reasonable doubt."

At the conclusion of this research study, it is my sincere wish and earnest hope that priests, both diocesan and religious, will be accorded the same justice on the fundamental principle, clearly and unequivocally established by the United Nations' Declaration of Human Rights that a person is innocent until proven guilty.

The following letter addressed to Joe Maher the president of *Opus Bono Sacerdotii*—an organization that is working diligently to uphold the rights of priests wrongly accused and regrettably left in *limbo*, accentuates the imperative need of a forum and a process that will ensure justice and the triumph of truth:

Dear Mr. Maher,

I don't know where to begin. A priest and friend gave me a flyer from Opus Bono two weeks ago and after I read of your ministry I felt I was given a direction or a glimpse of hope that someone might understand. And so, with all humility I extend my arm and hand to you.

Until a priest has to personally experience the pain and degradation of being removed from priestly service, there is no one who can possibly "understand." This year, I will observe (I cannot say celebrate) my 40th anniversary of ordination as a Roman Catholic priest. This past June, I had a surprise visit to my parish office by two officials from the chancery, the vicar for priests and a canon lawyer (who happens to be a classmate of mine). They asked to see me privately and I was extremely nervous because of their attitude and demeanor. When the three of us were alone, they proceeded to tell me that a "credible allegation of sexual abuse" was made against me and that I had an hour to pack a bag and to come with them. Few details were given to me when I asked.

They mentioned a name which I never heard of before and that this "victim" was deceased. His widow and attorney came to the diocese to bring this supposed abuse to their attention. This was to have occurred some thirty years ago. I have served in my parish as pastor for almost 20 years without the slightest hint of any impropriety.

As I left with them in utter disbelief, shame and humiliation, I discovered later that the diocese had already sent out a "Fax

Blast" concerning my removal. After the press and media extensively exposed my "credible allegation of sexual abuse" for two days, I found myself living in a hellish nightmare. After some two or three weeks later, the same two officials called me to another meeting and informed me that another "victim" came forth after the public disclosure to make a second allegation against me. (And I had thought that life could not have possibly gotten any worse.)

As God as my witness, I swear as I swore on a Bible before the diocesan officials, these allegations are totally and completely untrue. My mind and my soul are bruised, beaten and trampled down. My parishioners are most supportive but I am not permitted to visit them and I cannot afford to call them by telephone. My health is not good and I had avoided many appointments with my doctors. This past Christmas Eve and Christmas Day were the worst emotionally devastating events I have ever had to endure. I was close to suicide. I suffer panic attacks, acute anxiety and severe depression. Worst of all, there is nobody that can really understand or share this onerous burden that I bear.

I am in financial ruin "to put the icing on the cake." I have exhausted my life savings trying to pay monthly expenses for car lease payments, auto insurance, telephone, and many credit card companies to mention a few.

Even when the day for my exoneration and restoration does come, I have already seen the future. There is none. Two weeks ago a fellow priest of our diocese was accused of sexual misconduct which allegedly occurred forty years prior, was exonerated and was officially assigned to serve "in restricted ministry" at a convent motherhouse. When the media got hold of his new assignment, the public outcry that a "priest, accused of credible sexual abuse" would be assigned to an area which had schools and day-care centers nearby, our bishop, bowing to "public pressure and shepherdly concern" reversed and revoked his official assignment the very next day; not even twenty-four hours had elapsed.

Now I have abandoned all hope. I do not know where to turn for help, for someone who understands. I am ashamed. I am alone. I reach out for your hand.

"Father John"

Hailing as I do from Bombay (now Mumbai), India, I have the greatest respect and admiration for Mahatma Gandhi, a truly "great soul," the father of the Indian nation, a fearless and charismatic leader, an inspired and inspiring visionary, and the principal architect of Indian independence from the British. On one occasion this is what he said:

> "If I seem to take part in politics, it is only because politics encircles us today like the coil of a snake from which one cannot get out, no matter how much one tries. I wish, therefore, to wrestle with the snake . . . My work will be finished if I succeed in carrying conviction to the human family, that every man or woman, however, weak in body, is the guardian of his or her self-respect and liberty.[526]

In a similar vein, I will have considered my work finished if I too succeed, as he did, in carrying to the devoted, industrious, and self-sacrificing priests—both diocesan and religious—of our Catholic Church, this reassuring conviction: that their security will be sedulously safeguarded and the pursuit of justice will be vigorously upheld.

Indeed, *"A journey of a thousand miles begins with a single step."*[527]

---

[526] mkgandhi.org/momgandhi/chap.18
[527] The Way of Lao-tzu. Op.Cit.

POSTSCRIPT

[Immediately after the Crucifixion of Christ Jesus],
when the captain of the Roman military unit handling the executions
saw what had happened,
he was stricken with awe before God and said,
"Surely this man was innocent."
—Luke 23:48-49

Wednesday, July 19, 2011

I have e-mail. The librarian informs me that a book I requested has arrived. Promptly, I responded.

The title was captivating: *The Conspiracy.*[528] The subtitle was intriguing: *An Innocent Priest.* But what followed next was astounding: *Monsignor William McCarthy—A True Story.*[529]

So this was a candid firsthand account of a truly innocent priest who was falsely accused and completely exonerated but only after five harrowing years of vindictive malice, scurrilous innuendos, tyrannical persecution by the media, social ostracism, haunting uncertainty, humiliating and biased investigations, and a warped process that violated all laws—natural, canonical, and moral—and the dictates of both justice and charity.

When Msgr. McCarthy eventually confronted the former vicar general (VG) of the diocese, who was directly responsible for his gruelling

---

[528] Monsignor William McCarthy, *The Conspiracy, An Innocent Priest, A True Story* (Bloomington, IN: iUniverse, Inc., 2010).

[529] Monsignor William McCarthy was the pastor of St. Rose of Lima Church, East Hanover, New Jersey, in the Paterson Diocese New Jersey for 23 years.

ordeal and intended destruction (in conjunction with his former bishop and the promoter of justice), this is what the bungling cleric had to say in his defence: "Orders from Dallas, when they hastily put together that charter . . . Bill, we were acting in good faith."[530]

Looking the VG squarely in the eyes, Msgr. McCarthy bluntly informed him, "That's what they said at the Nuremburg Trials[531]: 'We were only following orders.'"

The VG was nonplussed and tongue-tied. So Msgr. McCarthy dealt him the punch line with justifiable indignation: "They were all convicted for crimes against humanity."

Very meekly, the VG confessed, "Sorry, Bill, we made a mistake." "Surely this man was innocent."[532]

Very magnanimously, Msgr. McCarthy responded, "I forgive you even though my life has been irreversibly tarnished."

Most regrettably, the high-ranking cleric, charged with a momentous responsibility in his diocese, had been operating with a dysfunctional compass—rational, legal, canonical, and moral. Over 2,000 years ago, he who is the Way, the Truth, and the Life very wisely instructed all:

> Don't criticize, and then you won't be criticized. For others will treat you as you treat them. And why worry about a speck in the eye of a brother when you have a board in your own? Should you say, "Friend, let me help you get that speck out of your eye," when you can't even see because of the board in your own? Hypocrite! First get rid of the board. Then you can see to help your brother.[533]

---

[530] Ibid., 317-318.

[531] At the Nuremberg trials, it was stated, "The crime which we seek to condemn and punish has been so calculated, so malignant, and so devastating, that civilization cannot tolerate their being ignored because it cannot survive their being repeated."

[532] Luke 23:48-49

[533] Matthew 7:1-5. We all suffer brokenness in our lives, in our relationships with God, and in our relationships with others. Brokenness tends to weigh us down and can easily lead us back into our addictions. Recovery isn't complete until all areas of brokenness are mended.

And again, "Your heavenly Father will forgive you if you forgive those who sin against you; but if you refuse to forgive them, he will not forgive you."[534]

Firing a final salvo, Msgr. McCarthy said to the dumbfounded VG: "So that my suffering will not be in vain, I want you to go public with an apology to the press—and further, that you write to the apostolic delegate in Washington DC, Archbishop Sambi, and demand that he make a concerted effort to review the weapon of mass destruction of our priests—that instrument known as the Dallas Charter."[535]

The VG sincerely and honestly resolved to do his best. He was truly contrite for what turned out to be a woeful and irretrievable miscarriage of justice—which the noble Msgr. McCarthy did gratefully appreciate.

This is how Jack Kraft, Esq., a close and trusted friend of Msgr. McCarthy describes this poignant, painful, and powerful story: "*The Conspiracy* chronicles the monumental struggles of an innocent priest, Monsignor William McCarthy, falsely accused in 2003 of molesting two young sisters more than 23 years earlier. On the eve of his retirement from a stellar career as a priest and pastor, for the next five tortuous years, he was the victim of an anonymous complaint that was accepted as true by his bishop and friend of 40 years. Share his travails and see how one's faith can overcome the worst injustices that man can heap on a holy and totally innocent person."

And Arthur N. Hoagland, MD, a practicing psychiatrist and devoted friend added, "Monsignor William McCarthy paints a picture embracing a situation that is almost impossible to comprehend. Had I not stood by him throughout the years of pure hell he experienced, I would not have believed the outright calumny by a detective, and how the subsequent action of his bishop and diocesan staff could have occurred. Child abuse is a terrible thing, but equally horrible is when innocent priests are unjustly condemned and destroyed by the hierarchy of the church."

In his classical Sermon on the Mount, Jesus said:

---

[534] Matthew 6:14-15. Much of recovery involves repairing the brokenness in our life. This requires that we make peace with God, with ourselves, and with others whom we have alienated. Unresolved issues in relationships can keep us from being at peace with God and ourselves.
[535] Op.Cit., 318.

Beware of false teachers who come disguised as harmless sheep, but are wolves and will tear you apart. You can detect them by the way they act, just as you can identify a tree by its fruit. You need never confuse grape-vines with thorn bushes or figs with thistles. Different kinds of fruit trees can quickly be identified by examining their fruit. A variety that produces delicious fruit never produces an inedible kind. And a tree producing an inedible kind can't produce what is good. [536]

Stated simply, there always is need to judiciously differentiate between what is sound and commendable and what is not. A sound and commendable principle cannot but produce positive and favourable results. If it doesn't, there is need for a change—the sooner the better, for, as the saying goes, "A stitch in time saves nine." The assumption "Innocent until proven guilty" is sound and commendable—it is a fundamental, sacrosanct, and inalienable right. The contradictory "Guilty until proven innocent," as we have just seen demonstrated, can have devastating, deplorable, and irreversible results. "Those who do not know their history are doomed to repeat it."[537]

Even as I write this particular paragraph, an e-mail from a priest-friend informs me that, just a month ago, a priest personally known to him, aged 42 and just six years in the pastoral ministry, tragically took his own life. All he left behind was a brief note that read: "I am innocent!" As is well known, scores of prisoners on death row have been fully exonerated on the basis of a new examination of the DNA evidence. And it was proved conclusively that they had nothing to do with the crimes for which they had been incarcerated for years and rashly condemned to the death penalty. "Those who do not know their history are doomed to repeat it."[538]

Again, Christ Jesus said, "Do for others what you want them to do for you. This is the teaching of the laws of Moses in a nutshell." [539] And as the Talmud says: "What is hateful to you, do not do to your neighbour. This

---

[536]   Matthew 7:15-18
[537]   George Santayana
[538]   Ibid.
[539]   Matthew 7:12

is the whole Torah; all the rest is commentary."[540] Confucius said, "One word which sums up the basis of all good conduct . . . loving-kindness. Do not do to others what you do not want done to yourself."[541] And the prophet Muhammad enjoined on his followers "Not one of you truly believes until you wish for others what you wish for yourself."[542]

And this very ideal is proposed by Hinduism, Buddhism, Taoism, Sikhism, Unitarianism, Native Spirituality, Zoroastrianism, Jainism, and the Baha'I Faith. That, in essence, is the Golden Rule. As is patently obvious, no right-thinking individual would ever want the heart-rending story of Msgr. William McCarthy to be ever visited upon an innocent son, brother, cousin, uncle, grand-uncle, or even distant relative. In the poignant words of George Santayana: *"Those who do not know their history are doomed to repeat it."*[543]

All's Well that Ends Well

The extraordinary story of Msgr. McCarthy will be incomplete if I do not relate one particularly salient event that figuratively places the icing on the cake. Much earlier, his former bishop had officially written to Cardinal Ratzinger, the prefect for the Congregation for Doctrine and Faith, suggesting "laicization," which is tantamount to dismissal from the priesthood. This would have been nothing short of the most devastating blow to one who had been so devotedly and selflessly committed to his priestly vocation and his pastoral ministry for 40 years. Providentially, the prefect then and Sovereign Pontiff now firmly and decisively turned it down; the case, as he saw it, lacked conclusive proof and certainly did not warrant such an excessively drastic and severe censure.

After Msgr. McCarthy was totally exonerated, restored to the priestly ministry, and honoured with the title of *pastor emeritus*,[544] there was a

---

[540] Hillel, Talmud, Shabbat 31a.

[541] Confucius, *Analects*, 15:23.

[542] The Prophet Muhammad, Hadith.

[543] George Santayana.

[544] "A pastor retired with honour"; "Emeritus" is defined by Webster's Dictionary as "a title for a person retired, but retaining one's title as an honour. The word 'emeritus' is derived from the Latin *merere*, meaning

celebratory dinner in his honour on June 3, 2008. About 150 priests were present as well as his former bishop—the very person who had earlier worked to destroy him. Msgr. McCarthy was seated at one extreme of the dining room and the bishop at the other.

Suddenly, the bishop rose from his chair and shuffled across the hall. As he approached the table of Msgr. McCarthy, he kept saying out loud: "Where is Liam?[545] Where is Liam?" On reaching Msgr. McCarthy, the bishop leaned across and embraced him. The emotional reunion was far too great for the elderly cleric who cried openly and unashamedly. "Surely this man was innocent."[546]

He was truly contrite as he unreservedly apologized publicly: "I'm very sorry, Liam! Congratulations! It is a resurrection for you."

To which, Msgr. McCarthy nobly responded, "Thank you!"

Said John Dryden (1631-1700), the English poet, critic, and playwright "Forgiveness to the injured does belong / But they ne'er pardon, who have done the wrong."[547]

Saturday, July 22, 2011

I have just received *The Tidings*, Southern California's Catholic weekly. On the second page is the customary and always thought-provoking letter of Archbishop Jose H. Gomez of Los Angeles. With a heart overflowing with Christ-like compassion and a distinctly fatherly love, this is what he writes as he reflects on the inspiring story of Mary Magdalene: "People make mistakes. They sin. Some people do evil that causes scandal and grave harm. We can condemn the offence and work for justice—without trying to destroy the person who committed the sin. We are called in all things to charity and truth, kindness and empathy. No matter whom we are dealing with . . . We need to reject every temptation to shame or

---

'to earn or deserve something.'" This was conferred on Msgr. McCarthy by the new bishop, Rt. Rev. Sarratelli, who was a staunch pillar of support and encouragement to Msgr. McCarthy during his agonizing nightmare for five grueling years.

[545] The Gaelic for William.

[546] Luke 23:48-49

[547] *The Conquest of Granada* (1670), part 2, act 4, scene 3.

condemn people. Let us never be the cause of turning someone away from seeking God's forgiveness and redemption."

Christus vincit!
May Christ Jesus, our Risen Lord and Saviour, triumph over evil and sin!

Christus regnat!
May he rule with his unfathomable wisdom and his almighty power!

Christus imperat!
And may his redemptive compassion and unconditional love ever reign supreme!

REFERENCES

Allen, Prudence. "Freedom and the Fatherhood of God." *Homiletic and Pastoral Review* (Jan. 2002): 18-27.

Applewhite, Monica. "The Impact of Abuse in the Church on Priests and Religious Men." An Address to the Clergy of the Archdiocese of Adelaide, South Australia (August 5, 2010).

Archdiocese of Los Angeles, *Report to the People of God: Clergy Sexual Abuse, 1930-2003.* Los Angeles, CA: Office of the Archbishop, 2004.

Austriaco, Nicanor, JG. "The Myth of the Gay Gene." *Homiletic and Pastoral Review* (Dec. 2003): 28-31, 48-51.

Balantyne, Hugh. "The Origin of Priestly Celibacy." *Homiletic and Pastoral Review* (Apr. 2003): 48-56.

Beal, John P., James A. Coriden, and Thomas J. Green. *New Commentary on the Code of Canon Law.* Mahwah, NJ: Paulist Press, 1998.

Beal, John P. "As Idle as a Painted Ship upon a Painted Ocean: A People Adrift in the Ecclesiological Doldrums." *Concilium* 3 (2004): 87-97.

Benedict XVI. *The Priesthood—Spiritual Thoughts Series.* Washington DC: United States Conference of Catholic Bishops (USCCB), 2009.

Besse, Gail. "Accused, Charged, Exonerated—Ousted Priest Wages Two-Year Battle to Clear Name, Return to Ministry." *National Catholic Register* (May 07, 2006).

Boyea, Earl. *John Samuel Foley, Third Bishop of Detroit—His Ecclesiastical Conflicts in the Diocese of Detroit 1888-1890.* Thesis submitted to the Graduate School of Wayne State University, Detroit, Michigan, in partial fulfilment of the requirements for the degree of master of arts, 1984.

Brachear, Manya A. "More Priests Likely to Sue—Clerics Say Court Is Only Defence." *Chicago Tribune* (December 3, 2006).

Brandon, Michael. "Freedom through Truth," *Homiletic and Pastoral Review* October 13, 2010.

Browder, Sue Ellen. "Helping Accused Priests Is His Calling." *National Catholic Register* (July 15, 2007).

—. "Accused Priest Hits Back with Lawsuit." *National Register* (January 14, 2007).

Byrne, Harry J., JCD. "Bishop as Cop, DA, Judge and Appellant Bench." *Justice for Priests and Religious* (May 5, 2010).

Cafardi, Nicholas P., JD, JCD. *Before Dallas—The U.S. Bishops' Response to Clergy Sexual Abuse of Children.* New York / Mahwah, NJ: Paulist Press, 1993.

Carey, Ann. *Sisters in Crisis—The Tragic Unravelling of Women's Religious Communities.* Huntington, IN: Our Sunday Visitor, Inc., 1997.

Carter, Stephen L. *Integrity.* Basic Books, New York Harper Collins, 1996.

Catechism of the Catholic Church. New York: Doubleday, 1995.

Chafee, Zechariah, Jr. *Three Human Rights in the Constitution.* Lawrence, KS: The University Press of Kansas, 1968.

Clark, William P. "Authority in the Church (Authority in the Church at All Levels Must Be Characterized by Balance." *Homiletic and Pastoral Review* (June 2008): 66-69.

Clowes, Brian W., and David L. Sonnier. "Child Molestation by Homosexuals and Heterosexuals. "*Homiletic and Pastoral Review* (May 2005): 44-54.

Coleridge, Mark. "Sexual Abuse of the Young in the Catholic Church." *Justice for Priests* (May 23, 2010).

Conde, H. Victor. *A Handbook of International Human Rights Terminology.* 2nd Ed. Lincoln: University of Nebraska Press, 2004.

Coriden, James A., Thomas J. Green, and Donald E. Heintschel. *The Code of Canon Law—A Text and Commentary.* Mahwah, NJ: Paulist Press, 1985.

Covey, Stephen R. *The 8th Habit—From Effectiveness to Greatness.* New York: Free Press, Simon & Schuster, Inc., 2004.

Cozzens, D.B. *The Changing Face of the Priesthood.* Collegeville, MN: The Liturgical Press, 2002.

—. *Sacred Silence: Denial and Crisis in the Church.* Collegeville MN: The Liturgical Press, 2002.

D'Arienze, Camille, RSM. "Mercy toward Our Fathers." *America* (August 18, 2008).

De Marco, Donald. "The Primacy of Truth." *Homiletic and Pastoral Review* (July 2002): 44-46.

Dilanni, Albert. "Religious Vocations: Decline and Revival." *Homiletic and Pastoral Review* (April 2002): 23-31.

Dolan, Archbishop Timothy M. *Called to be Holy.* Huntington, IN: Our Sunday Visitor Publishing, 2005.

Due Process, Law and Love—Justice for Priests and Deacons. Vol. 1, no. 1 (September 2007).

Due Process, Law and Love—Justice for Priests and Deacons. Vol. 2, no. 1 (January 2010).

Dulles, Avery. "Rights of Accused Priests—Toward a Revision of the Dallas Charter and the 'Essential Norms.'" *America*, 190 (June 21, 2004): 19.

Father X. "The Renewal of the Episcopacy—(The Church's Flourishing Depends on the Strength of Her Bishops)." *Homiletic and Pastoral Review* (Aug./Sept. 2008): 64-67.

Ference, Damian J. "Why We're Different: Bridging the Priesthood's Generation Gap." *Commonweal* (May 23, 2008).

Feuerherd, Joe. "Clergy Witch Hunt? Due Process for Accused Priests Is a Sham—Critics Say." *National Catholic Reporter* (April 25, 2007).

Fisichella, Rino. "The Identity of the Priest." *Homiletic and Pastoral Review* (June 2004): 17-22.

Figueiredo, Anthony J., STD. "Charity and Mission of the Priest." *Homiletic and Pastoral Review* (Dec. 2010): 51-58.

Fitsgibbons, Richard P., and Peter Rudegeair. "A Letter to the Bishops." *Homiletic and Pastoral Review* (Nov. 2002): 53-61.

Fladder, John. "Primacy of Conscience." *The Catholic Weekly.* Vol. 69, no. 4523 (June 6, 2010): 11.

Gibbs, Nancy. "Zero Tolerance, Zero Sense." *Time* (March 28, 2011): 59.

Gilchrist, Michael. "Struggling to Survive." *The Catholic World Report* (June 2006): 42-45.

Gimenez, Mark. *Accused.* www.markgimenez.com

Girard, Peter M. "Holding Jesus with Imperfect Hands." *Homiletic and Pastoral Review* (Aug./Sept. 2002): 73-75.

Gomez, Archbishop Jose H. *The Virtue of Courage in the Priestly Life.* Huntington, IN: Our Sunday Visitor Publishing, 2009.

Groeshcel, Benedict, CFR, "The Life and Death of Religious Life." *First Things* (June-July 2007): 12-15.

Harter, Kevin. "He Inspires Fear in the Church, Hope for Victims." Pioneer Press (January 28, 2007).

Hawkins, David R. *Power Vs. Force—the Hidden Determinants of Human Behaviour.* California: Hay House Inc., 2006.

Henningsen, Catharine. "The Second Wave of Abuse: the Fate of Our Accused Priests." *Voice of the Faithful* (VOTF) (February 5, 2004).

Herboelte, Hermann. "Shepherding Troubled Shepherds." *Homiletic and Pastoral Review* (Nov. 2007): 60-65.

Heuser, Frederick. "A Resigned Priest on His Death Bed." *Homiletic and Pastoral Review* (May 2002): 31, 44-45.

Hopkins, Nancy Myer, and Mark Laaser. *Restoring the Soul of a Church—Healing Congregations Wounded by Clergy Sexual Misconduct.* Collegeville, MN: The Liturgical Press, 1995.

Hull, Michael. "Priestly Identity and the Danger of Democratism." *Homiletic and Pastoral Review* (July 2005): 8-13.

Hurley, Thomas. "The Importance of the Hierarchy of the Church." *Homiletic and Pastoral Review* (June 2005): 56-6.

Integrity in Ministry—A Document of Principles and Standards for Catholic Clergy & Religious in Australia (June 2004).

Irish Bishops' Conference / Conference of Religious of Ireland / Irish Missionary Union. *Our Children, Our Church: Child Protection Policies and Procedures of the Catholic Church in Ireland.* Dublin: Veritas, 2005, chapters 8 and 9.

Irish Catholic Bishops' Conference. *Pastoral Reflections for Lent—2005, Towards Healing.* Dublin: Veritas, no. 2 (February 2005).

Jordan, Harry J. "Our Bishops Have Abandoned Us." *Homiletic and Pastoral Review* (May 2004): 62-66.

Kane, Michael. "Investigating Attitudes of Catholic Priests toward the Media and the US Conference of Catholic Bishops' Response to the Sexual Abuse Scandals of 2002." *Mental Health, Religion & Culture.* Vol. 11, no. 6 (September 2008): 579-595.

—. "A Qualitative Study of the Attitudes of Catholic Priests toward Bishops and Ministry Following the Sexual Abuse Revelations of 2002." *Pastoral Psychology*, Vol. 57 (2008): 183-198.

—. "Codes of Conduct for Catholic Clergy in the United States: The Professionalization of the Priesthood." *Mental Health, Religion & Culture*. Vol. 9, no. 4 (September 2006): 355-377.

—. "Risk Management for Catholic Priests in the United States: A New Demand from the Code of Pastoral Conduct." *Journal of Religion & Spirituality in Social Work*. Vol. 25, no. 1 (2006): 47-67.

Kasper, Walter. "Leadership in the Church: Traditional Roles Can Serve the Christian Community Today." New York: Crossroad, 2003, 47-48.

Kippley, Sheila. "The Influence of One Priest." *Homiletic and Pastoral Review* (Jan. 2007): 62, 66.

Konvitz, Milton R. *Fundamental Rights—History of a Constitutional Doctrine*. New Brunswick: Transaction Publishers/Rutgers University, 2001, 49-50.

Kouzes, James M., and Barry Z. Posner. *The Leadership Challenge*. San Francisco, Jossey-Bass, A Wiley Company, 2002.

LoBaugh, Marnie. *Fear of False Accusation (in Priests)*. PhD Dissertation, Fielding University.

Landry, Roger J. "False Accusations." *CatholiCity* (July 9, 2010).

Larson, Thomas. "Training Priests Today." *Homiletic and Pastoral Review* (Aug./Sept. 2002): 64-72.

Lawler, Philip E. "Two New Documents, One Glaring Omission." *The Catholic World Report* (July 2011): 24-25.

Lytton, Timothy. *Holding Bishops Accountable*. Cambridge, MA: Harvard University Press, 2008.

McBride, Alfred, O. Praem. *A Priest Forever—Nine Signs of Renewal and Hope*. Cincinnati, Ohio: St. Anthony Messenger Press, 2010.

MacDonald, Ryan Anthony. *Truth in Justice*. *www.thesestonewalls.com/* **truth-in-justice/**

McCarthy, Monsignor William. *The Conspiracy—An Innocent Priest (A True Story)*. Bloomington, IN: iUniverse, Inc., 2010.

McChesney, Kathleen. "What Caused the Crisis?" *America*, Vol. 204 (June 6-13, 2011): 13-15.

McKeating, Michael P. "The Problem Is Pederasty, not Paedophilia." *Homiletic and Pastoral Review* (July 2002): 59-62.

—. "Is the Church Homophobic?" *Homiletic and Pastoral Review* (June 2003): 56-58.

McKenna, Kevin E. "The Battle for Rights in the United States Catholic Church." Mahwah, NJ: Paulist Press, 2007.

Mandal, Ananya, MD. "Bad Jobs Can Make One Mentally Ill: Study." *Medical News*. Online. March 14, 2011, at 11:20 p.m.

Meconi, David Vincent, SJ. "The Joy of Vulnerability." *Homiletic and Pastoral Review* (Feb. 2003): 28-32, 45-47.

Meng, Barbara. "Gossip: Killing One Softly." *Homiletic and Pastoral Review* (Oct. 2008): 26-31.

Murphy, Austin G. "The Importance of the Priesthood." *Homiletic and Pastoral Review* (Jan. 2005): 20-25.

Neuhaus, Richard John. "Scandal Time I." *First Things* (April 2002).

—. "Scandal Time II." *First Things* (June/July 2002).

—. "The Public Square—Scandal Time (Continued)." *First Things* (June-July 2002): 75-83.

—. "Scandal Time III." *First Things* (August/September 2002).

—. "The Public Square—The Embarrassment of Sin and Grace." *First Things* (December 2002): 67-70.

—. "The Bishops in Charge." *First Things* (Jan. 2003).

—. "Nasty and Nice in Politics and Religion." *First Things* (March 2004).

—. "The Catholic Reform I." *First Things* (May 2004).

—. "The Catholic Reform II." *First Things* (June/July 2004).

—. "A Kafkaesque Tale." *The Public Square* (Sept. 2008).

—. "In the Aftermath of Scandal." *First Things*, 140 (Feb. 2004): 60.

"The Vulnerable Priest—The Official State of *Opus Bono Sacerdotii* on the Crisis in the United States of America." *Opus Bono Sacerdotii* (Work for the Good of the Priesthood).

Orsi, Michael P. "Priests' Privacy and Reputation Need Protection." *Homiletic and Pastoral Review* (Oct. 2003): 54-57.

—. "I Have Confidence in Holy Orders." *Homiletic and Pastoral Review* (May 2005): 2-31, 43-45.

—. "The Bishops Offer a 'Vioxx Solution' for Societal Ills (Identifying the Root Cause of a Problem)." *Homiletic and Pastoral Review* (July 2005): 62-64.

—. "Correction: Father's Job." *Homiletic and Pastoral Review* (Oct. 2007): 56-59.

—. "Calumny in the Blogosphere." *Homiletic and Pastoral Review* (June 2008): 12-17.

—. "Reckless Bishops Ruin Priests' Reputations" *Homiletic and Pastoral Review* (Jan. 2009): 44-49.

Peter, Val J. "How They Market Homosexuality." *Homiletic and Pastoral Review* (Dec. 2006): 18-22.

Pierre, David F., Jr. *Double Standard—Abuse Scandals and the Attack on the Catholic Church.* Copyrighted Material—Published in the United States of America, 2009.

Rediger, G. Lloyd. *Clergy Killers—Guidance for Pastors and Congregations under Attack.* Grove Heights, MN: Logos Productions Inc., 1997.

Rice, David. *Shattered Vows—Priests Who Leave.* New York: William Morrow & Co. Inc., 1990.

Rabinowitz, Dorothy. *No Crueller Tyrannies—Accusations, False Witnesses, and Other Terrors of Our Time.* A Wall Street Journal Book. New York: Free Press, 2004.

Rose, Michael S. *Goodbye, Good Men! How Liberals Brought Corruption into the Catholic Church. Washington,* Aquinas Publishing, 2002.

Rossetti, Stephen J. "Priestly Life and Morale Today." *The Priest,* 61 (October 2005): 12-21, 47.

—. "Post-Crisis Morale among Priests." *America,* 191, no. 6 (2004): 8-10.

—. *The Joy of Priesthood.* Notre Dame, IN: Ave Maria Press, 2005.

—. *Why Priests Are Happy: A Study of the Psychological and Spiritual Health of Priests.* Notre Dame, IN: Ave Maria Press, 2011.

Ruddy, Christopher. "The American Church's Sexual Abuse Crisis." *America* (June 3, 2002).

Scerbo, Joe, SA, PhD. *Reconciliation: The Purpose of Spirit-directed Therapy.* University Microfilms International, Michigan, USA, 1984.

Schuth, Katarina. "A View of the Priesthood in the United States." *Louvain Studies,* 30 (2005): 8-24.

Silverglate, Harvey A. "Fleecing the Shepherd: Will the Church Settle the Sexual-Abuse Cases This Time Around?" *The Boston Phoenix.*

Sofield, S.T., and Carroll Juliano, SHCJ. *Principled Ministry: A Guidebook for Catholic Church Leaders.* Notre Dame, IN: Ave Maria Press, 2011.

"For Critics, the Study Raises More Questions than It Answers." The John Jay Report. *The Catholic World Report* (July 2011): 22-23.

Stefanski, Jacek. "The Ingredient for Priestly Vocations." *Homiletic and Pastoral Review* (May 2009): 8-13.

"Influential Pastor Pledges to Fight Sexual Allegations." The *Wall Street Journal* (September 27, 2010).

Zero Tolerance, Zero Sense, Time (October 11, 2010): 32.

Towards Healing, Principles and Procedures in Responding to Complaints of Abuse against Personnel of the Catholic Church in Australia (January 2004).

Towards Healing, Principles and Procedures in Responding to Complaints of Abuse against Personnel of the Catholic Church in Australia (January 2010).

Treacy, David (pseudonym). "Guilty until Proven Innocent (A First-hand Account of a Priest Falsely Accused of Sexual Abuse)." *Homiletic and Pastoral Review* (June 2009): 28-31, 41-44.

Varacalli, Joseph A. "Dissecting the Anatomy of the Sexual Scandal." *Homiletic and Pastoral Review* (Jan. 2004): 44-49.

Vitz, Paul C., and Daniel Vitz. "Priests and the Importance of Fatherhood." *Homiletic and Pastoral Review* (Dec. 2008): 16-22.

Von Hiddebrand. "From Defeat to Victory: We Need a Supernatural Response to Evil." *Homiletic and Pastoral Review* (June 2002): 15-22.

Wronka, Joseph. *Human Rights and Social Policy in the 21st Century: A History of the Idea of Human Rights and Comparison of the United Nations Universal Declaration of Human Rights with United States Federal and State Constitutions*. New York: University Press of America, Inc., 1998.

Yeung, Bernice. "Children of the Church." *Legal Affairs Magazine* (October 2, 2006).